Abstracts of Parker County, Texas Pre-emption Land Records 1850–1858

Compiled by

Jerry Wright Jordan

HERITAGE BOOKS
2013

HERITAGE BOOKS
AN IMPRINT OF HERITAGE BOOKS, INC.

Books, CDs, and more—Worldwide

For our listing of thousands of titles see our website at
www.HeritageBooks.com

Published 2013 by
HERITAGE BOOKS, INC.
Publishing Division
100 Railroad Ave. #104
Westminster, Maryland 21157

Copyright © 1988 Jerry Wright Jordan

Other Heritage Books by the author:

Abstracts of Parker County, Texas
Pre-emption Land Records, 1850–1858

Cherokee by Blood
Volumes 1-9

All rights reserved. No part of this book may be reproduced or transmitted in any form or by any means, electronic or mechanical, including photocopying, recording or by any information storage and retrieval system without written permission from the author, except for the inclusion of brief quotations in a review.

International Standard Book Numbers
Paperbound: 978-1-55613-132-5
Clothbound: 978-0-7884-6971-8

CONTENTS

PREFACE   v

INTRODUCTION:
    Facts about Parker County;   vi
    Texas Land Grants; terms

Maps: xiii
    Parker County Rivers and Creeks
    Robertson County, 1845
    Northwest Texas Frontier, 1850
    Parker County Abstract Map - SW Section - Pt. 1
    Parker County Abstract Map - SW Section - Pt. 2

Milam Land District 1850-1857   1

Robertson Land District 1852-1853   5

Denton Land District 1854-1855   10

Denton Land District, Record Book "B" 1855   24

Denton Land District 1854-1857   49

Denton Land District Index Records A, C, D   72

Parker County Record Book B 1856-1858   77

Parker County Record Book C 1856-1858   128

Parker County Record Book D 1857   143

APPENDIX I - Tarrant County: Petition for New County   183

APPENDIX II - Legislative Act Creating Parker County   186

INDEX   188

PREFACE

The original records from which these abstracts were made are housed in a regional branch of the Texas State Archives at the Mary Couts Burnett Library, Texas Christian University, Fort Worth, Texas. This branch archives is small and contains records primarily of Tarrant and Parker Counties, with a few records from Hood, Johnson, and Somervell counties. There is no archivist at this time and the records have been placed under the Special Collections Dept. of the Mary Couts Burnett Library.

The records are filed in a box marked "Parker County - PAR 223 - Pre-emption Records 1850-58" and divided into 9 file folders. The last three folders were not abstracted for this book as they are not preemption records and belong to a later time period. The contents of each folder and the condition of the records are as follows:

(1) Pre-emption Record "A";
    Robertson Land District, 1852 - 1853   19 pp
    DESCRIPTION: unbound pages approx. 8 x 12 water-soaked and faded but legible

(2) Three divisions:
    [A] Pre-emption Record
        Milam Land District, 1850 - 1857   13 pp
    [B] Denton Land Office, 1854 - 1855   50 pp
        (Transcript)
    [C] Parker Co Pre-emption Record "C" 1856 - 1858 69 PP
    DESCRIPTION: unbound pages approx. 8 x 12 - brittle and edges torn

(3) Pre-emption Record "B" Parker Co, 1856 - 1858   223 pp
    DESCRIPTION: loosely bound - pages approx. 8 x 12

(4) Pre-emption Record "B" Transcript Book "B" 1855
    Denton Land Dist.   81 PP
    DESCRIPTION: loosely bound - pages approx. 8 x 12

(5) Two Divisions:
    [A] Pre-emption Record "D" 1854 - 1857
        Transcript Denton Land Office   98 pp
    [B] Pre-emption Record "D", 1857 - Parker Co. 181 pp
    DESCRIPTION: loosely bound - pages approx 8 x 12 1st part of book is for Denton Land Dist. the second part is the same book but begins with page "1" and is for Parker Co. TX

(6) Index to Pre-emption Records, A, C, D
    Denton Land District   23 pp
    DESCRIPTION: pages approx 7" x 12" - loose, very brittle, corners torn or folded, some pages taped

(7) Survey Record 1873-1874   4 pp

(8) Homestead Applications 1880

(9) Land Appraisals 1880-1882   34 pp

In addition the box contains the front & back covers of a record book, and the front or back of a larger record book.

One cover of the smaller record book has written on the inside

> "Book F Purchased by
> George N. Heifrin
> ____?____ Surveyor Parker
> Co Texas
> May 6th 1874"

    In abstracting the preemption records I included the land district and/or the county the land was situated in; any creeks or rivers mentioned; and adjoining land owners; chain carriers; and witnesses. Distances included in the surveys were omitted with the exception of the ones pertaining to a nearby town. I have also arranged the records in a chronological order rather than the one listed above.

    I would like to express appreciation to Mrs. Laura Dubiel, of the Special Collection Dept., Mary Couts Burnett Library; and to Mrs. Evlyn Broumley, head of the Genealogy Dept. of the Weatherford Public Library and editor of "Trails West", publication of the Parker County Genealogical Society, who has given me much assistance and provided the photostatic copy of the original petition for the creation of Parker County which appears in Appendix I.

INTRODUCTION

SOME FACTS ABOUT PARKER COUNTY:

Parker County lies in the north central region of the state of Texas just west of Fort Worth, Tarrant County. Settlement in the area began in the mid to late 1840's and grew rapidly. In the summer & fall of 1855 ISAAC PARKER, the State Representative for the residents of the Western Territory of Tarrant County, Texas, began circulating a petiton seeking the creation of a new county. This petition was presented to the State Legislature and on the 12th of December 1855, an act creating the County of Parker was passed. Prior to its creation, the area encompassed within its limits fell under the jurisdiction of three different Land Districts (Milam, Robertson, and Denton). The District Surveyors of these three districts made transcripts of all surveys in their offices which fell within the new county's boundaries and sent them to the office of the Parker County Surveyor. All subsequent surveys were then made by surveyor and deputy surveyors of the new county.

In the early morning of May 13, 1874, a fire broke out in the clerk's office in the southeast corner of the County Courthouse. There was no equipment to extinquish even small fires, much less the one that spread so quickly through the building. Two men were in the courthouse when the fire broke out. GEORGE PLOWMAN, a lawyer who was sleeping in the office he shared with his partner Mr. SHANNON on the second floor of the courthouse, and GEORGE HEIFRIN, a deputy surveyor who was asleep in the surveyor's office on the first floor. Both men escaped the blazing building. Mr HEIFRIN got away with all the plans and the surveyor's books and maps, but lost his gold watch in the fire. The destruction of the building was complete and with it the records of 19 years. The official papers of County Judge F. A. LEACH and the county tax books were also saved, but everything else was destroyed - deeds, county minutes, marriage records, will & probate records, court cases, etc. There were approximately 100 original deeds in the clerk's office waiting for the owners to pay the recording fee.[1]

[NOTE: On the inside cover of one of the record books is written GEORGE HEIFRIN's name and the date May 6, 1874 one week prior to the courthouse fire - see PREFACE]

---

[1] Smythe, H. _Historical_ _Sketch_ _of_ _Parker_ _County_ _and_ _Weatherford_ _Texas_ [Louis C. Lavat Book and Job Printers, St. Louis, 1877] 293-296.

Several years ago, Mr. FRED COTTON, a note historian & civic leader of Parker County, located the original petition asking the State Legislature for a new county. All major sources cite Navarro & Bosque as the parent counties of Parker County, yet after having gone through many, many boxes of records the petition was finally located in a box marked "Tarrant County" in the State Archives in Austin, TX. A photostatic copy of the original was made and placed in the Genealogy Dept. of the Weatherford Public Library. A typescript of the petition was printed in "Trails West", Vol. 3 No. 3 (Spring, 1973), the quarterly publication of the Parker County Genealogical Society. I compared this typescript with the photostatic copy of the original and was able to clarify several names which had been misprinted in the typescript. This petition is included to show those people whose names do appear in the preemption records plus additional residents, temporary or permanent, not included in the Abstracts. [See APPENDIX 1]

TEXAS LAND GRANTS:

Land was the only commodity the young Republic of Texas possessed after the successful war for independence from Mexico. The war was short, but the debt incurred was tremendous, approximately $10,000,000. Some means had to be found to repay this huge debt and the enormous amount of land appeared to be the answer. First and foremost, however, those citizens who had been living in Texas and had obtained land from Spain and then from Mexico had to be guaranteed the titles to their land if it had been obtained legally and without fraud. Secondly, and just as important, the men who had fought for the young republic's independence had been promised land as recompense for their services. Thirdly, the young nation needed new people and land was a good means of securing them. A General Land Office was established by the Republic on December 22, 1836 but did not become completely functional until 1844. While land was intended to be utilized in adding money to the treasury it is estimated that Texas gave away slightly more than half of all the public lands that she possessed at the time she became independent. Office fees and the surveyor's fees were the only money generated and they covered the expenses only.²

The deficit of the Treasury of the Republic was carried over when Texas was annexed as a State in the United States in 1845. A previous attempt at annexation to the Union had been defeated by the Congress of the United States when the govern-

----
2. Lang, Aldon Socrates, Financial History of the Public Lands in Texas [The Baylor Bulletin, Baylor University, Waco & Dallas TX, 1932] 79

ment had been asked to assume the $10,000,000 debt of the republic. When annexation was finally agreed upon, Texas was left with her debt but also with the power over her large public domain. The debt was finally alleviated in 1850 when an estimated 72,892,000 acres were transferred to the United States for a sum of $10,000,00 in bonds and an additional $2,750,000 in cash received in 1855.[3]

It is not within the scope of this work to give an entire history of the distribution of the Texas Public Domain. Rather a brief explanation of the various grants, particularly those mentioned in the records abstracted for Parker County will be given to offer some understanding of what each type of grant meant.

HEADRIGHTS:

FIRST CLASS HEADRIGHTS: The Republic of Texas decided to offer Headright grants to those citizens who were in Texas on March 2, 1836 (the date of the Declaration of Independence) and who had not received title to any lands prior to this date. These grants were for 1 league + 1 labor of land (4,605 acs.) for every head of household and 1/3 this amount (1,536 acs.) for all single men over the age of 17. An individual receiving this type of headright was not required to settle upon or make improvements on the land thus granted, but were required to mark it.

First Class recipients were required to take the following oath:

> "I do solemnly swear, that I was a resident of Texas at the date of the declaration of independence, that I did not leave the country during the campaigns of the spring of 1836, to avoid a participation in the struggle, that I did not refuse to participate in the war, and that I did not aid or assist the enemy, that I had not previously received a title to any quantum of land, and that I conceive myself justly entitled, under the Consti- tution and Laws to the quantity of land for which I now apply."

In addition, two creditable witnesses were required to offer proof of residence prior to March 2, 1836.

----

3. Webb, Walter Prescott, <u>The Handbook of Texas</u> [The Texas State Historical Association, Austin, 1952] II, pp 23, 24

Military service was not part of the conditions for the above headrights, however, soldiers who had been in Texas prior to March 2, 1836, and whose families were expected to arrive within 12 months, plus volunteers arriving after March 2, 1836 and served in the military until August 1, 1836, received an honorable discharge, or had died, were also granted FIRST CLASS status. Special headrights were granted to the heirs of those men who had fallen with Colonels J. W. FANNIN, F. W. JOHNSON, W. B. TRAVIS, and Dr. JAMES GRANT in the spring of 1836. Another special headright was granted to those men permanently disabled while in the service of Texas.

SECOND CLASS HEADRIGHTS: Free white immigrants who arrived in Texas after March 2, 1836 and before October 1, 1837 were offered the following amounts of land: Head of household - 1280 acs.; single men - 640 acs. Recipients of this grant had to remain in the Republic for three years and provide proof of this residency.

THIRD CLASS HEADRIGHTS: Free white immigrants arriving in Texas after Oct 1, 1837 and before January 1, 1840. Heads of families to receive 640 acs.; single men over the age 17 to receive 320 acs. In addition, any resident citizen attaining the age of 17 during this period was also entitled to 320 acs. plus any soldiers who were in the service prior to March 1, 1837. Same conditions as to 3 years residency within the republic were required.

FOURTH CLASS HEADRIGHTS: Free white immigrants arriving after January 1, 1840 and prior to January 1, 1842. Heads of families to receive 640 acs.; single men over 17 years of age 320 acs. More stringent conditions required actually settling upon the land claim and cultivation of at least 10 acres.

The headright grants were issued in the counties which the recipient resided in. The land they claimed could be any unappropriated Public domain.

BOUNTY WARRANTS:

Several acts were passed by the Republic of Texas to reward those men who had served during the war for independence from Mexico. These various acts were confusing as to the exact amount of land a soldier was entitled to. Finally on December 4, 1837 an act was passed, over the veto of President Houston, which clarified all previous acts offering bounty to men who had given military service. Under this act, 320 acres of land were offered for each three months service up to one year with the maximum amount offered being 1280 acs. for any one enlistment. There was one exception to this guideline which gave 320 acs. to any who had participated in the siege of Be`xar from Dec 5 through Dec 10, 1835, even if their service had been less than 3 months.

There were still dangers to the frontier of Texas after Independence was won and various acts were passed offering bounty lands to men who would render military service on the frontier. On December 10, 1841, an act granting 240 acs. of bounty land to these men was passed. The land could be located on any unappropriated Public domain but could not be transferred.

DONATION GRANTS:

Donation grants are offered for service *after* military service is rendered. Texas passed two such donation acts - the first were to the men who had participated in the Battle of San Jacinto, the skirmish the day preceeding it, and to those who had remained at Harrisburg to care for the sick & wounded; to those involved in the siege of Be`xar; and to the heirs of those who fell at the Alamo,. This Donation grant offered 640 acs. to the recipients. The second type of "Donation Grants" were passed in 1879 granting to indigent veterans of the war for independence 640 acs. which was increased to 1280 acres in 1881.

[NOTE: THERE ARE AFFIDAVITS IN THE PARKER COUNTY PRE-EMPTION RECORDS WHICH CLAIM LAND BY RIGHT OF THE "DONATION LAW" PASSED FEB 13 1854 - THIS WAS NOT A DONATION GRANT BUT RATHER A PRE-EMPTION GRANT - SEE NEXT SECTION]

PRE-EMPTION GRANTS:

A pre-emption grant entitled a person and/or family to settle upon unappropriated land and gave them the option to purchase that land when it became available for sale. The first pre-emption act in Texas was passed on January 22, 1845, permitting settlers to claim 320 acres of land, live on it for three years and begin making improvements. After the 3 year occupation of the land the title could be obtained by paying anywhere from $.50 to $2.00 per acre. This pre-emption grant was later (Feb 7, 1853) changed to become an outright gift requiring only the 3 year occupancy.

The amount of land granted by pre-emption grants was later reduced to 160 acs. There were several other acts passed by the Texas State Legislature regarding pre-emption grants.

The State Legislature passed an Act on Feb 13 1854 "donating to actual settlers" 160 acs. of land. This act required the testimony of "two respectable witnesses" that the claimant had been "bonafide settled upon vacant land", had resided & cultivated it for three years and was a citizen of the state at the date the act was passed. Upon presenting to the General Land Office the field notes of the survey along with an authenticated duplicate of the affidavit, the claimant could pay the usual patent fee "and no more" and would then be given a patent to the land.[4] There are surveys in the Parker Co. pre-emption records which were made on the basis of the "Donation Law", however, the testimony of the witnesses are not included. This act was a pre-emption grant but was referred to in the affidavits of the applicants as the "Donation Law". Usually this type of claim also mentioned the Feb 13 1854 date which helps to avoid confusing this particular type of grant with the "Donation Grants" which were given for military service

THE MISSISSIPPI & PACIFIC RESERVE:

Texas also designated certain land for internal improvements. On December 31, 1853, the State legislature created the Mississippi & Pacific Reserve hoping to encourage the building of a railroad across the state to connect with other lines reaching ultimately across the continent. A sixty mile wide stretch across the state was set aside. Twenty sections of land for each mile, including all timber and mineral rights were offered to the Railroads with the exception of alternate sections which were reserved for the state. A series of complicated events followed the passage of this act and a further complication was enacted when the State legislature opened the Mississippi & Pacific Reserve to location and sale on the 26th of August 1856. Many litigations were initiated in later years regarding this Reserve and its opening for settlement, the effect upon the Parker County residents who claimed their land through this act is unknown at this time.

Throughout the pre-emption books of Parker County are references to the act of August 26, 1856, offering the Mississippi & Pacific Reserve for location and sale.[5] The testimony of two respectable witnesses were not specifically required by this act, but every instance in the records includes the testimony of two people. The claimant was required to pay $.50 an acre for the land so claimed, after which a land patent would be issued by the General Land Office.

---

4. Gammell, H. P. N., The Laws of Texas 1822-1897 [Austin, The Gammel Book Co., 1898] III, pp 1550-1552.
5. Ibid., IV, 474

COUNTY SCHOOL LANDS:

It will also be noticed throughout the locations of the surveys contained in this book, mention of certain county school lands. Texas set aside a certain amount of land for public institutions, i.e., public schools, a university system, and institutions for the blind, deaf, insane & orphans. More land was allowed for the public schools than for any other appropriation. At first each county was allowed 3 Leagues for its school lands, 1 additional league was added later. As will be noted in Parker County, a county's school land alottment did not have to be within its boundaries. These lands could be sold to individuals with the proceeds going into a Public School Fund. This was perhaps one of the most farsighted arrangements made by the governing powers of the Republic & State of Texas. In 1942 there was close to $73,000,000 in the Public School Fund of Texas. This amount was derived from the sale of these lands plus mineral royalties.

TERMS:

Texas adopted the Spanish and Mexican Land Measure when it became a republic. However, both Spanish & English standards were recognized. The following equivalents are given for a clearer understanding:

```
            1 vara*     = 33 & 1/3 inches = 2.778 feet
 1.806.520 square varas = 320 acres
 3.613.040 square varas = 640 acres = 1 square mile
 1.000.000 square varas = 177 & 1/7 ac. = 1 labor
25.000.000 square varas = 4,428.3 acres = 1 Leauge
26,000.000 square varas = 4,605 acres = 1 League & 1 labor
```

* vara is abbreviated as vr. or vrs.

SUGGESTED READING ON TEXAS LAND POLICIES:

1. Lang, Aldon Socrates, Financial History of the Public Lands in Texas [The Baylor Bulletin, Baylor University, Waco & Dallas TX, 1932]

2. Miller, Thomas Lloyd, The Public Lands of Texas; 1519-1970 [University of Oklahoma Press, Norman, 1971]

3. Webb, Walter Prescott, The Handbook of Texas [The Texas State Historical Association, Austin, 1952] II,

Map of Parker County

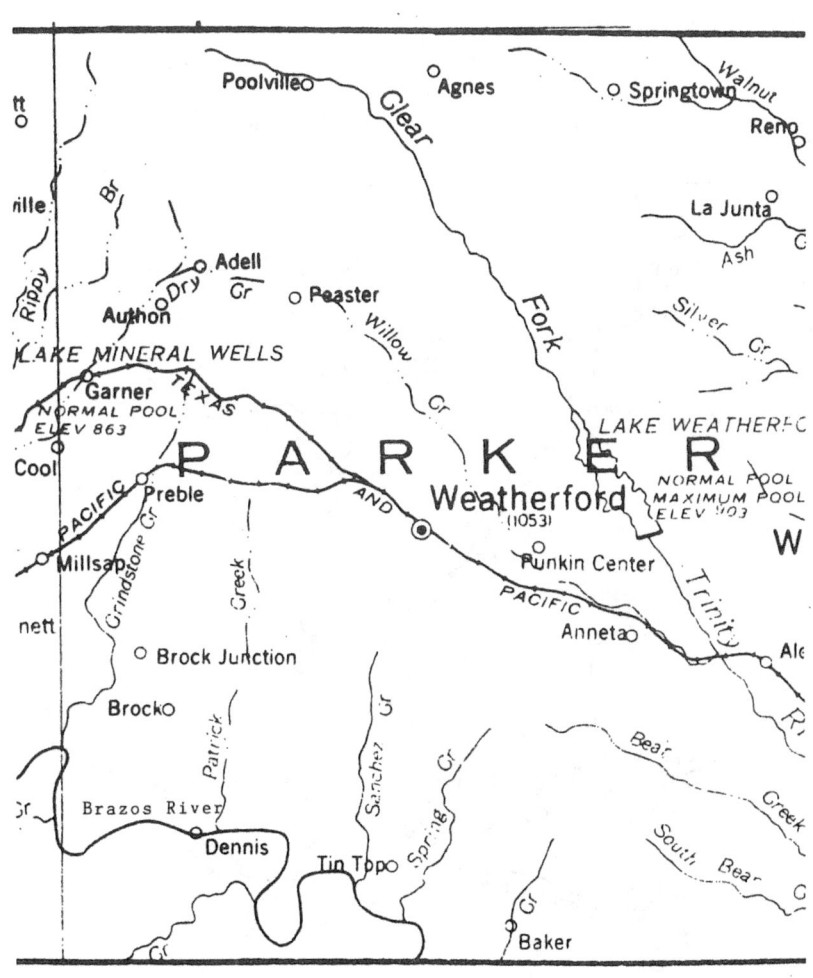

Rivers and creeks in Parker County, Texas

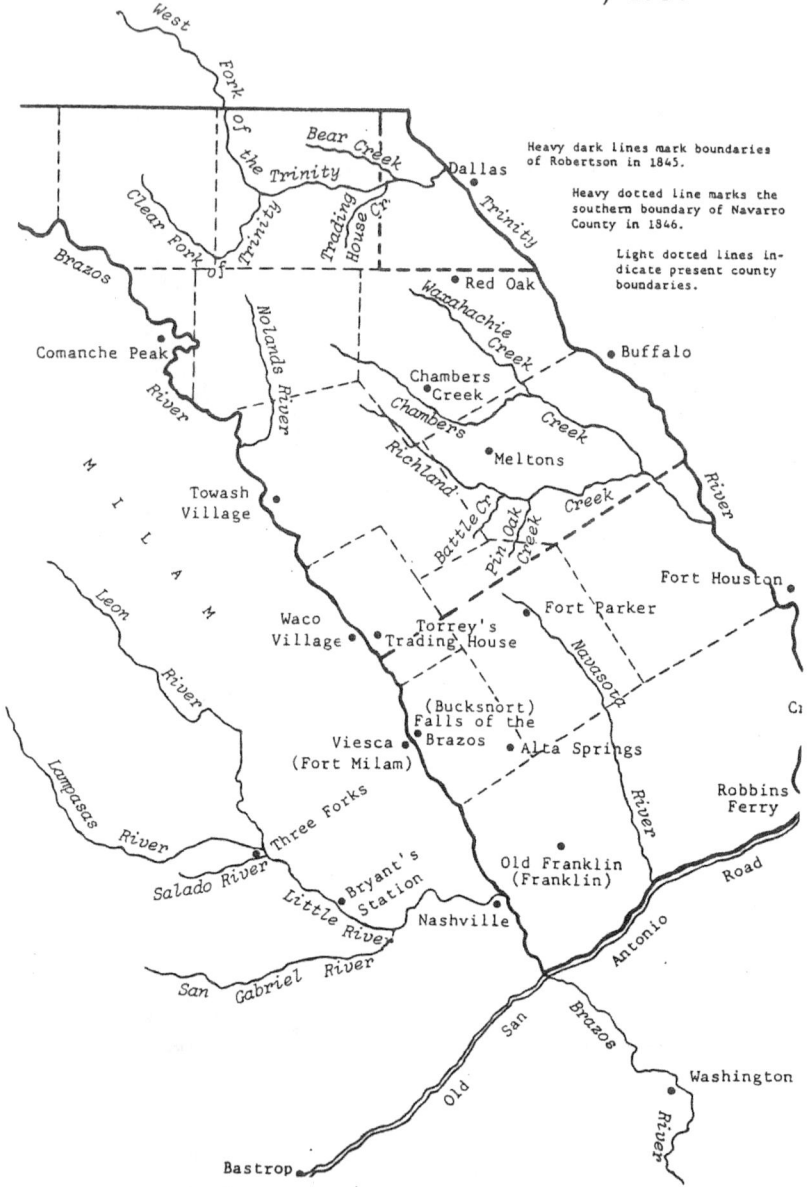

Reprinted from Nancy Timmons Samuels *Old Northwest Texas* [Fort Worth Genealogical Society, Fort Worth, Texas, 1980] 1A, p 7

NORTHWEST TEXAS FRONTIER, 1850

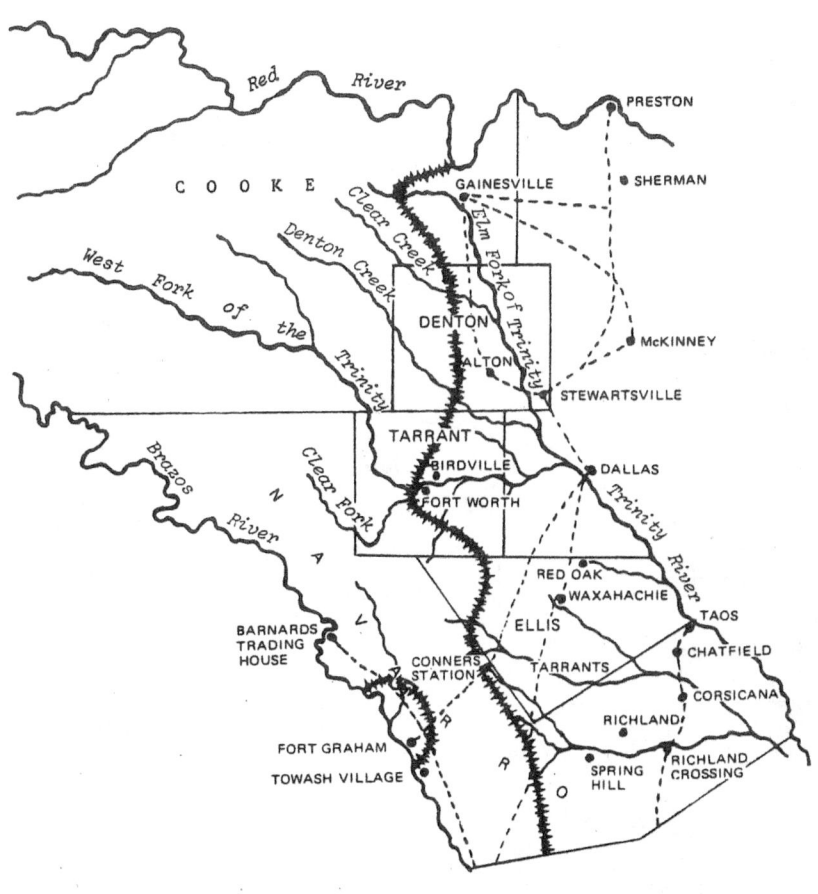

Reprinted from Nancy Timmons Samuels *Old Northwest Texas* [Fort Worth Genealogical Society, Fort Worth, Texas, 1980] 1A, p 8

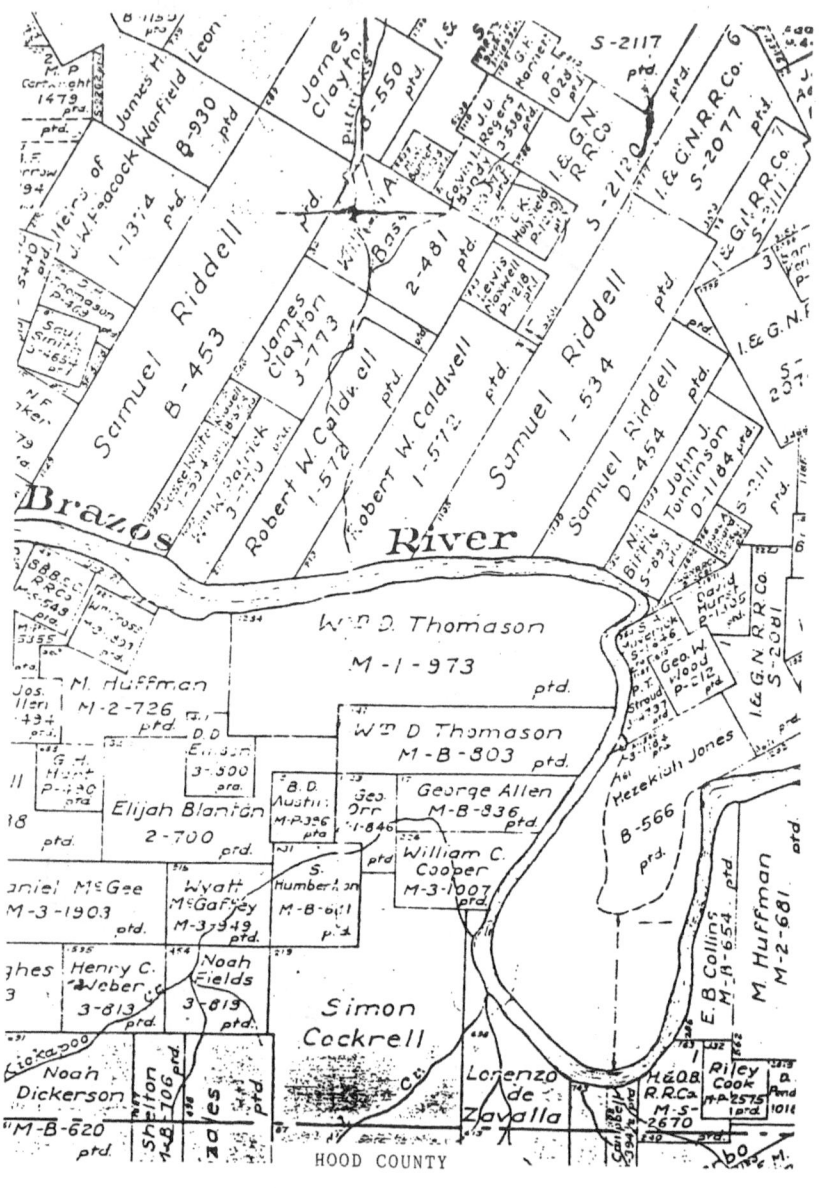

Abstract map of Parker County, Texas – southwest section – pt. 1

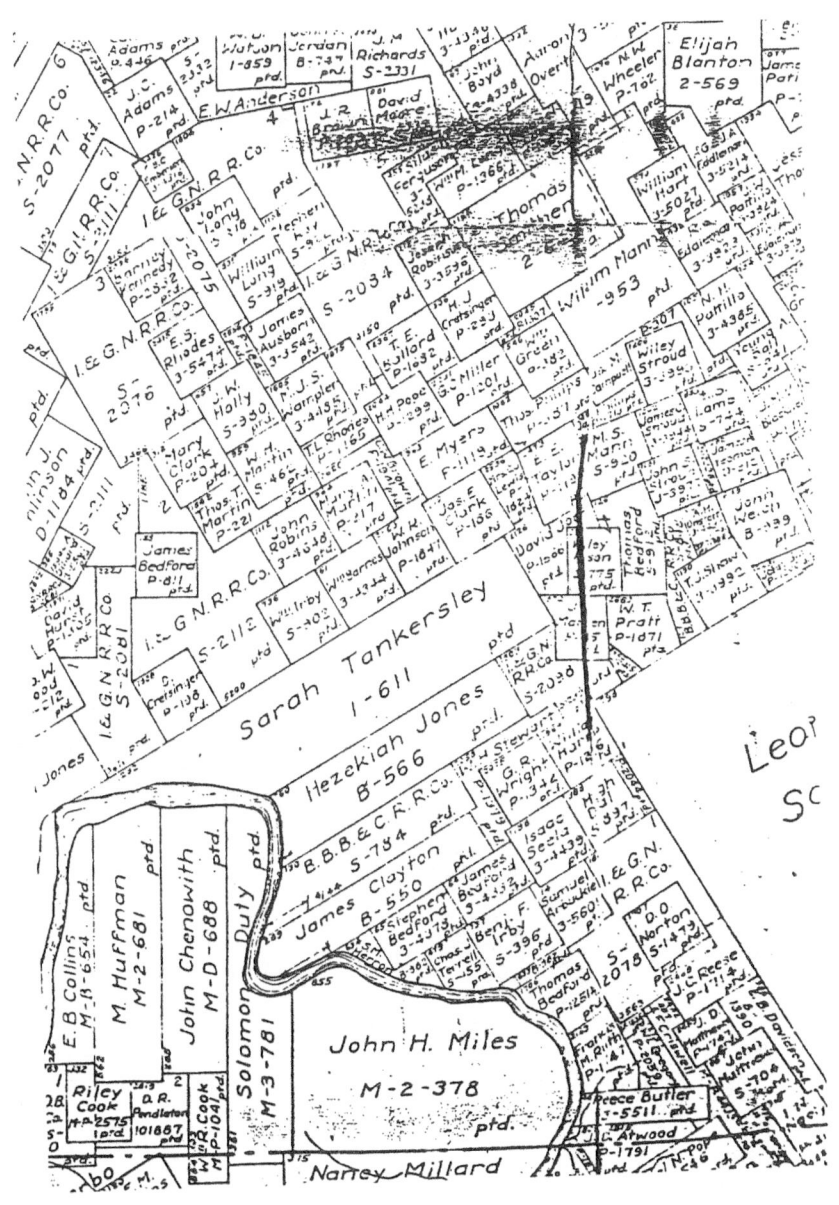

Abstract map of Parker County, Texas - southwest section - pt. 2

MILAM LAND DISTRICT
1850 - 1857

[NOTE: This volume begins with page numbered "7" in the middle of a previous entry dated Jul 2 1850]

[7] [in pencil] Pre-emption Book "C" begins next page after page 68 this volume [remainder in ink]

The State of Texas | Survey for JOHN CHENAWORTH of 8 1/3
District of Milam | Labors of Land Situate on the Brazos
River about 8 1/2 miles above the mouth of the Paloney (?) being the quantity of Land to which he is entitled by virtue of Cert. No. 366 issued in Harris County - Beginning at the NE cor. of a survey made for WHORY (?) ADAMS for the SE cor. of this survey -

[8]   Containing all areable land
Surveyed: Jun 16 1847 - GEORGE GREEN, Dept. Surveyor
Chain Carriers: A. CLOYES, UNA MC KENNEY

[in pencil]   CERTIFICATE WANTED

Milam Dist TX - Survey for GEORGE ALLEN - 320 acres in McLennan Co on SW Bank of Brazos Riv. about 14 mi. above Comanche Peak - being quantity entitled to by virtue of Bounty Cert. No. 715 issued by BEN F. HILL adjutant General on the 13th day of Oct 1850 - Beg. at NE cor. of GEORGE ORR labor survey for the NW cor. this survey - NE cor. of WM. C. COOPER survey -
Dated: Jun 1 1851 - WM. ARMSTRONG, Dept. Surv. for Milam Land Dist.
Chain Carriers: SILAS PERKIN, HIRAM BALES

[9]   Milam Dist. TX - Survey for 320 acs for NOAH FIELDS decd [or deed ?] on Kickapoo Creek waters of Brazos Riv. in Milam Dist. being the quantity entitled to by Virtue of Headright Cert. No. 127 Class 4th granted by Board of Land Commrs. for Liberty Co. for 320 acs. - Beg. NE cor. of ? C. WEBER 320 ac. survey -
Surveyed: Apr 18 1850 - WM. ARMSTRONG

[10]   Chain Carriers: JAMES BICHARELS, HIRAM BALES
Jul 23 1850 - JAMES HAWTER, Dist. Surveyor, certifies above as true copy of original

Milam Dist. TX - Survey for J. SHELTON 320 acs Land on waters of Kickapoo Cr. about 3 1/2 mi from junction with Brazos Riv. - being quantity entitled to by Virtue of Land Warrant No 728 dated 26th Nov 1850 - Beg. NE cor. of NOAH DICKENSON survey for NW cor. this sur....South with line of D. GONZALAS Survey

1

Surveyed: May 10 1851 - G. B. ERATH, Dept. Surv. Milam Dist.

[11] Chain Carriers: DAN RICHARDSON, H. BIBBES (?)
Jun 9 1851 - WM. ARMSTRONG, Dist. Surveyor, certifies above to be correct & according to law.

[12]   Milam Dist. TX - Survey of 3.612.800 sq. varas for the Heirs of NOAH DICKENSON Junr. on Saline Creek waters of Brazos Riv. in Milam Dist. being part of the quantity they are entitled to by virtue of Headright Cert. No. 10 issued from Gen. Land Office Jun 13 1850 & signed by BEN F. HILL adjutant General for 1/3 League - Beg. N from NE cor. of A. PHYMER 640 ac. survey for the N.W. cor. this survey -

[13]   contains 2 1/2 labors areable residue pasture land.
Surveyed: Apr 29 1850 - WM. ARMSTRONG, Dept. Surv. Milam Dist.
Chain Carriers: JAMES RICHARDS, HIRAM BOWLES
Jul 26 1850 - JAMES HAWTER, Dist. Surveyor, certifies above true copy of original

Milam Dist. TX - Surveyed 7 5395117/10,000,00 Labors of Land for JOHN H. MILES in McLennan Co. on W. Bank Brazos Riv. about 14 mi above Comanche Peak, being part of quantity entitled to by virtue of Cert. No. 130 class 2nd issued by Board of Commrs. for Austin Co for 1/3 League - Beg. NE cor. of N. MILLAND Survey -

[14]   NE cor. of S. DUTY - containing five labors areable residue pasture land.
Surveyed: Apr 14th 1850 - WM. ARMSTRONG, Dept. Surv. Milam Dist.
Chain Carriers: JAMES RICHARDS, HIRAM BOLES
Mar 8 1851 - Camron (?) - WM. ARMSTRONG certifies copy

[15]   JOSEPH B. WALDRON
Milam Dist. TX - Field notes of Survey of 8 1/3 Labors made for CHAS. S. WALDRON administrator of JOSEPH B. WALDRON being the land entitled to by virtue of Headright Cert. No. 107 issued by Board of Land Commrs. for Washington Co. Sd. survey situated in McLennan Co on Pigeon Creek, a branch of Brazos "about miles above Comanche Peak" - Beg. SW cor. League No. 4 made for Burleson County School Lands - Contains 5 Labors areable residue pasture lands -
Surveyed: Apr 2_th 1850.
Chain Carriers: none given
Oct 6 1853 - WM. ARMSTRONG, Dist. Surv. Milam Dist., certifies above survey made on sd. date & <u>refiled</u> his office Oct 6 1853

[16]   Heirs of A. L. CARRINGTON
Milam Dist. TX - Field notes of survey for A. L. CARRINGTON being land entitled to by virtue of Headright Cert. No. 603

2

issued by Board of Land Commrs. of Washington Co....situate in McLennan Co on W. side Brazos Riv & "about miles" above Comanche Peak - Beg. E from SW cor. Survey No. 4 made for Burleson Co. School Lands -
Surveyed: Apr 24th 1850
Chain Carriers: HIRAM BOWLS, JAS. RICHARDS
Oct 6 1853 - WM. ARMSTRONG certifies above survey made on sd. date & refiled his office Oct 6 1853

[17]   Milam Dist. TX - 320 ac Survey for WM. C COOPER on SW Bank of Brazos "about miles above Comehe [sic] Peak" being quantity entitled to by virtue of Headright Cert. No. 19 granted to him by Board of Land Commrs. for Jasper Co...Beg. SE cor. WM. HERRINGTON survey - past SE cor. GEOR. ORR 1 Labor survey -
Surveyed: Apr 19 1850 - WM. ARMSTRONG, Dept. Surv.
Chain Carriers: HIRAM BOWLES, JAMES RICHARDS

[18]   Jul 24 1850 - JAMES HAWTER, Dist. Surv., certifies true copy of original

[new sheet - no number]

State of Texas | I, H. E. BRADFORD, Dist. Surv. for
District of Milam | Milam Land Dist. ___?___ hereby
certify that the foregoing is a true & correct transcript of the field notes of the original [lined through in original] surveys made & Returned of the portion of Parker County Laying within the bounds of Milam Land District - Together - with the Surveyors Certificate thereunto - appended.
        Given under my hand at Belton on this the 12th day of January A. D. 1857
                            H. E. BRADFORD
                            Dist. Surveyor for
                            Milam Land District

State of Texas | I, J. C. CADDELL Clerk of the County
County of Bell | Court in and for said county hereby
certify that the foregoing Pages from One to Eighteen contains a true and correct transcript of the Field Notes of the surveys in the portion of Parker County lying in Milam Land District as appears of Record in the District Surveyors Office of Milam Land District.
        In testimony whereof I hereunto Set my hand & affix the Seal of said court at office in Belton this the 12th day of January A. D. 1857
                            J. C. CADDELL
                            Clk. Co. Ct. Bell Co.

[next 2 pages blank]

[79] [sic] Denton Land Dist. TX - JESSE R. CLIFTON personally appeared before LEWELLEN MURPHY, a Dept. surveyor of Denton Land District, and took the following oath to wit "I do Solemly Swear that I believe the land on which I am Settled to be vacant Public domain so help me God"
Signed: JESSE R. CLIFTON
Dated: 1 Feb 1855

Denton Land Dist. TX - Survey of 160 acs made for JESSE R. CLIFTON by virtue of foregoing affidavit attached. Situate in Tarrant County Territory on waters of Ash Creek a tributary of the West Fork of the Trinity River. Beg. NE from SE cor. of WILLIAM PENNINGTON 160 ac. preemption survey

[NOTE: This volume ends with the above entry from the Denton Land District which is apparently continued elsewhere]

PRE-EMPTION RECORD "A"
ROBERTSON LAND DISTRICT
1852 - 1853

[NOTE: This volume begins with page "23" in the middle of a previous entry dated May 21 1852 and signed by B. J. CHAMBER, District Surveyor "R. D."]

[23]   "A"   [in pencil]

"   ?   R L D p 294" [left margin beside the next entry]
The State of Texas
Robertson Land District   I have surveyed one-third of a
                           League of Land in Robertson
Dist. on the East Bank of Brasos [sic] River about 18 miles North of Comanche Peak by virtue of part of certificate issued by decree of the District Court of Limestone County at the Spring Term A. D. 1850 - Beg. on bank of River at upper corner of HEZEKIAH JONES 640 acres survey-

[24] in all 4774 vs. - Five Labors areable the balance pasture Land
Surveyed: May 31 1852 - B. J. CHAMBERS, Dept. Surv. Robertson Land Dist.
Chain Carriers: NATHANIEL G. KEER, JOHN SMITH
Recorded: Mar 29 1853 - B. J. CHAMBERS, Dist. Surv. R. D.

[25]   "Trans R. L. D. p 416" [left margin]
Robertson Land Dist. TX - Surveyed 640 acs for J. BERLINAN (?) "W. A. BASS" [written in pencil] Situate in Ellis Co. on Patrick's Creek, a tributary of Brazos, by virtue Cert. #359 issued by Board of Land Commissioners for Galveston Co. Mar 7 1851 - Beg. SW from cor. SAMUEL RIDDLE's 1920 ac. survey, in line of same - line of ROBT. W. CALDWELL's lower survey -
Surveyed May 27 1852 - JOHN PATRICK D.S.R.L.D
Chain Men: WM. SINCLAIR, JOHN SMITH

[26] Recorded Sep 25 1852 - B. J. CHAMBERS Dist Surv R.L.D.

"Trans R. L. D. p 424" [left margin]
Robertson Land Dist. TX - Surveyed for E VINY (?) WILSON 320 acs. by virtue of Headright Cert. # [blank] issued by the Board of Land Commissioners Robertson Co. a Duplicate from Gen. Land Off. # 2113/2114 dated Jun 26 1851 - Situate in Robertson Land Dist. on "Eastern Margin" Brazos Riv. about 15 mi. N. from Comanche Peak - Beg. on Bank of River as upper cor. JAMES CLAYTON 320 ac. survey.

[24]   Surv May 30 1852 - B. J. CHAMBERS, Dept. Surv. R. L. D.
Chain Men: NATHL. G. REER, JOHN SMITH
Recorded Mar 29 1853 - B. J. CHAMBERS, Dist. Surv. R. D.

5

[28]   "688" [beside page number - lined through]

"Trans R. L. D. p 689" [left margin]
Robertson Land Dist. - Surveyed 640 ac. for SAMUEL RIDDLE -
Situate in [blank] Co. on NE bank Brazos Riv. being quantity
entitled to by virtue Donation Warrant #270 issued by H. P.
BREWSTER, acting Adj. Genl. Mar 28 1851 - Beg. NW from NE cor.
MARY MILLSAPP 13 Labor survey
Surveyed: Sep 29 1851 - JOHN PATRICK, D. S. R. L. D.
Chain Men: IRA PROCTOR, JOHN SMITH

[29]   Recorded: Oct 14 1851 J. P. PHILPOTT, D. S.

"Trans R. L. D. p 705" [left margin]
Robertson Land Dist. TX - Surveyed 640 acs. for George GREENs
Donation Warrant #303 dated Jun 7 1851 in Robertson Dist. near
Brazos Riv. in Upper Cross Timbers - Beg. at SE of RICHD.
STARR 1/3 League survey in N. boundary of ROBT. EVANS -
Signed: B. J. CHAMBERS, Dept. Surveyor R. L. D. [no date]

[30]   Chain Men: JOHN B. BEULEU (?), NATHL. G. REER
Jun 9 1852 - CHAMBERS certifies foregoing "made" May 21 1852
Recorded Apr 16 1853 - B. J. CHAMBERS, Dept. Surveyor R. L. D.

"Trans R L D p 709" [left margin]
Robertson Land Dist. TX - Surveyed 640 acs. for WILLIAM LONG -
Situate on Patrick's Creek about [blank] mi. from Brazos Riv.
in Ellis Co. by virtue Cert. # [blank] issued by Board of Land
Commissioners for Galveston Co Jan 6 1846 - Beg. N cor. JAMES
CLAYTON's 640 ac. survey on SE boundary line of 960 ac. Leon
Co. School land survey -
Surveyed: May 28 1852 - JOHN PATRICK, D.S.R.L.D.
Chain Men: WM. SINCLAIR, JOHN SMITH
Recorded: Sep 25 1852 - B. J. CHAMBERS, Dist. Surv. R. L. D.

[32]   "Trans R L D p 712" [left margin]
Robertson Land Dist. TX - Surveyed 320 acs. for WILLIAM W.
PATRICK - Situate in Ellis Co. by virtue Cert. # [blank] is-
sued by Board of Land Commissioners of Robertson Co. Oct 2
1843 - Beg. upper cor. of upper survey of ROBT. W. CALDWELLs
4.166.666 sq. vs. on NE bank Brazos Riv. -
Surveyed: Oct 1 1851 - JOHN PATRICK, D. S. R. L. D
Chain Men: IRA PROCTOR, JOHN SMITH

[33]   Recorded: Dec 30 1852 - B. J. CHAMBERS, Dist. Surv. R.
L. D.

"Trans R L D p 713" [left margin]
Robertson Land Dist. TX - Surveyed 320 acs. for WM. MILLS
Junr. in Ellis Co. on NE Bank Brazos Riv. by virtue Cert #426
issued by Board Land Commissioners of Montgomery Co. - Beg. NW
& SW from NW cor. MARY MILLSAPPS 13 Labor survey -

[34]   Surveyed: May 29 1852 - JOHN PATRICK, D. S. R. L. D.
Chain Men: JOHN SMITH, WILLIAM SINCLAIR
Recorded: Dec 30 1852 - B. J. CHAMBERS, Dist. Surv. R. L. D.

[NOTE: The following was written in large letters across the bottom of this page and was crossed out]

"END OF SURVEYS MADE BEFORE THE PASSAGE OF THE 'PACIFIC RAILROAD RESERVATION' ACT SHOWN ON MAP NO. 2"

[35]   320 acre preemptions
"N.E. cor of J. H. MAYS's 320 ac survey is Situate 2483 vs S 64 1/2° W from the S.W.cor. of a 320 ac. survey in the name of WM. ADAMS" [left margin]

"trans   ?   B D 122" [left margin]

[NOTE: the next entry begins with an affidavit by a preemptionist and his statement is given verbatim]

State of Texas
Robertson Land District | I, JAMES H MAYS do Solemnly swear
                              that on or about the 14th day of
December 1853 I was on the Land I now claim as a preemptionor and I believe the same to be vacant and unappropriated this March 22nd 1854
                                        JAMES H. MAYS
Sworn to and subscribed before me.
                                        J. E. JENKINS
                                        Deputy Surveyor
                                        Robertson Land District

Robertson Land Dist. TX - Surveyed 320 acs. for JAMES H. MAYS of the Dist. of Tarrant lying on waters of Clear Fork of Trinity by virtue of his preemption claim - Beg. SW of WILLIAM ADAMS NW cor. -
Signed: J. E. JENKINS, Dept. Surveyor R. L. D. [no date]
Chain Carriers: JAMES COOK, THOMPSON MASON

[36]   Jun 15 1854 - J. E. JENKINS, Dept. Surv. R. L. D. swears foregoing survey "made by me on the date above mentioned"
Recorded: Oct 17 1855 - R. W. ALLEN, Dist. Surv. D.L.D. [sic]

"   ?   Book 2 p 130" [left margin]
Tarrant Co TX - WILLIAM J. MAYS swears he was on land now claimed on Dec 14 1853 - claims to be vacant & unappropriated - claims 320 acs by virtue preemption law
Signed: WILLIAM J. MYERS
Sworn to & subscribed before J. E. JENKINS, Dept. Surv. R. L. D. Mar 22 1854

[37]   Robertson Land Dist. TX - Survey for WILLIAM J. MAYSS of Dist. of Tarrant Co. 320 acs. lying on waters of Clear Fork of the Trinity by virtue his pre-emption claim - Beg. NE cor. JAMES H. MAYES 320 ac. survey
Signed: J. E. JENKINS, Dept. Surveyor R. L. D. [no date]
Chain Carriers: THOMPSON MASON, JAMES COOK
Jun 13 1854 - JENKINS swears foregoing survey made on "date above mentioned"
Recorded: Oct 27 1855 - R. W. ALLEN, Dist. Surveyor D. L. D.

[38]   Robertson Land Dist. TX - WILLIAM ADAMS   swears - on or about Dec 19 1853 -   settled on land now   claimed as preemptionist believe same to be vacant & unappropriated
Signed: WILLIAM "X" ADAMS
Sworn to & subscribed before J. E. JENKINS, Dept. Surveyor R. L. D. Aug [no day] 1854

"   ?   Bk D 126" [left margin]
Robertson Land Dist. TX - Survey for WILLIAM ADAMS in Dist. of Tarrant Co. 320 acs. lying on waters of Clear Fork of Trinity by virtue his preemption claim - Beg. W of NW cor. J. M. SOWELL 320 ac. survey -
Surveyed: Mar 16 1854 - J. E. JENKINS, Dept. Surv. Robertson Land Dist.
Chain Carriers: WILLIAM SEWELL, JOHN ADAMS

[39] Recorded: Oct 17 1855 - R. W. ALLEN, Dist. Surv. D.L.D.

"Surveys made before the passage of the 'Pacific Railroad Reservation'"

[NOTE: The following Plat is drawn beside the next 3 surveys]

30	31	32
27	26	25

"Trans R L D p 181" [left margin]
Robertson Land Dist. TX - Field notes of survey of 320 acs. by virtue Bounty Warrant #69 for 320 acs. issued from Adjutant General's Office of Texas Jun 3 1846 to PLEASANT MC ANNELLY - said survey is # 27 made by me on Silver Creek, a SW tributary of Trinity Riv. in Roberson Land Dist. - Beg. SW cor. Survey # 26 of 320 acs. in name of JAMES THOMPSON -

[40]   Surveyed Sep 14 1851 - RICHARD BEALL, Dept. Surveyor R. L. D.
Chain Men: JOSEPH DUNKIN (?), G. W. COTRELL
Recorded: Jan 28 1852

[41]   "Trans R L D p 184" [left margin]
Robertson Land Dist. TX - Field notes & survey of 320 ac. made

by virtue Bounty Land Warrant # 345 for 320 acs. issued from Adjutant General's Office Nov 23 1847 to F. B. TURNER - said survey is # 31 made by me on waters of Silver Creek, tributary of Trinity Riv. in Robertson Land Dist. - Beg. SE cor. Survey # 30 of 320 acs. in name of F. B. TURNER ass. of JOSEPH L. WALKER & NW cor. Survey # 26 of 320 acs. in name of JAS. THOMPSON

[42] Surveyed: Sept 15 1851 - RICHARD BEALL, Dept. Surveyor R. L. D.
Chain Men: JOSEPH JUNKIN, G. W. COTRELL
Recorded: Feb 10 1852 - J. P. PHILPOTT

Robertson Land Dist. TX - Field notes of survey of 320 acs. by virtue Bounty Warrant # 423 issued from Adj. General's Office Jun 10 1848 to F. B. TURNER ass. of JOSEPH L. WALKER. said survey is No. 30 made by me on Silver Creek a SW tributary of Trinity Riv. in Robertson Land Dist. - Beg. N of NE cor. Survey # 28 640 acs in name of JACOB WILCOX

[NOTE: End of this volume for Robertson Land District]

DENTON LAND OFFICE
1854 - 1855

[Page 1 - number torn off]

State of Texas | I, William [torn] do Solemnly swear
Denton Land District | [torn] or about the 1st day of
December 185[torn] I S[torn] upon
the Land I now claim as a preemptionist and b[torn] the same
to be vacant and unappropiated [sic]. And [torn] clame [sic]
the Same by virtue of the Donation Land this Dec 20th 1854
WILLIAM D. HARRISON
Sworn to and subscribed before me this Dec 20th 1854
J. E. JENKINS Dept Surveyor
Denton Land District

Denton Land Dist. TX - Dec 14 1854 - Survey for WILLIAM D. HARRISON of 160 acres of Land Lying on Walnut Creek [acreage & creek inserted in original] by virtue of [torn] his preemption claim. - Beg. at SW cor. of G. L. LEONARD 160 ac. Survey - pass H. R. LEONARD [torn] cor. - NE cor. J. L. LEONARDs -
Signed: J. E. JENKINS, Dept. Surv. D. L.
Chain Carriers: A. HARRIS, M. E. HARRIS
Recorded: Aug 18 1855 - R. W. ALLEN, De[torn] S. D. L. DIST.

[Page 2 - no page number]
[torn] Land Dist., TX - I, ACHILES MORRIS, do Solemnly Swear that on or about the 15th December 1854 I settled upon the Land I now claim as a preemptionist and believe the same to be vacant & unappropiated & claim the same by virt[torn] of the Donation Law this January 1st 1855
Signed: ACHILES MORRIS
Dated: Jan 15 1855 - J. C. JENKINS Dept Surv Denton Land Dist

Denton Land Dist. TX - Jan 15 1855 - Survey for ACHILES MORRIS 160 acs Land lying on Walnut Creek, waters of the Trinity, by virtue of his preemption Claim. Beg. N of NE cor. JOHN DUNKINS 160 ac survey - SW cor. W D HARRISONs - E line J. DUNKINS
Surveyed: by J. E. JENKINS, Dept. Surveyor Denton Land Dist.
Chain Carriers: M. E. HARRISON (?), M. R. MORRIS
[RE]corded: Aug 17 1855 - R. W. ALLEN, Dist. Surv. D. L. D.

[Page 3 - upper right corner torn off and missing. The page is in two pieces, torn diagonally and has a strip of yellowed tape across a previous tear]

Denton Land Dist TX - JAMES PEIRCE swears on or about Nov 1 1854 settled on land now claimed as app[torn] & believes same to be vacant & unappropriated and [torn] the same by virtue of the Donation Law this January 2[torn] 1855
Signed: JAMES PEIRCE
Dated: Jan 2 1855 - J. E. JENKINS, Dept. Surv. D. L. D.

Denton Land Dist TX - Survey for JAMES PEIRCE for 160 ac on waters of Ash Creek, waters of the Trin[covered with tape] Riv. by virtue of his preemption claim - Beg. N of W. H. BAYLOR's - DE__ THERILL, M. A. REYNOLDS - NW cor. W. H. BAYLEY
Chain Carriers: WILLIAM BAYLEY, WILLIAM BURROW (?)
Jan 2 18[torn] - J. E. JENKINS swears survey made on date stated

[Page 4 - upper left corner torn]
Recorded: Jul 27 1855 - R. W. ALLEN, Dist. Surv. Denton Land Dist.

Denton Land Dist. TX - JOSEPH RASH appears before LEWELLEN MURPHY, Dept. Surveyor Denton Land Dist. - took oath - believe land settled on is vacant Public domain
Signed: JOSEPH RASH
Dated: Feb 27 1855 - LEWELLEN MURPHY

Denton Land Dist. TX - Survey of [torn] hundred & sixty ac. for JOSEPH RASH by virtue of foregoing affidavit - Situate in Tarrant Co. Territory - waters of Ash Creek, tributary of the West Fork of the Trinity Riv. - Beg. N of NE cor JESSE R. CLIFTON Preemption survey -

[NOTE: bottom of page torn]

[NOTE: Page numbers begin]

[22] Mar 28 1855 - LEWELLEN MURPHY declares foregoing survey made by him Feb 27 1855
Recorded: May 15 1855 - R. W. ALLEN, Dist. Surv. D. L. Dist.

Denton Land Dist. TX - JOHN G. REYNOLD appeared before LEWELLEN MURPHY, Dept. Sur. of Denton Land Dist. - took oath - believe land settled on to be vacant Public domain
Signed: JOHN G. REYNOLDS
Dated: Mar 1 1855 - LEWELLEN MURPHY

Denton Land Dist. TX - Survey of 160 acs for JOHN G. REYNOLD by virtue foregoing affidavit - Situate in Tarrant Co. Territory on waters of Ash Creek, tributary of West Fork of Trinity Riv. - Beg. S [torn] preemption survey CHRISTOP[torn]

[23] Surveyed: Mar 1 1855 - LEWELLEN MURPHY
Chain Carriers: JAMES HAZARD, G. (?) B. MASSEGEE (?)

[NOTE: Bottom of page torn]

[NOTE: Pages missing or misnumbered]

[28] Surveyed: Feb 27th 1855 - LEWELLEN MURPHY
Chain Carriers: WILLIAM D. CAL___Y, CHRISTOPHER BEDWELL

Denton Land Dist. TX - WILLIAM F. FLETCHER appeared before LEWELLEN MURPHY, Dept. Surv. Denton Land Dist. - took oath - believe land settled on to be vacant Public domain
Signed: WILLIAM F. "X" FLETCHER [his mark]
Dated: Feb 29 [sic] 185_5_ - LEWELLEN MURPHY

Denton Land Dist. TX - Survey of 160 acs made for WILLIAM F. [or "K"] FLETCHER by virtue foregoing affidavit - Situate in Tarrant Co. Territory on Ash Creek, tributary of West Fork Trinity Riv.- Beg. E [torn] W cor. JOSEPH RASHEs preemption survey -

[29] Surveyed: Feb 27 1855
Chain Carriers: WILLIAM D. CALLAWAY, CHRISTOPHER BEDWELL
Mar 28 1855 - LEWELLEN MURPHY swears to foregoing survey

Denton Land Dist. TX - ROBERT WRIGHT swears that on or about Aug 24 1854 settled upon land now claimed as a preemptionist - believe same to be vacant & unappropriated & claim same by virtue of Donation Law this Jan 13 1855
Signed: ROBERT WRIGHT
Dated: Jan 15 1855 J. E. JENKINS, Dept Surv Denton Land Dist

[30] "C 166" [left margin]
Denton Land Dist. TX - Jan 12 1855 - Survey made for ROBERT WRIGHT for 160 acs lying on [illegible] Creek, waters of Trinity Riv. by virtue of preemption claim - Beg. W & N of NW cor. D. C. CENTO (?) 160 ac survey & S of NW cor. S. WRIGHT 160 ac. survey -
Chain Carriers: C. GILDAN, JAMES ALMON
Jun 12 1855 - J. E. JENKINS swears to above
Recorded: Aug 18 1855 - R. W. ALLEN Dist Surv Denton Land Dist

Denton Land Dist. TX - ROBERT J. BILLINGSLEY appeared before LEWELLEN MURPHY, Dept. Surveyor Denton Land Dist. - believe land settled on to be vacant Public domain & "I am" citizen of this state at date of present preemption law

[31] Signed: ROBERT J. BILLINGSLEY
Sworn to & subscribed May 2 1855 before LEWELLEN MURPHY

Denton Land Dist. TX - Field notes of survey of 160 acs. made for ROBERT BILLINGSLEY by virtue of foregoing affidavit - Situate in Tarrant Co. Territory on Walnut Creek, tributary of W Fork of Trinity River - Beg. NW of NW cor JAMES WIMBLY 160 ac preemption survey -
Surveyed: Jul 20 1855 - LEWELLEN MURPHY
Chain Carriers: WILLIAM HALL, HOWARD HAYES

[32] Recorded: Aug 9 1856 - R. W. ALLEN Dist Surv Denton Land Dist

Denton Land Dist. TX - EDWARD LANG [or LONG] appeared before LEWELLEN MURPHY, Dept. Surveyor Denton Land Dist. - took oath - believe land settled to be vacant Public domain - was citizen of this state at time of enactment of present preemption Law.
Signed: EDWARD "X" LONG [his mark]
Dated: Apr 26 1855 - LEWELLEN MURPHY

Denton Land Dist. TX - Survey of 160 acs made for EDWARD LANG by virtue of foregoing affidavit - Situate in Tarrant Co. Territory on waters of Silver Creek, tributary of W Fork Trinity Riv. - Beg. N of SW cor. Momucan HUNT 160 acs Survey No. 29

[33] Surveyed: Apr 26 1855 - LEWELLEN MURPHY
Chain Carriers: JOHN J. JOHNSON, JAMES P. JOHNSON
Recorded: Jul 24 1855

Denton Land Dist. TX - WILLIAM D. CALAWAY appeared before LEWELLEN MURPHY, Dept. Surveyor Denton Land Dist. - took oath - believe land settled on to be vacant Public domain
Signed: WILLIAM D. CALAWAY
Sworn to & subscribed Feb 27 1855 before LEWELLEN MURPHY

[34] Territory of Tarrant, Denton Land Dist. TX - Survey of 160 acs. made for WILLIAM D. CALAWAY by virtue of foregoing affidavit - Situate in Tarrant Co. Territory on waters of Ash Creek, tributary of West Fork of Trinity Riv. - Beg. S from SW cor. CHRISTOPHER BEDWELL 160 ac. preemption survey -
Surveyed: Feb 28 1855 - LEWELLEN MURPHY
Chain Carriers: WILLIAM K. FLETCHER, CHRISTOPHER BEDWELL
Recorded: Jun 30 1855 - R. W. ALLEN, Dist. Surv. Denton Land Dist

[35] Denton Land Dist. TX - JOHN MC CLERRAN appeared before CHAS. C. LACY, Dept. Surveyor Denton Land Dist. - took oath - believe land settled on is vacant & "I am entitled to same by virtue of an Act of the Legislature of the State of Texas ap- proved Feb 13 1854 Donating to actual settlers 160 acs of land"
Signed: JOHN "X" McCLERRIN [his mark]
Dated: Oct 17 1855 - CHAS. C. LACY

Tarrant Territory, Dist. of Denton, TX - Field notes of survey of 160 acs for JOHN MC CLERRAN by virtue of "this" affidavit No. 53 dated Nov 17 1855 - Situate in Territory of Tarrant on Briny Branch, tributary of Trinity Riv. - about 20 1/2 mi. N 51° W from Birdwell - Beg. at SE cor. J. MATTHEWS survey -
Surveyed: Oct 17 1855 - CHAS. C. LACY
Chain Carriers: B. ?. MATTHEWS, J. M. YOUNG

[36] Sep 11 1855 [sic] R. W. ALLEN, Dist. Surv. for Denton Land Dist., certifies he has examined foregoing & find them

correct & they are recorded in "my office" in Alton correctly in Book G page 4

Territory of Tarrant, Dist. of Denton, TX - ARTETIOUS O. MILLER appeared before CHAS. C. LACY, Dept. Surveyor "in & for the Land Dist." - took oath - believe land settled on is vacant - entitled to same by virtue of Act of the legislature of State of TX approved Feb 13 1855 Donating to actual Settlers 160 acs.
Signed: ARTETIOUS O. MILLER
Dated: Nov 19 1855 - CHAS. C. LACY

Territory of Tarrant, Dist. of Denton TX - Field notes of survey of 160 acs. made for ARTETIOUS O. MILLER by virtue of affidavit No. 56 taken Nov 19 [no year] - Situate in Territory of Tarrant on waters Brieny Creek, tributary of Trinity Riv. -

[37] about 21 1/2 mi N 52° W from Birdwell - Beg. S of NW cor. Z. G. MATTHEWS to SW cor. of same - NW cor. JOHN MC CLERRAN - SE cor. M. L. JOHNSON -
Surveyed: Nov 19 1855 - CHAS. C. LACY
Chain Carriers: RICHARD H. MATTHEWS, Z. G. MATTHEWS
Sep 11 1856 - CHAS. C. LACY, Dist. Surv. Denton Land Dist., certifies foregoing correctly recorded "my office" in Alton Bk. G, p. 8

[38] "J 12 & 13" [left margin]
Denton Land Dist. TX - JOHN T. PASCHALL appeared before CHAS. C. LACY, Dept. Surveyor Denton Land Dist. - took oath - believe land settled on is vacant - am entitled to same by virtue of Act of Legislature of the State of TX approved Feb 13 1854 Donating to Actual Settlers 160 acs land
Signed: JOHN T. PASCHALL
Sworn to & subscribed Sep 24 1855 before CHAS. C. LACY

Territory of Tarrant, Dist. of Denton, TX - No. 31 - Field notes of 160 ac. survey made for JOH [sic] T. PASCHALL by virtue of affidavit # 31 dated Sep 24 1855 - Situate in Territory of Tarrant on headwaters Ash Creek, tributary of Trinity Riv. about 26 mi. N 57° W from Town of Birdville [lined through] Ft. Worth - Beg. SE cor. REIGHNEY (?) L. FRANCIS - SW cor. JOHN FRANCIS survey - NW cor. SAMUEL WOODY Survey - S line R. L. FRANCIS -
"Made" Sep 24 1855 - CHAS. C. LACY
Chain Carriers: J. C. PASCHALL, R. T. PASCHALL

[39] "G 30" [left margin]
Sep 12 1856 - CHAS. C. LACY, Dist. Surv. Denton Land Dist., certifies he has examined foregoing & finds correct as recorded in office in Alton Book G pp 12 & 13

Territory of Tarrant, Dist. of Denton, TX - RICHARD H.

MATTHEWS appeared before CHAS. C. LACY, Dept. Surveyor Denton. Land Dist. took oath - believe land settled on is vacant & am entitled to same by virtue of Act of the Legislature of State of TX approved Feb 13 1854 donating to actual settlers 160 acs. land
Signed: RICHARD H. MATTHEWS
Sworn to & subscribed Nov 17 1855 before CHAS. C. LACY

[40] Territory of Tarrant, Dist. of Denton, TX - Field notes of survey of 160 acs. made for RICHARD H. MATTHEWS by virtue affidavit # 52 dated Nov 17 1855 - Situate in Territory of Tarrant on Brieny Branch, tributary of Trinity Riv. about 20 mi. N 51° W from Birdville - Beg. E of SW cor. JOSEPH M. YOUNG
Surveyed Nov 17 1855 - CHAS. C. LACY
Chain Carriers: JOHN MC CLERRAN, ARTITIOUS O. MILLER
Recorded: Sep 16 [no year] CHAS. C. LACY, Dist. Surv. Denton Land Dist.

"D.328" [left margin]
Denton Land Dist. TX -J. G. [or "H"] TATE appeared before ISAAC O. HEADLEY, Dept. Surveyor Denton Land Dist. - took oath - believe land settled on is vacant & said settlement made on or about 11th Jun 1855
Signed: J. G. [or "H"] TATE
Sworn to & subscribed Nov 16 1855 - ISAAC O. HEADLEY

[41] Denton Land Dist. TX - Plat & field notes of survey made for J. H. TATE "children" [inserted below TATE's name] - Situate in Tarrant Co. in the upper Crosstimbers - Beg. ? from SE cor. ISAAC TEETER 160 ac. survey
Surveyed: Nov 16 1855 - ISAAC O. HEADLEY
Chain Carriers: WILLIAM C. MC ADAMS, J. A. STEPHENS
Recorded: Mar 20 1856 - R. W. ALLEN, Dist. Surv. Denton Land Dist.

"D320" [left margin]
Denton Land Dist. TX - J. S. STEPHENS appeared before ISAAC O. HEADLEY, Dept. Surveyor Denton Land Dist - took oath - believe land settled on is vacant & said settlement made on or about Oct 1 1855
Signed: J. S. STEPHENS
Sworn to & subscribed Nov 16 1855 before ISAAC O. HEADLEY

[42] Denton Land Dist. TX - Plat & field notes of survey made for J. S. STEPHENS by virtue his affidavit - Situate in Tarrant Co. in upper Crosstimbers - Beg. NW from SW cor W. C. MC ADAMS 160 ac. survey -
Surveyed: Nov 13 1855 - ISAAC O. HEADLEY
Chain Carriers: WM. C. MC ADAMS, G. (?) C. F__CHER
Recorded: Mar 20 1856 - R. W. ALLEN, Dist. Surv. Denton Land Dist.

"D 293" [left margin]
Denton Land Dist. TX - WILLIAM UPTON appeared before LEWELLEN MURPHY, Dept. Surveyor Denton Land Dist. - took oath - believe land settled on to be vacant Public domain - settled on said land [on or about] 10th day Dec 1855 - was citizen of State of TX at date of enactment of present pre-emption Law

[next page - no number]
Signed: WILLIAM UPTON
Sworn to & subscribed Dec 17 1855 before LEWELLEN MURPHY

Denton Land Dist. TX - Field notes of 160 ac. survey for WILLIAM UPTON by virtue foregoing affidavit - Situate in Denton Land Dist. Tarrant Co. Territory on waters of Brazos Riv. - Beg. NE from NE cor Pleasant H. MAG_ORS 160 ac pre-emption survey -
Surveyed: Dec 19 1855 - LEWELLEN MURPHY
Chain Carriers: JAMES M. UPTON, Pleasant H. MAGERS
Recorded: Mar [no day] 1856 - R. W. ALLEN, Dist. Surv. Denton Land Dist.

[44] Denton Land Dist. TX - H. "YRAM" [inserted above] PINNELL appeared before ISAAC O. HEADLEY, Dept. Surv. Denton Land Dist. - took oath - believe land settled on is vacant & said settlement made on or about Aug 20 1854
Signed: H. PINNELL
Sworn to & subscribed Nov 7 1854 before ISAAC O. HEADLEY

Denton Land Dist. TX - Plat & Field notes of 160 ac. survey made for HYRAM PINNELL by virtue of above affidavit - Situate in Tarrant Co. at head of Grindstone Creek, tributary of Brazos Riv. - Beg. NW from SW cor. JOHN SHEEN 320 ac. survey -
Surveyed: Nov 7 1854 - ISAAC O. HEADLEY
Chain Carriers: ISAAC LYNN, PETER LYNN
Recorded: [torn] A. D. 1856 - R. W. ALLEN, Dist. Surv. Denton Land Dist.

Denton Land Dist. TX - PETER MEDLAN * appeared before LEWELLEN MURPHY, Dept Surveyor Denton Land Dist. - took oath - believe land settled on to be vacant Public domain - settled on said land as a preemptionist on 3rd day Aug 1855 - was citizen of the State at date of enactment of present preemption Law
Signed: PETER MEDLAN
Sworn to & subscribed Nov 19 1855 before LEWELLEN MURPHY

[* 1st letter looks like an "M", maybe "W" - see next entry]

Denton Land Dist. TX - Field notes of survey of 160 acs. in name of PETER WALDON by virtue foregoing affidavit - Situate in Denton Land Dist. waters of Grindstone Creek, tributary of Brazos Riv - Beg. NW from NW cor. Silas BARNS 160 ac. pre-emption survey

[46]   [no survey date]
Chain Carriers: SILAS BARNS, NOAH S. BARNS
Recorded: Nov 30 1855 - R. W. ALLEN, Dist. Surv.   Denton Land Dist.

"p 119" [left margin]
Denton Land Dist. TX - SILAS BARNS appeared before LEWELLEN MURPHY, Dept. Surveyor Denton Land Dist - took oath - believe land settled on to be vacant Public domain - settled on said land on Nov 7 1854 - was citizen of the state at date of enactment of present preemption Law
Signed: S. BARNS
Sworn to & subscribed Sep 14 1855 before LEWELLEN MURPHY

Denton Land Dist. TX - Field notes of survey of 160 acs. in name of SILAS BARNES by virtue foregoing affidavit - Situate in Denton Land Dist. waters of Grindstone Creek, tributary of Brazos Riv. - Beg. N of NE cor. -

[47]   PERRY M. BARNS 160 ac. preemption survey -
Surveyed: Sep 14 1855 - LEWELLEN MURPHY
Chain Carriers: CANUMEL (?) LARIMORE, PERRY M. BARNES
Recorded: Oct 17 1855 - R. W. ALLEN, Dist. Surv. Denton Land Dist.

"p. 141" [left margin]
Denton Land Dist. TX - J. B. MITCHEL appeared before ISAAC O. HEADLEY, Dept. Surveyor Denton Land Dist. - took oath - believe land settled on is vacant - said settlement made on or about Oct 5 1854
Signed: JOHN B. MITCHEL[torn]

[48]   Sworn to & subscribed Oct 21 1854 before ISAAC O. HEADLEY

Denton Land Dist. TX - Field Notes of 160 ac. survey made for JOHN R. MITCHELL by virtue of his affidavit - Situate in Tarrant Co. on south prong Clear Fork of Trinity Riv - Beg. at SW cor. JAMES H. MAYS 320 ac. survey -
Surveyed: Oct 21 1854 - ISAAC O. HEADLEY
Chain Carriers: PETER LYNN, JOHN E. FALDER
Recorded: Oct 31 1855 - R. W. ALLEN, Dist. Surv. Denton Land Dist.

[49]   "p 151" [left margin]
Denton Land Dist. TX - LEWIS WHITE appeared before ISAAC O. HEADLEY, Dept. Surveyor Denton Land Dist. - took oath - believe land settled on is vacant - settled upon same on or about Dec 2 1854
Signed: LEWIS WHITE
Sworn to & subscribed Aug 31 1855 before ISAAC O. HEADLEY

Denton Land Dist. TX - Plat & field notes of survey of 160 acs. for LEWIS WHITE by virtue of above affidavit - Situate in Tarrant Co. on waters of Brazos Riv. - Beg. SW from SW cor JAMES KIDWELL [or "BIDWELL"] 160 ac survey -
Surveyed: Aug 30 1855 by ISAAC O. HEADLEY
Chain Carriers: STEPHEN BEDWELL, PRESTON WHITE
Recorded: Oct 31 1855 - R. W. ALLEN Dist. Surv. Denton Land Dist.

[50] "p. 268" [left margin]
Denton Land Dist. TX - JAMES WHITE appeared before LEWELLEN MURPHY, Dept. Surveyor Denton Land Dist. - took oath - believe land settled on to be vacant Public domain - settled on said land as a preemptionist on Oct 12 1855 - was citizen of state at enactment of present preemption Law
Signed: JAMES "X" WHITE [his mark]
Sworn to & subscribed Nov 13 1855 before LEWELLEN MURPHY

Denton Land Dist. TX - Field notes of survey of 160 acs. in name of JAMES WHITE by virtue of foregoing affidavit - Situate in Tarrant Co. Territory on waters of Ash Creek, tributary of W Fork of Trinity Riv. - Beg. E of SW cor. WILLIAM THOMAS REYNOLDS 320 ac. preemption survey & S boundary line of said survey -
Surveyed: Nov 18 1855 - LEWELLEN MURPHY
Chain Carriers: JAMES WOODY, THOMAS GULKER

[51] Recorded: Mar 3 1856 - R. W. ALLEN, Dist. Surv. Denton Land Dist.

"p. 148" [left margin]
Denton Land Dist. TX - ELIZABETH DOSS appeared before LEWELLEN MURPHY, Dept. Surveyor Denton Land Dist. - took oath - believe land settled on to be vacant Public domain - settled said land as pre-emptionist on or about Jan 8 1856 - was citizen of state at date of enactment of present preemption Law
Signed: ELIZABETH DOSS
Sworn to & subscribed Jan 8 1856 before LEWELLEN MURPHY

Denton Land Dist. TX - Field notes of survey of 160 acs. in name of ELIZABETH DOSS by virtue foregoing affidavit - Situate in Denton Land Dist. in Tarrant Co. Territory on waters of Grindstone Creek, tributary of Brazos Riv. - Beg. SE cor. ROBERT S. POTER 160 ac. preemption survey -

[52] NE cor. JOSEPH REEVES preemption - S to cor. in JOSEPH REEVES E boundary line - E boundary line of ROBERT S. POTERs preemption -
Surveyed: Jan 8 1856 by LEWELLEN MURPHY
Chain Carriers: ALFORD J. DYCHE, WILLIAM P. WISON
Recorded: March 3 1856 - R. W. ALLEN, Dist. Surv. Denton Land Dist.

"p. 255" [left margin]
Denton Land Dist. TX - JOHN F. POTER appeared before LEWELLEN MURPHY, Dept. Surveyor Denton Land Dist. - took oath - believe land settled on to be vacant Public domain - settled on said land as preemptionist on or about Dec 20 1855 - was citizen of state at date of enactment of present preemption Law
Signed: JOHN F. POTER

[53] Sworn to & subscribed Jan 2 1856 before LEWELLEN MURPHY

Denton Land Dist. TX - Field notes of survey of 160 acs. in name of JOHN F. POTER by virtue of foregoing affidavit - Situate in Denton Land Dist. in Tarrant Co. Territory on waters of Grind- stone Creek, tributary of Brazos Riv. - Beg. E of NE cor. JOHN C. HIGHTOWER preemption survey -
Surveyed: Jan 2 1855 by Lewlellen MURPHY
Chain Carriers: THOMAS M. CLGTON (?), JOHN C. HIGHTOWER
Recorded: Mar 3 1856 - R. W. ALLEN, Dist. Surv. Denton Land Dist.

[54] "p. 157" [left margin]
Denton Land Dist. TX - JOHN HITTSON appeared before LEWELLEN MURPHY, Dept. Surveyor Denton Land Dist. - took oath - believe land settled on to be vacant Public domain - settled as preemptionist on or about Oct 7 1855 - was citizen of state at enactment of present preemption Law
Signed: JOHN HITTSON
Sworn to & subscribed Nov 17 1855 before LEWELLEN MURPHY

Denton Land Dist. TX - Field notes of survey of 160 acs. in name of JOHN HITTSON by virtue foregoing affidavit - Situate in Denton Land Dist. in Tarrant Co. Territory waters of Grindstone Creek, tributary of Brazos Riv. - Beg. NW cor. ALFORD J. DYET (?) 160 ac. preemption survey - SW cor. A. J. DYER's preemption

[55] W boundary line A. J. DYEKE (?) preemption -
Surveyed: Nov 17 1855 by LEWELLEN MURPHY
Chain Carriers: BENJAMIN JOHNSON, JAMES DULENS
Recorded: Mar 3 1856 - R. W. ALLEN, Dist. Surv. Denton Land Dist.

"p. 251" [left margin]
Denton Land Dist. TX - CHRISTOPHER C. POTER appeared before LEWELLEN MURPHY, Dept. Surveyor Denton Land Dist. - took oath - believe land settled on to be vacant Public domain - settled as preemptionist on or about Nov 4 1855 - was citizen of state at date of present preemption Law
Signed: CHRISTOPHER C. POTER
Sworn to & subscribed Nov 21 1855 before LEWELLEN MURPHY

Denton Land Dist. TX - Field notes of survey of 160 acs. in

name of CHRISTOPHER C. POTER by virtue of foregoing affidavit - Situate in Denton Land Dist in -

[56] Tarrant Co Territory waters of Grindstone Creek, tributary stream of Brazos Riv. - Beg. N of NW cor WILLIAM C. BAKER 160 ac preemption survey -
Surveyed: Nov 21 1855 by LEWELLEN MURPHY
Chain Carriers: JOHN C. HIGHTOWER, JOHN F. POTER
Recorded: Mar 3 1856 - R. W. ALLEN, Dist. Surv. Denton Land Dist.

"p. 251" [left margin]
Denton Land Dist. TX - WILLIAM C. BAKER appeared before LEWELLEN MURPHY, Dept. Surveyor Denton Land Dist. - took oath - believe land settled on to be vacant Public domain - settled on said land Dec 10 1854 - was citizen of state at enactment present preemption Law

[57] Signed: WILLIAM C. BAKER
Sworn to & subscribed Aug 21 1855 before LEWELLEN MURPHY

Denton Land Dist. TX - Field notes of survey of 160 acs. made for WILLIAM C. BAKER by virtue foregoing affidavit - Situate in Denton Land Dist. on waters of Brazos Riv. - Beg. NW from NW cor. ROBERT P. BAKER 160 ac. preemption survey -
Surveyed: Aug 22 1855 by LEWELLEN MURPHY
Chain Carriers: ASHLY N. DENTON, MONROE UPTON
Recorded: Oct 17 1855 - R. W. ALLEN, Dist. Surv. Denton Land Dist.

[58] "p. 242" [left margin]
283 [top line of page]

Denton Land Dist. TX - MONROE UPTON appeared before LEWELLEN MURPHY, Dept. Surveyor Denton Land Dist. - took oath - believe land settled on to be vacant Public domain - settled as preemptionist on or about last day March 1855 - was citizen of state at enactment present preemption Law
Signed: MONROE UPTON
Sworn to & subscribed Dec 14 1855 before LEWELLEN MURPHY

Denton Land Dist. TX - Field Notes of survey of 160 acs. in name of MONROE UPTON by virtue of foregoing affidavit - Situate in Denton Land District in Tarrant Co. Territory waters of Brazos Riv. - Beg. NW from NW cor. R. P. BAKER preemption survey -

[59] Surveyed: Dec 14 1855 - LEWELLEN MURPHY
Chain Carriers: MILTON IKARD, JOSEPH H. HEWITT
Recorded: Mar 3 1856 - R. W. ALLEN, Dist. Surv. Denton Land Dist.

"p. 266" [left margin]
Denton Land Dist. TX - JOSEPH H. HEWITT appeared before LEWELLEN MURPHY, Dept. Surveyor Denton Land Dist. - took oath - believe land settled on to be vacant Public domain - settled as pre- emptionist on or about Aug 12 1855 - was citizen of state at enactment present preemption Law
Signed: JOSEPH H. HEWITT
Sworn to & subscribed Dec 14 1855 before Lewelen MURPHY

[60]   Denton Land Dist. TX - Field notes of survey of 160 acs. in name of JOSEPH H. HEWITT by virtue of foregoing affadavit - Situate Denton Land Dist. in Tarrant Co. Territory on waters of Brazos Riv. - Beg. W Boundary line of ROBERT P. BAKER 160 ac. preemption survey & N of SW cor. of said survey
Surveyed: Dec 14 1855 by LEWELLEN MURPHY
Chain Carriers: MONROE UPTON, MILTON IKARD

[61] Recorded: Mar 3 1856 - R. W. ALLEN, Dist. Surv. Denton Land Dist.

"p. 115" [left margin]
Denton Land Dist. TX - ROBERT P. BAKER appeared before LEWELLEN MURPHY, Dept. Surveyor Denton Land Dist. - took oath - believe land settled on to be vacant Public domain - settled on Dec 12 1855 - was citizen of state at enactment present preemption Law
Signed: ROBERT P. BAKER
Sworn to & subscribed Aug 21 1855 [sic] before LEWELLEN MURPHY

Denton Land Dist. TX - Field notes of survey of 160 acs. for ROBERT P. BAKER by virtue foregoing affidavit - Situate Denton Land Dist. on waters of Brazos Riv. - Beg. NW from N cor. of survey of 960 acs. made & denominated for Leon Co. School Land

[62]   Surveyed Aug 21 1855 - LEWELLEN MURPHY
Chain Carriers: ASHLEY N. DENTON, WILLIAM C. BAKER
Recorded: Oct 17 1855 - R. W. ALLEN, Dist. Surv. Denton Land Dist.

[NOTE THE CHANGE IN LAND DISTRICT NEXT ENTRY]

"p. 26" [left margin]
The State of Texas
Robertson Land District | I, RICHARD C. EDDLEMAN do Solemnly swear that on or about the 14TH ["1" lined through] day of December 1854 I settled upon the land I now claim as a preemptionist and believe the same to be vacant and unappropriated this February 13th 1854
RICHARD C. EDDLEMAN
Sworn to and subscribed before me this May 10th 1854 - J. E. JENKINS, Dept. Surveyor Robertson Land District

The State of Texas | February 13th 1854
County of Tarrant | Survey for RICHARD C. EDDLEMAN
320 acres of land lying on the waters of Clear Fork of Trinity River by virtue of his preemption claim - Beg. S of NW cor. A. B. (?) SMITH - E boundary line J. W. SPEARMAN -
Chain Carriers: L. B. LEDBETTER, JOHN G. REY
Signed: J. E. JENKINS, Dept. Surv., R. L. DIST [sic]

[NOTE THE NEXT ENTRIES ARE FOR DENTON LAND DISTRICT AGAIN]

[63] "B. G. P 30" [left margin]
Territory of Tarrant, Dist. of Denton, TX - RICHARD H. MATTHEWS appeared before CHAS. C. LACY, Dept. Surveyor Denton Land Dist. took oath - believe land settled vacant - am entitled to same by virtue of Act of the Legislature of State of TX approved Feb 13 1854 donating to actual settlers 160 ac. land
Signed: [no signature shown]
Sworn to & subscribed Nov 17 1855 before CHAS. C. LACY

Territory of Tarrant, Dist. of Denton, TX - Field notes of survey of 160 acs. made for RICHARD H. MATTHEWS by virtue affidavit # 52 dated Nov 17 1855 - Situate in Territory of Tarrant on Brieny Branch, tributary Trinity Riv. about 20 mi. N 51° W from Birdville - Beg. E of SW cor. JOSEPH M. YOUNG -

[64] Surveyed: Nov 17 1855
Chain Carriers: JOHN MC CLAREN, ARTITIOUS O. MILLER
CHAS. C. LACY, Dept. Surveyor Denton Land Dist., certifies foregoing survey "made by me" on date mentioned

Recorded: Sep 16 [no year] - CHAS. C. LACY, Dist. Surv. Denton Land Dist

[65] J. E. JENKINS Solemnly swears survey designated by foregoing "made by me" on date above written - Jun 12 1854 - J. E. JENKINS, Dept. Surveyor of R. L. DIST
Recorded: Aug 24 1855 - R. W. ALLEN

"p 158" [left margin]
Denton Land Dist. TX - STEPHEN TRIMBLE appeared before ISAAC O. HEADLEY, Dept. Surveyor Denton Land Dist. - took oath - believe land settled on is vacant - settlement made on or about Nov 15 1854
Signed: STEPHEN TRIMBLE
Sworn to & subscribed Sep 14 1855 before ISAAC O. HEADLEY

Denton Land Dist. TX - Plat & field notes of survey of 160 acs. made for STEPHEN TRIMBLE by virtue his affidavit - Situate in Tarrant Co. on Clear Fork Trinity Riv. - Beg. SW from S(?)E cor. WM. TRIMBLE 160 ac. survey -

[66]   Surveyed: Sept 14 1855 - ISAAC O. HEADLEY
Chain Carriers: JOHN TRIMBLE, JOSEPH TRIMBLE
Recorded: Oct 31 1855 - R. W. ALLEN, Dist. Surv. Denton Land Dist.

"Bo. B. P. 50" [left margin]
Denton Land Dist. TX - ISAAC BRISCO appeared   before LEWELLEN MURPHY, Dept. Surveyor Denton Land Dist - took   oath - believe land settled on is vacant Public domain
Signed: ISAAC "X" BRISCO [his mark]
Sworn to & subscribed Mar 6 1855 before LEWELLEN MURPHY

[67]   Denton Land Dist. TX - survey of 160 ac. for ISAAC BRISCO by virtue foregoing affidavit in Tarrant Co. Territory on dividing   ridge (?)   between   (?) Clear   and West Fork of Trinity Riv. - Beg. SW from SW cor. JOHN H. W. NEWLY 160 ac. preemption survey
Surveyed: Mar 6 185<u>6</u> [ink blot - but looks like "6"] by LEWELLEN MURPHY
Chain Carriers: EDWARD M. HARRIS, THOMAS J. WAUGH (?)

[68]   Recorded May 12 1855

State of Texas
Denton Land District   I, CHAS. C. LACY, District Survey-
                           or of Denton Land Dist., do hereby certify that the foregoing 49. pages from 19 to 68 inclusive is a true and correct coppy [sic] of the original Record of Surveys of my office
                Given under my Hand at Alton this the 21st
                day of March 1857
                    CHAS. C. LACY District
                    Surveyor of Denton Land District

State of Texas
County of Denton   I, A. P. LLOYD, Clerk of the
                        County Court of Denton County, Texas, hereby certify that I have assisted in Examining the foregoing Transcript and   believe the Same to be a Correct & true Copy from the Original Records in the   Office of the Dis- trict Surveyor of the Denton Land District at Alton of the Surveys herein Described
                Given under my hand and Seal of Office at
                Alton March 21st 1857
                    A. P. LLOYD Clerk
                    County Court D. Co. T [sic]

PRE-EMPTION RECORD "B"
DENTON LAND DISTRICT
1855

[NOTE: The first sheet is a cover page for book with "BOOK B" written across the top. The second sheet is torn in half with the bottom half missing]

Transcript Book B
83 Pages

AUSBURN, JAS. A	41	INMAN, J. M.		[torn]
		INMAN, HENRY		[torn]
BROWN, ELI	66			
BAWCOM, G. W.	29	JAMESON, JOHN		[torn]
BURROWS, ISRAEL	5	JONES G. B.		[torn]
		JOHNSON, JAMES		[torn]
COFFEY, WM.	74			
CAMPBELL, J. R.	77	KIDWELL, STEPH	[torn]	
COPELAND, WM.	69	KING, W. D.	[torn]	
COZART, W. N.	58	KING, W. S	[torn]	
COFFMAN, J. P.	[torn]			
CROP, REBECCA	[torn]			
CROP, J. H.	[torn]			
CHILDERS	[torn]			

[Back side of torn sheet]

ROBBINS, JOHN	39
ROWLAND, P.	42
RIGHTMER, E.	46
RASH, JNO. N.	75

SHIRLEY, Z. P.	64
SILLIVANT, WM	67
SPARKS, WM	57
SISK, D. H.	37
SHAW, T. J.	10
SPROULS, JAMES	24
SANCHES, F.	15
SKIDMORE, L. D.	11
SHIRLEY, W. V. D.	65

[NOTE: THIS SIDE BLANK]

TUBB, W. M. T.	50
TRIMBLE, JOHN	62
[Torn]MBLE, JOSEPH	63
[Torn]BLE, W.	83
[Torn]	27

[next page - No. torn off]

24

The State of Texas
Denton Land District | Personally appeared before me
LEWELLEN MURPHY Dept. Surveyor of
Denton Land District ROBERT S. PORTER who took and Subscribed the following oath "to wit" I do Solemnly Swear that I believe the Land on which I am Settled to be vacant Public Domain and that I Settled on said land on the 20th day of December A. D. 1854 and moreover that I was a citizen of this State at the date of the Enactment of the present preemption Law. So help Me God   Signed: R. S. PORTER
Sworn to and Subscribed Aug 17 1855 - LEWELLEN MURPHY   Dept. Surv. D. L. Dist.

"P. B. E. P. 4, 5 & 6" [left margin]
Denton Land Dist. TX - Field notes of survey of 160 acs. made for ROBERT S. PORTER by virtue of foregoing affidavit - Situate in Denton Land Dist. on waters of Grindstone Creek, tributary of Brazos Riv. - Beg. NE from NW cor. WILLIAM C. BAKER 160 ac. preemption survey -
Signed: LEWELLEN MURPHY, Dept. Surv. Denton L. D. [no date]
Chain Carriers: A. J. DYCHE, JOHN C. HIGHTOWER
Recorded: Oct 1 1855 - R. W. ALLEN - Dist. Surv. D. L. D.

[Next page - Number torn]

"P B E P 6, 7 & 8" [left margin]
Denton Land Dist. TX - JAMES. H. PORTER before LEWELLEN MURPHY , Dept. Surveyor Denton Land Dist. - took oath - believe land settled on to be vacant Public domain - settled on or about Dec 20 1854 - was citizen of State at date of enactment of present preemption Law
Signed: JAMES H. PORTER
Sworn to & subscribed before LEWELLEN MURPHY Aug 17 1855

Denton Land Dist. TX - Field notes of survey of 160 acs. for JAMES H. PORTER by virtue of foregoing affidavit - Situate in Denton Land Dist. on waters of Grindstone Creek, tributary Brazos Riv. - Beg. SE from NW cor. ROBERT S. PORTER 160 ac preemption survey -
Surveyed: Aug 17 1855 - LEWELLEN MURPHY Dept. Surveyor
[no chain carriers]
Recorded: Oct 17 1855 - R. W. ALLEN Dist. Surv. Denton Land Dist.

[5]   "P B E P 12 & 13" [left margin]
Denton Land Dist. TX - ISRAEL BURROW before LEWELLEN MURPHY - took oath - believe land settled to be vacant Public domain - settled on or about Dec 20 1854 - was citizen of state on date of enactment of present preemption Law
Signed: ISRAEL BURROWS
Sworn to & subscribed before Aug 23 1855 before LEWELLEN MURPHY, Dept. Surv. Denton Land Dist.

Denton Land Dist. TX - Field notes of survey of 160 acs. made for ISRAEL BURROWS by virtue of foregoing affidavit - Situate in Denton Land Dist. on waters of Grindstone Creek, tributary Brazos Riv. - Beg. SW from SE cor. ROBERT S. PORTER 160 ac. preemption survey -
Surveyed: Aug 23 1855 - LEWELLEN MURPHY Dept. Surv. Denton L.D.
Chain Carriers: YOUNG WARREN, WILLIAM P. WILSON
Recorded: Oct 17 1855 - R. W. ALLEN Dist. Surv. Denton Land Dist.

[6]   "P B E P 84 & 5" [left margin]
Denton Land Dist. TX - S. P. MULKIN before ISAAC O. HEADLEY - took oath - believe land settled on is vacant - settled on or about Mar 30 1855
Signed: S. P. MULKIN
Sworn to & subscribed before Oct 3 1855 - ISAAC O. HEADLEY Dept. Surv. Denton Land Dist.

Denton Land Dist. TX - Field notes of survey of 160 acs made for S. P. MULKIN by virtue of above affidavit - Situate in Tarrant Co. on Clear Fork Trinity Riv. - Beg. NW cor J. B. [or I. B.] HIBBERT -
Surveyed: Oct 3 1855 - ISAAC O. HEADLEY, Dept. Surv. Denton Land Dist.
Chain Carriers: K. P. WILLIAMS, JOHN MULKIN
Recorded: Oct 29 1855 - R. W. ALLEN, Dist. Surv. Denton Land Dist.

[7]   "P. B. E. P 89 & 90" [left margin]
Denton Land Dist. TX - ISAIAH MULKIN before ISAAC O. HEADLEY - took oath - believe land settled on is vacant - settled on or about Mar 30 1855 -
Signed: ISAIAH MULKIN

Denton Land Dist. TX - Field notes of survey of 160 acs. made for ISAIAH MULKIN by virtue his affidavit - Situate in Tarrant Co. on Clear Fork of Trinity Riv. - Beg. NW cor. S. P. MULKIN 160 ac survey -
Surveyed: Oct 3 1855 - ISAAC O. HEADLEY, Dept. Surv. Denton Land Dist.
[Chain Carriers] - R. P. WILLIAMS, JOHN MULKIN
Recorded: Oct 29 1855 - [not signed]

[8]   "P. B. E. P 86 & 7" [left margin]
Denton Land Dist. TX - JAMES FISHER before ISAAC O. HEADLEY - took oath - believe land settled on to be vacant - settled on or about Nov 2 1854
Signed: JAMES FISHER
Sworn to & subscribed Nov 2 1854 before ISAAC O. HEADLEY, Dept. Surv. Denton Land Dist.

Denton Land Dist. - Field notes of survey of 160 acs. made for JAMES FISHER by virtue above affidavit - Situate in Tarrant Co. on Clear Fork of Trinity Riv. - Beg. at NW cor. R. C. EDDLEMAN 320 ac. survey in E. boundary line of J. G. WRAY 320 ac. survey
Surveyed: Nov 2 1854 - ISAAC O. HEADLEY, Dept. Surv. Denton Land Dist.
Chain Men: JOHN H. PHELPS, THOMAS H. TOLEN
Recorded: Oct 29 1855 - R. W. ALLEN, Dist. Surv. Denton Land Dist.

[9] "P B E P 115 & 16" [left margin]
Denton Land Dist. TX - JASON LORANCE before ISAAC O. HEADLEY - took oath - believe land settled on to be vacant - settled on or about Dec 1 1854
Signed: JASON LORANCE
Sworn to & subscribed May 7 1855 before - ISAAC O. HEADLEY Dept. Surv. Denton Land Dist.

Denton Land Dist. - Field notes of survey of 160 acs. for JASON LORANCE by virtue above affidavit - Situate in Tarrant Co. on Clear Fork of Trinity Riv. - Beg. [torn] from NW cor. S. DERRITT 320 ac. survey -
Surveyed: May 7 1855 - ISAAC O. HEADLEY, Dept. Surv. Denton Land Dist.
Chain Men: JASON LORANCE, R. W. DERRETT
Recorded: OCT 30 1855 - R. W. ALLEN, Dist. Surv. Denton Land Dist.

[10] "P B E P 121 & [torn]" [left margin]
Denton Land Dist. TX - T. J. SHAW before ISAAC O. HEADLEY - took oath - believe land settled on to be vacant - settled on or about Nov 1 1854
Signed: T.J. SHAW
Sworn to & subscribed Mar 27 1855 before ISAAC O. HEADLEY Dept. Surv. Denton Land Dist.

Denton Land Dist. TX - Field notes of survey of 160 acs. for T. J. SHAW by virtue above affidavit - Situate in Tarrant Co. on Spring Creek, branch of Brazos Riv. - Beg. NE from NW cor. of survey of 43,356,408 Sq. vs. of land surveyed for Leon County [school lands ?]
Surveyed: Mar 27 1855 - ISAAC O. HEADLEY Dept. Surv. Denton Land Dist.
Chain Men: BENJAMIN GALE, T. J. SHAW
Recorded: Oct 31 1855 - R. W. ALLEN, Dist. Surv. Denton Land Dist.

[NOTE: PAGES MISSING OR MISNUMBERED]

[17] "P B E P 143 & 4 [left margin]
Denton Land Dist. TX - MILTON MILLS before ISAAC O. HEADLEY -

took oath - believe land settled on is vacant - settled on or about Jul 15 1855
Signed: MILTON MILLS
Sworn to & subscribed Jul 3 1855 [sic] before ISAAC O. HEADLEY

Denton Land Dist. TX - Field notes of survey of 160 acs. for MILTON MILLS by virtue above affidavit - Situate in Tarrant Co. on Clear Fork of Trinity Riv. - Beg. at SE cor. EZRA MULKIN 160 ac. survey in W. boundary line of WM. COLE 320 ac. survey -
Surveyed: Oct 3 1855 ISAAC O. HEADLEY Dept. Surv. Denton Land Dist.
Chain Men: R. P. WILLIAMS, JOHN MULKIN
Recorded: Oct 31, 1855 - R. W. ALLEN, Dist Surv. Denton L. D.

[18] "B P E P 145 & 6" [left margin]
Denton Land Dist. TX - G. K. ELKINS before ISAAC O. HEADLEY - took oath - believe land settled on is vacant - settled on or about Dec 28 1854
Signed: G. K. ELKINS
Sworn to & subscribed Apr 21 1855 before ISAAC O. HEADLEY Dept. Surv. Denton Land Dist.

Denton Land Dist. TX - Field notes of survey of 160 acs. for G. K. ELKINS by virtue his affidavit - Situate in Tarrant Co. on Clear Fork of Trinity Riv. - Beg. SE cor. J. M. FROMAN 320 ac. survey in N. boundary line of WILSON WOODS 320 ac. survey - JAMES OXIER 320 ac. survey
Surveyed: Apr 21 1855 - ISAAC O. HEADLEY Dept. Surv. Denton L. D.
Chain Men: WILSON WOODS, A. E. TOLEN
Recorded: Oct 31 1855 - R. W. ALLEN, Dist. Surv. D. L. D.

[19] "P B E P 139 & 40" [left margin]
Denton Land Dist. TX - J. H. CROP [CROSS ?] before ISAAC O. HEADLEY - took oath - believe land settled is vacant - settled on or about Feb 13 1855
Signed: J. H. CROP
Sworn to & subscribed Feb 13 1855 before ISAAC O. HEADLEY Dept. Surv. Denton Land Dist.

Denton Land Dist. TX - Field notes of survey of 160 acs. for J. H. CROP by virtue above affidavit - Situate in Tarrant Co. on waters of Longs Creek, branch of Brazos Riv. - Beg. SE from NE cor. Leon Co. 43,358,408 sq. vs. survey -
Surveyed: Feb 13 1855 - ISAAC O. HEADLEY Dept. Surv D. L. D.
Chain Men: GEORGE CRUM, SAMUEL T. CRUM
Recorded: Oct 31 1855 - R. W. ALLEN, Dist. Surv. D. L. D.

[20] "P B E P 148 & 9" [left margin]
Denton Land Dist. TX - EZRA MULKIN before ISAAC O. HEADLEY - took oath - believe land settled on is vacant - settled on or

about Oct 3 1855
Signed: EZRA MULKIN
Sworn to & subscribed Oct 3 1855 before ISAAC O. HEADLEY Dept. Surv. Denton Land Dist.

Denton Land Dist. TX - Field notes of survey of 160 acs. for EZRA MULKIN by virtue above affidavit - Situate in Tarrant Co. on Clear Fork of Trinity Riv. - Beg. at NW cor. WM. COLE 320 ac. survey -
Surveyed: Oct 3 1855 - ISAAC O. HEADLEY Dept. Surv. D. L. D.
Chain Men: MILTON MILLS, JOHN WILKIN
Recorded: Oct 31 1855 - R. W. ALLEN, Dist. Surv. D. L. D.

[21]   "P B E P 138" [left margin]
Denton Land Dist. TX - JAMES HUDSON before ISAAC O. HEADLEY - took oath - believe land settled on is vacant - settled on or about Dec 20 1854
Signed: JAMES HUDSON
Sworn to & subscribed Oct 1 1855 before ISAAC O. HEADLEY, Dept. Surv. Denton Land Dist.

Denton Land Dist. TX - Field notes of survey of 160 acs. for JAMES HUDSON by virtue above affidavit - Situate in Tarrant Co. on Clear Fork of Trinity Riv. - Beg. W & S from SW cor. A. PIPKIN 160 ac. survey -
Surveyed: Oct 1 1855 - ISAAC O. HEADLEY Dept. Surv. D. L. D.
Chain Men: A. SPARKS, JOHN MILLER
Recorded: Oct [no day] 1855 - R. W. ALLEN, Dist Surv D. L. D.

[22]   "P B E P 88" [left margin]
Denton Land Dist. TX - J. M. MOORE before ISAAC O. HEADLEY - took oath - believe land settled on is vacant - settled on or about Nov 1 1854
Signed: J. M. MOORE
Sworn to & subscribed Dec 15 1854 before ISAAC O. HEADLEY, Dept. Surv. D. L. D.

Denton Land Dist. TX - Field notes of survey of 160 acs. for J. M. MOORE by virtue his affidavit - Situate in Tarrant. Co. on Clear Fork of Trinity Riv. - Beg.SE from SW cor C. C. MC CARVER 320 ac. survey -
Surveyed: Dec 15 1855 - ISAAC O. HEADLEY Dept. Surv. D. L. D.
Chain Carriers: DAVID EDDLEMAN, I. C. EDDLEMAN
Recorded: Oct 29 1855 - R. W. ALLEN, Dist. Surv. Denton L. D.

[23]   "P B E P 157" [left margin]
Denton Land Dist. TX - LEWIS KIDWELL before ISAAC O. HEADLEY - took oath - believe land settled on is vacant - settled on or about Aug 8 1855
Signed: LEWIS KIDWELL
Sworn to & subscribed Sep 1 1855 before ISAAC O. HEADLEY, Dept. Surv. Denton Land Dist.

Denton Land Dist. TX - Field notes of survey of 160 acs. for LEWIS KIDWELL by virtue above affidavit - Situate in Tarrant. Co. on waters of Brazos Riv. - Beg. at NW cor. PRISTON WHITE 160 ac. survey -
Surveyed: Sep 1 1855 - ISAAC O. HEADLEY Dept. Surv. D. L. D.
Chain Men: JAMES KIDWELL, BENJ. REYNOLDS
Recorded: Oct 31 1855 - R. W. ALLEN, Dist. Surv. D. L. D.

[24]   "P B E P 26" [left margin]
Denton Land Dist. TX - JAMES SPROULS before LEWELLEN MURPHY - took oath - believe land settled on to be vacant Public domain
Signed: JAMES SPROULS
Sworn to & subscribed Feb 22 1855 before LEWELLEN MURPHY, Dept. Surv. Denton Land Dist.

Denton Land Dist. TX - Survey of 160 acs. for JAMES SPROULS by virtue foregoing affidavit - Situate in Tarrant Co. on waters of Walnut Creek, tributary stream of West Fork of Trinity Riv. - Beg. N of NE cor ANDREW JACKSON CALDWELL 160 ac. survey -
Surveyed: Feb 22 1855 - LEWELLEN MURPHY Dept. Surv. D. L. D.
Chain Carriers: JESSE W. FRANKLIN, WILLIAM COPELAND
Recorded: Oct 19 1855 - R. W. ALLEN, Dist. Surv. D. L. D.

[25]   "P B E P 141" [left margin]
Denton Land Dist. TX - WESLEY WHITE before ISAAC O. HEADLEY - took oath - believe land settled on is vacant - settled on or about Mar 1 1855
Signed: WESLEY WHITE
Sworn to & subscribed Aug 31 1855 before ISAAC O. HEADLEY, Dept. Surv. Denton Land Dist.

Denton Land Dist. TX - Field notes of survey of 160 acs. for WESLEY WHITE by virtue above affidavit - Situate in Tarrant Co. on waters of Brazos Riv. - Beg. NE & NE from NE cor. JOHN JENKINS 160 ac. survey -
Surveyed: Aug 31 1855 - ISAAC O. HEADLEY Dept. Surv. D. L. D.
Chain Men: LEWIS WHITE, JOHN JONES
Recorded: Oct 31 1855 - R. W. ALLEN, Dist. Surv. Denton L. D.

[26]   "P B E P 290" [left margin]
Denton Land Dist. TX - STEPHEN F. JONES before ISAAC O. HEADLEY took oath - believe land settled on is vacant - settled on or about Jun 27 1855
Signed: STEPHEN F. JONES
Sworn to & subscribed Dec 8 1855 before ISAAC O. HEADLEY, Dept. Surv. Denton Land Dist.

Denton Land Dist. TX - Field notes of survey of 160 acs for STEPHEN F. JONES by virtue above affidavit - Situate W of Tarrant Co. on head of Red Bear Creek, tributary of Brazos Riv. Beg. W & S from SW cor. REYNOLD REYNOLDS 750 ac. survey -
Surveyed: Dec 8 1855 - ISAAC O. HEADLEY Dept. Surv. D. L. D.

Chain Carriers: SAMUEL R. BARBER, SOLOMON P. BARBER
Recorded: Apr 18 1856 - R. W. ALLEN, Dist. Surv. Denton L. D.

[27]   "P B E P 286" [left margin]
Denton Land Dist. TX - JOHN S. WHITE before ISAAC O. HEADLEY - took oath - believe land settled on is vacant - settled on or about Nov 6 1855
Signed: JOHN S. WHITE
Sworn to & subscribed Dec 8 1855 before ISAAC O. HEADLEY, Dept. Surv. Denton Land Dist.

Denton Land Dist. TX - Field notes of survey of 160 acs for JOHN S. WHITE by virtue above affidavit - Situate W of Tarrant Co. on Red Bear Creek, tributary of Brazos Riv. - Beg. at NW cor. STEPHEN F. JONES 160 ac. survey -
Surveyed: Dec 8 1855 [no surveyors signature]
Chain Carriers: STEPHEN F. JONES, SOLOMON P. BARBAR
Recorded: Apr 18 1856 - R. W. ALLEN, Dist. Surv. Denton L. D.

[28]   "P B E P 302" [left margin]
Denton Land Dist. TX - AMOS PERRY before ISAAC O. HEADLEY - took oath - believe land settled on is vacant - settled on or about Nov 5 1855
Signed: AMOS PERRY
Sworn to & subscribed Dec 8 1855 before ISAAC O. HEADLEY, Dept. Surv. Denton Land Dist.

Denton Land Dist. TX - Field notes of survey of 160 acs for AMOS PERRY by virtue above affidavit - Situate W of Tarrant Co. on head Red Bear Creek, tributary of Brazos Riv. - Beg. at SW cor. STEPHEN F. JONES 160 ac. survey - cor. JOHN D. WHITE 160 ac. survey -
Surveyed: Dec 8 1855 - ISAAC O. HEADLEY Dept Surv Denton L. D.
Chain Carriers: S. R. BOOKER, S. P. BARBER
Recorded: Apr 21 1856 - R. W. ALLEN, Dist. Surv. Denton L. D.

[29]   "P B E P 339" [left margin]
Denton Land Dist. TX - J. W. BAWSCOM before ISAAC O. HEADLEY - took oath - believe land settled on is vacant - settled on or about Jan 1 1854
[no signature]
Sworn to & subscribed Mar 28 1854 before ISAAC O. HEADLEY, Dept. Surv. Denton Land Dist.

Denton Land Dist. TX - I have surveyed for J. W. BAWCOM 160 acs. Situate in Parker Co. on Red Bear Creek, tributary of Brazos Riv. - Beg. SW cor. JOSEPH ROBINSON 160 ac. survey - passing SW cor. MAHALA HART 160 ac. survey -
Surveyed: Mar 28 1856 - ISAAC O. HEADLEY, Dept. Surv. D. L. D.
Chain Carriers: BARTLEY ADKINS, JOSEPH ROBINSON
Recorded: Apr 26 1856

[30]   "P B E P 346" [left margin]
Denton Land Dist. TX - MAHALA HART before ISAAC O. HEADLEY - took oath - believe land settled on is vacant - settled on or about Oct 8 1855
Signed: MAHALA HART
Sworn to & subscribed Jan 15 1855 before ISAAC O. HEADLEY, Dept. Surv. Denton Land Dist.

Denton Land Dist. TX - Field notes of survey of 160 acs. for MAHALA HART by virtue above affidavit - Situate in Tarrant Co. about 5 mi. from Brazos Riv. - Beg. SE & SW from NW cor. HUMPHREY PRICE 160 ac. survey -
Surveyed: Jan 15 1856 - ISAAC O. HEADLEY Dept. Surv. D. L. D.
Chain Carriers: STEPHEN HART, ROBERT HART
Recorded: Apr 28 1856 - R. W. ALLEN, Dist. Surv. Denton L. D.

[31]   "P B E P 320" [left margin]
Denton Land Dist. - JOSEPH HART before ISAAC O. HEADLEY - took oath - believe land settled on is vacant - settled on or about Mar 10 1856
Signed: JOSEPH HART
Sworn to & subscribed Mar 31 1856 before ISAAC O. HEADLEY, Dept. Surv. Denton L. D.

Denton Land Dist. TX - Surveyed for JOSEPH HART 160 acs. by virtue above affidavit - Situate in Parker Co. on Red Bear Creek, tributary of Brazos Riv. - Beg. SW from SE cor. MAHALA HART 160 ac. survey -
Surveyed: Mar 31 1856 - ISAAC O. HEADLEY Dept. Surv. D. L. D.
Chain Carriers: STEPHEN HART, R. C. HART
Recorded: Apr 24 1856 - R. W. ALLEN, Dist. Surv. Denton L. D.

[32]   "P B E P 325" [left margin]
Denton Land Dist. TX - R. C. HART before ISAAC O. HEADLEY - took oath - believe land settled on is vacant - settled on or about Oct 10 1856
[no signature - no date]

Denton Land Dist. TX - Have surveyed for R. C. HART 160 acs. - Situate in Parker Co. on Red Bear Creek, tributary of Brazos Riv. - Beg. at NE cor. MAHALA HART 160 ac. survey - W. boundary line UMPHREY PRICE 160 ac. survey -
Surveyed: Mar 29 1856 - ISAAC O. HEADLEY Dept. Surv. D. L. D.
Chain Carriers: GABRIEL HART, JOSEPH HART
Recorded: Apr 25 1856 - R. W. ALLEN, Dist. Surv. Denton L. D.

[NOTE: PAGES MISSING OR MISNUMBERED]

[37]   "P B E P 269" [left margin]
Denton Land Dist. TX - D. H. SISK before ISAAC O. HEADLEY - took oath - believe land settled on is vacant - settled on or about Oct 1 1855

Signed: D. H. SISK
Sworn to & subscribed Jan 15 1855 before ISAAC O. HEADLEY, Dept. Surv. Denton Land Dist.

Denton Land Dist. TX - Field notes of survey of 160 acs. for D. H. SISK by virtue above affidavit - Situate in Tarrant Co. at head of Spring Creek, tributary Brazos Riv. - Beg. NE & N from SE cor. J. P. DOLLARHIDE 160 ac. survey -
Surveyed: Jan 15 1856 - ISAAC O. HEADLEY Dept. Surv. D. L. D.
Chain Carriers: WALTER BATY, R. E. BYRD
Recorded: Apr 11 1856 - R. W. ALLEN, Dist. Surv. Denton L. D.

[38] "P B E P 282" [left margin]
Denton Land Dist. TX - N. H. PATILLO before ISAAC O. HEADLEY - took oath - believe land settled on is vacant - settled on or about Jan 30 1856
Signed: N. H. PATILLO
Sworn to & subscribed Apr 1 1856 before ISAAC O. HEADLEY Dept. Surv. Denton L. D.

Denton Land Dist. - Have surveyed for N. H. PATILLO 160 acs. by virtue above affidavit - Situate in Parker Co. on Spring Creek, tributary Trinity Riv. - Beg. at NW cor. C. A. EDDLEMAN 160 ac. survey in boundary line of R. C. EDDLEMAN 160 ac. survey -
Surveyed: Apr 1 1856 - ISAAC O. HEADLEY Dept. Surv. D. L. D.
Chain Carriers: J. C. PREWETT (?), JAMES DEATON [or DEASON]
Recorded: Apr 14 1856 - R. W. ALLEN, Dist. Surv. Denton L. D.

[39] "P B E P 318 - 19 & 20" [left margin]
Denton Land Dist. TX - JOHN ROBINS before ISAAC O. HEADLEY - took oath - believe land settled on is vacant - settled on or about Dec 20 1854
Signed: JOHN ROBINS
Sworn to & subscribed Dec 20 1855 before ISAAC O. HEADLEY, Dept. Surv. Denton L. D.

Denton Land Dist. TX - Field notes of survey of 160 acs. for JOHN ROBINS by virtue above affidavit - Situate in Tarrant Co. on Red Bear Creek, branch of Brazos Riv. - Beg. at E. cor. F. SANCHES 160 ac. survey -
Surveyed: Jan 17 1856 - ISAAC O. HEADLEY Dept. Surv. D. L. D.
Chain Carriers: M. J. S. WAMPLER (?), WM. R. ROBINS
Recorded: Apr 23 1856 - R. W. ALLEN, Dist. Surv. Denton L. D.

[40] "P B E P 263" [left margin]
Denton Land Dist. TX - W. J. S. WAMPLER before ISAAC O. HEADLEY took oath - believe land settled on is vacant - settled on or about Oct 15 1855
Signed: W. J. S. WAMPLER
Sworn to & subscribed Jan 18 1856 before ISAAC O. HEADLEY, Dept. Surv. Denton L. D.

Denton Land Dist. TX - Field notes of survey of 160 acs. for W. J. S. WAMPLER by virtue above affidavit - Situate in Tarrant Co. on Red Bear Creek, tributary of Brazos Riv. - Beg. NE cor. JOHN ROBINS 160 ac. survey -
Surveyed: Jan 18 1856 - ISAAC O. HEADLEY Dept. Surv. D. L. D.
Chain Carriers: R. R. WAMPLER, JOHN ROBINS
Recorded: April 11 1856 - R. W. ALLEN, Dist. Surv. Denton L. D.

[41] "P B E P 317" [left margin]
Denton Land Dist. TX - J. A. AUSBURN before ISAAC O. HEADLEY - took oath - believe land settled on is vacant - settled on or about Oct 15 1855
Signed: JAMES A. AUSBURN
Sworn to & subscribed Mar 21 1856 before ISAAC O. HEADLEY, Dept. Surv. Denton Land Dist.

Denton Land Dist. TX - Field notes of survey of 160 acs. for JAMES A. AUSBURN by virtue above affidavit - Situate in Tarrant Co. on Red Bear Creek, tributary of Brazos Riv. - Beg. NW cor. M. J. S. WAMPLER 160 ac. survey -
Surveyed: Mar 29 1856 - ISAAC O. HEADLEY Dept. Surv. D. L. D.
Chain Carriers: B. V. EMBERSON, JAMES A. AUSBURN
Recorded: Apr 23 1856 - R. W. ALLEN, Dist. Surv. Denton L. D.

[42] "P B E P 309" [left margin]
Denton Land Dist. TX - PLEASANT ROLAND before ISAAC O. HEADLEY - took oath - believe land settled on is vacant - settled on or about Oct 15 1855
Signed: PLEASANT ROLAND
Sworn to & subscribed Mar 27 1856 before ISAAC O. HEADLEY, Dept. Surv. Denton L. D.

Denton Land Dist. TX - Field notes of survey of 160 acs. for PLEASANT ROWLAND by virtue above affidavit - Situate W. of Tarrant Co.on Red Bear Creek, tributary of Brazos Riv. - Beg. NE of NW cor. J. A. Ausburn 160 ac survey -
Surveyed: Mar 27 1856 - ISAAC O. HEADLEY Dept. Surv. D. L. D.
Chain Carriers: JOSEPH ROBINSON, DAVID MOORE
Recorded: Apr 22 1856 - R. W. ALLEN, Dist. Surv. Denton L. D.

[43] "P B E P 267" [left margin]
Denton Land Dist. TX - J. JIMMERSON before ISAAC O. HEADLEY - took oath - believe land settled on is vacant - settled on or about Jul 15 1855
Signed: JOHN JIMERSON
Sworn to & subscribed Dec 4 1855 before ISAAC O. HEADLEY Dept. Surv. Denton L. D.

Denton Land Dist. TX - Field notes of survey of 160 acs. for JOHN JIMERSON by virtue above affidavit - Situate in Tarrant Co. on Patricks Creek, tributary of Brazos Riv. - Beg. NE & NW

from NW cor. WM. LONG 640 ac survey -
Surveyed: Dec 4 1855 -ISAAC O. HEADLEY Dept. Surv. D. L. D.
Chain Carriers: JOHN B. PINKSON, JAMES BUTTLER
Recorded: Apr 11 1856 - R. W. ALLEN, Dist. Surv. Denton L. D.

[44]   "P B E P 265" [left margin]
Denton Land Dist. TX - ALDERSON DODSON before ISAAC O. HEADLEY
- took oath - believe land settled on is vacant - settled on
or about Jul 3 1855
Signed: ALDERSON DODSON
Sworn to & subscribed Dec 6 1855 before ISAAC O. HEADLEY,
Dept. Surv. Denton L. D.

Denton Land Dist. TX - Surveyed for ALDERSON DODSON 160 acs.
by virtue his affidavit - Situate in Tarrant Co. on Patricks
Creek, tributary of Brazos Riv. - Beg. W of NW cor Eli BROWN
160 ac sur
Surveyed: Dec 6 1855 - ISAAC O. HEADLEY Dept. Surv. D. L. D.
Chain Men: J. J. HAMILTON, JOHN JIMERSON
Recorded: Apr 11 1856 - R. W. ALLEN, Dist. Surv. Denton L. D.

[45]   "P B E P 306" [left margin]
Denton Land Dist. TX - J. J. HAMILTON before ISAAC O. HEADLEY
- took oath - believe land settled on is vacant - settled on
or about Jul 3 1855
Signed: J. J. HAMILTON
Sworn to & subscribed Dec 6 1855 before ISAAC O. HEADLEY,
Dept. Surv. Denton L. D.

Denton Land Dist. TX - Have surveyed for J. J. HAMILTON of 160
acs. by virtue his affidavit - Situate in Tarrant Co. on
Patrick's Creek, tributary of Brazos Riv. - Beg. [torn]
Surveyed: Dec 6 1855 - ISAAC O. HEADLEY Dept. Surv. D. L. D.
Chain Men: ALDERSON DODSON, JOHN JAMISON
Recorded: Apr 22 1856 - R. W. ALLEN, Dist. Surv. Denton L. D.

[46]   "P B E P 274" [left margin]
Denton Land Dist. TX - EDWIN RIGHTMER before ISAAC O. HEADLEY
- took oath - believe land settled on is vacant - settled on
or about May 1 1855
Signed: EDWIN RIGHTMER
Sworn to & subscribed Nov 27 1855 before ISAAC O. HEADLEY,
Dept. Surv. Denton L. D.

Denton Land Dist. TX - Field notes of survey of 160 acs. for
EDWIN RIGHTMER by virtue affidavit - Situate in Tarrant Co. on
Brazos Riv. - Beg. at SE cor. W. MILLER 320 ac. survey -
Surveyed: Nov 27 1855 - ISAAC O. HEADLEY Dept. Surv. D. L. D.
Chain Carriers: E. S. EMBERSON, JAMES CALDEROUS [?]
Recorded: Apr 12 1856 - R. W. ALLEN, Dist. Surv. Denton L. D.

[47]   "P B E P 235" [left margin]
Denton Land Dist. TX - G. W. FOX before ISAAC O. HEADLEY - took oath - believe land settled on is vacant - settled on or about Sep 15 1855
Signed: GEORGE W. FOX
Sworn to & subscribed Oct 17 1855 before ISAAC O. HEADLEY, Dept. Surv. Denton L. D.

Denton Land Dist. TX - Field notes of survey of 160 acs. for G. W. FOX by virtue above affidavit - Situate Tarrant Co. on Clear Fork Trinity Riv. - Beg. SW from SE cor. J. M. MOORE 160 ac. survey -
Surveyed: Oct 17 1855 - ISAAC O. HEADLEY, Dept. Surv. D. L. D.
Chain Carriers: WESLEY FRANKLIN, G. W. FOLLY
Recorded: Apr 7 1856 - R. W. ALLEN, Dist. Surv. Denton L. D.

[48]   "P B E P 233" [left margin]
Denton Land Dist. TX - LYDIA FOLLY before ISAAC O. HEADLEY - took oath - believe land settled on is vacant - settled on or about Jan 15 1856
Signed: Lydia FOLLY
Sworn to & subscribed Feb 28 1856 before ISAAC O. HEADLEY, Dept. Surv. Denton Land Dist.

Denton Land Dist. TX - Field notes of survey of 160 acs. for LYDIA FOLLY by virtue above affidavit - Situate in Tarrant Co. on Clear Fork Trinity Riv. - Beg. SW from SE cor. J. M. MOORE 160 ac. survey -
Surveyed: Feb 28 1856 - ISAAC O. HEADLEY, Dept. Surv. D. L. D.
Chain Carriers: G. W. FOX, WESLEY FRANKLIN
Recorded: Apr 7 1856 - R. W. ALLEN, Dist. Surv. Denton L. D.

[49]   "P BOOK E P 225" [left margin]
Denton Land Dist. TX - THOS. M. OWEN before ISAAC O. HEADLEY - took oath - believe land settled on is vacant - settled on or about Dec 28 1855
Signed: THOS. M. OWEN
Sworn to & subscribed Dec 28 1855 before ISAAC O. HEADLEY, Dept. Surv. Denton L. D.

Denton Land Dist. TX - Field notes of survey of 160 acs. for THOS. M. OWEN by virtue above affidavit - Situate in Tarrant Co. on Clear Fork of Trinity Riv. - Beg. at SE cor. M. M. T. TUBB 160 ac. survey -
Surveyed: Dec 28 1855 - ISAAC O. HEADLEY, Dept. Surv. D. L. D.
Chain Carriers:J. B. WINN, J. H. (?) OWEN
Recorded: Apr 7 1856 - R. W. ALLEN, Dist. Surv. Denton L. D.

[50]   "P Book E P 232" [left margin]
Denton Land Dist. TX - W. M. T. TUBB before ISAAC O. HEADLEY - took oath - believe land settled on is vacant - settled on or about Feb 15 1855

Signed: W. M. T. TUBB
Sworn to & subscribed Dec (?) 19 1855 before ISAAC O. HEADLEY,
Dept. Surv. Denton L. D.

Denton Land Dist. TX - Field notes of survey of 160 acs. for
W. M. T. TUBB by virtue above affidavit - Situate in Tarrant
Co. on Clear Fork of Trinity Riv. - Beg. E & N of SE cor. M.
F. FOLDER (?) 160 ac. survey -
Surveyed: Dec 19 1855 -ISAAC O. HEADLEY, Dept. Surv. D. L. D.
Chain Carriers: J. B. CAFFMAN, M. J. HOLDER
Recorded: Apr 7 1856 - R. W. ALLEN, Dist. Surv. Denton L. D.

[51]   "P B E P 241" [left margin]
Denton Land Dist. TX - W. T. KING before ISAAC O. HEADLEY -
took oath - believe land settled on is vacant - settled on or
about Jul 16 1855
Signed: W. T. KING
Sworn to & subscribed Dec 26 1855 before ISAAC O. HEADLEY,
Dept. Surv. Denton L. D.

Denton Land Dist. TX - Field notes of survey of 160 acs. for
W. T. KING by virtue above affidavit - Situate in Tarrant Co.
on Clear Fork of Trinity Riv. - Beg. SE & SE from SE cor. W.
?. KING 160 ac. survey -
Surveyed: Dec 20 1855 - ISAAC O. HEADLEY, Dept. Surv. D. L. D.
Chain Carriers: J. B. WYNN, G. H. HORTON
Recorded: Apr 9 1856 - R. W. ALLEN, Dist. Surv. Denton L. D.

[52]   "P B E P 244" [left margin]
Denton Land. Dist. TX - W. D. KING before ISAAC O. HEADLEY -
took oath - believe land settled on is vacant - settled on or
about Jul 14 1855
Signed: W. D. KING
Sworn to & subscribed Dec 26 1855 before ISAAC O. HEADLEY,
Dept. Surv. Denton L. D.

Denton Land. Dist. TX - Field notes of survey of 160 acs. for
W. D. KING by virtue above affidavit - Situate in Tarrant Co.
on Clear Fork of Trinity Riv. - Beg. NE & SE & S of NE cor. G.
(?) B. WYNN 160 ac. survey -
Surveyed: Dec 20 1855 - ISAAC O. HEADLEY, Dept. Surv. D. L. D.
Chain Carriers: T. (?) W. HORTON, T. B. WYNN
Recorded: Apr 9 1856 - R. W. ALLEN, Dist. Surv. Denton L. D.

[53]   "P B E P 240" [left margin]
Denton Land Dist. TX - T. (?) B. WYNN before ISAAC O. HEADLEY
- took oath - believe land settled on is vacant - settled on
or about Jun 26 1855
Signed: T. (?) B. WYNN
Sworn to & subscribed Dec 15 1855 before ISAAC O. HEADLEY,
Dept. Surv. Denton L. D.

Denton Land Dist. TX - Field notes of survey of 160 acs. for
T. B. WYNN by virtue above affidavit - Situate in Tarrant Co.
on Clear Fork of Trinity Riv. - Beg. at SE cor. J. B. COFFMAN
160 ac. survey -
Surveyed: Dec 19 1855 - ISAAC O. HEADLEY, Dept. Surv. D. L. D.
Chain Carriers: N. B. HEALLN (?), T. P. COFFMAN
Recorded: Apr 9 1856 - R. W. ALLEN, Dist. Surv. Denton L. D.

[54]   "P B E P 246" [left margin]
Denton Land Dist. TX - J. P. COFFMAN before ISAAC O. HEADLEY -
took oath - believe land settled on is vacant - settled on or
about Jun 23 1855
Signed: J. P. COFFMAN
Sworn to & subscribed Dec 19 1855 before ISAAC O. HEADLEY,
Dept. Surv. Denton L. D.

Denton Land Dist. TX - Field notes of survey of 160 acs. for
J. P. COFFMAN by virtue above affidavit - Situate in Tarrant
Co. on Clear Fork of Trinity Riv. - Beg. NE & SE from SE cor.
W. B. HOLDER 160 ac. survey -
Surveyed: Dec 19 1855 - ISAAC O. HEADLEY, Dept. Surv. D. L. D.
Chain Carriers: W. B. HOLDER, J. B. WYNN
Recorded: Apr 9 1856 - R. W. ALLEN, Dist. Surv. Denton L. D.

[55]   "P B E P 249" [left margin]
Denton Land Dist. TX - N. B. HOLDER before ISAAC O. HEADLEY -
took oath - believe land settled on is vacant - settled on or
about Nov 1 1855
Signed: N. B. HOLDER
Sworn to & subscribed Dec 19 1855 before ISAAC O. HEADLEY,
Dept. Surv. Denton L. D.

Denton Land Dist. TX - Field notes of survey of 160 acs. for
N. B. HOLDER by virtue above affidavit - Situate in Tarrant
Co. on Clear Fork of Trinity Riv. - Beg. N from SE cor. H.
HALFULL 160 ac.survey -
Surveyed: Dec 19 1855 - ISAAC O. HEADLEY, Dept. Surv. D. L. D.
Chain Carriers: J. B. WYNN, J. P. COFFMAN
Recorded: Apr 28 1856 - R. W. ALLEN, Dist. Surv. Denton L. D.

[56]   "P B E P 230" [left margin]
Denton Land Dist. TX - N. J. HOLDER before ISAAC O. HEADLEY -
took oath - believe land settled on is vacant - settled on or
about Nov 22 1855
Signed: N. J. HOLDER
Sworn to & subscribed Dec 17 1855 before ISAAC O. HEADLEY,
Dept. Surv. Denton L. D.

Denton Land Dist. TX - Field notes of survey of 160 acs. for
N. J. HOLDER by virtue above affidavit - Situate in Tarrant
Co. on Clear Fork of Trinity Riv. - Beg. at SE cor. WM. M.
COZORT 160 ac. survey -

Surveyed: Dec 17 1855 - ISAAC O. HEADLEY, Dept. Surv. D. L. D.
Chain Carriers: W. B. HOLDER, J. P. COFFMAN
Recorded: Apr 28 1856 - R. W. ALLEN, Dist. Surv. Denton L. D.

[57]   "P B E P 250" [left margin]
Denton Land Dist. TX - JOHN SHANKS before ISAAC O. HEADLEY -
took oath - believe land settled on is vacant - settled on or
about Nov 1 1855
Signed: JOHN SHANKS
Sworn to & subscribed Dec 18 1855 before ISAAC O. HEADLEY,
Dept. Surv. Denton L. D.

Denton Land Dist. TX - Field notes of survey of 160 acs. for
JOHN SHANKS by virtue above affidavit - Situate in Tarrant Co.
on Clear Fork of Trinity Riv. - Beg. SW from SW cor. J. C.
HALFELL 160 ac. survey -
Surveyed: Dec 18 1855 - ISAAC O. HEADLEY, Dept. Surv. D. L. D.
Chain Carriers: J. C. HALFELL, J. C. SHANKS
Recorded: Apr 28 1856 - R. W. ALLEN, Dist. Surv. Denton L. D.

[58]   "P B E P 228 " [left margin]
Denton Land Dist. TX - WM. N. COZART before ISAAC O. HEADLEY -
took oath - believe land settled on is vacant - settled on or
about Aug 15 1855
Signed: WM. N. COZART
Sworn to & subscribed Dec 11 1855 before ISAAC O. HEADLEY,
Dept. Surv. Denton L. D.

Denton Land Dist. TX - Field notes of survey of 160 acs. for
WM. N. COZART by virtue above affidavit - Situate in Tarrant
Co. on Clear Fork of Trinity Riv. - Beg. at SW cor. H. PEPKIN
160 ac. survey - SE cor. JAMES HUDSON 160 ac. survey
Surveyed: Dec 11 1855 - ISAAC O. HEADLEY, Dept. Surv. D. L. D.
Chain Carriers: ASER PIPKIN, P. B. PIPKIN
Recorded: Apr 27 1856 - R. W. ALLEN, Dist. Surv. Denton L. D.

[59]   "P B E P 240" [left margin]
Denton Land Dist. TX - ASER PEPKIN before ISAAC O. HEADLEY -
took oath - believe land settled on is vacant - settled on or
about Jan 1 1856
Signed: A. PEPKIN
Sworn to & subscribed Feb 16 1856 before ISAAC O. HEADLEY,
Dept. Surv. Denton L. D.

Denton Land Dist. TX - Field notes of survey of 160 acs. for
ASER PEPKIN by virtue above affidavit - Situate in Tarrant Co.
on Clear Fork of Trinity Riv. - Beg. at SW cor. Oliver DAVIS
160 ac. survey - W. boundary of A. SPARKS 160 ac. survey -
Surveyed: Feb 16 1856 - ISAAC O. HEADLEY, Dept. Surv. D. L. D.
Chain Carriers: OLIVER DAVIS, HENRY INMON
Recorded: APR 7 1856 - R. W. ALLEN, Dist. Surv. Denton L. D.

[60]   "P B E P 238" [left margin]
Denton Land Dist. TX - G. W. HOLLINGSWORTH before ISAAC O. HEADLEY - took oath - believe land settled on is vacant - settled on or about Oct 10 1855
Signed: G. W. HOLLINGSWORTH
Sworn to & subscribed Dec 15 1855 before ISAAC O. HEADLEY, Dept. Surv. Denton L. D.

Denton Land Dist. TX - Field notes of survey of 160 acs. for G. W. HOLLINSWORTH by virtue above affidavit - Situate in Tarrant Co. on Clear Fork of Trinity Riv. - Beg. S & W from SW cor. HENRY INMON 160 ac. survey -
Surveyed: [no date] - ISAAC O. HEADLEY Dept Surv Denton L. D.
Chain Carriers: E. H. CRUMPTON, ASER PEPKIN
Recorded: Apr 7 1856 - R. W. ALLEN, Dist. Surv. Denton L. D.

[61]   "P B E P 224" [left margin]
Denton Land Dist. TX - J. M. INMAN before ISAAC O. HEADLEY - took oath - believe land settled on is vacant - settled on or about Dec 15 1855
Signed: J. M. INMAN
Sworn to & subscribed Jan 4 1856 before - ISAAC O. HEADLEY Dept. Surv. Denton L. D.

Denton Land Dist. TX - Field notes of survey of 160 acs. for J. M. INMON by virtue above affidavit - Situate in Tarrant Co. on Clear Fork of Trinity Riv. - Beg. at SW cor. HENRY INMAN 160 ac. survey -
Surveyed: Jan 4 1856 - ISAAC O. HEADLEY Dept. Surv. D. L. D.
Chain Carriers: HENRY INMAN, F. A. MOORE
Recorded: Apr 7 1856 - R. W. ALLEN, Dist. Surv. Denton L. D.

[62]   "P B E P 291" [left margin]
Denton Land Dist. TX - JOHN TRIMBLE before ISAAC O. HEADLEY - took oath - believe land settled on is vacant - settled on or about Sep 30 1855
Signed: JOHN TRIMBLE
Sworn to & subscribed Mar 25 1856 before ISAAC O. HEADLEY Dept. Surv. Denton L. D.

Denton Land Dist. TX - Have surveyed for JOHN TRIMBLE 160 acs by virtue above affidavit - Situate in Parker Co. on Clear Fork of Trinity Riv. - Beg. S from NE cor. Joseph TRIMBLE 160 ac. survey
Surveyed: Mar 21 1856 - ISAAC O. HEADLEY Dept. Surv. D. L. D.
Chain Carriers: [none shown]
Recorded: Apr 14 1856 - R. W. ALLEN, Dist. Surv. Denton L. D.

[63]   "P B E P 269" [left margin]
Denton Land Dist. TX - JOSEPH TRIMBLE before ISAAC O. HEADLEY - took oath - believe land settled on is vacant - settled on or about May 1 1855

Signed: JOSEPH TRIMBLE
Sworn to & subscribed May 21 1855 before ISAAC O. HEADLEY
Dept. Surv. Denton L. D.

Denton Land Dist. TX - Have surveyed for JOSEPH TRIMBLE 160 acs. by virtue above affidavit - Situate in Parker Co. on Clear Fork of Trinity Riv.- Beg. SE & E of SE cor A. M. KINSLEY 160 ac. sur
Surveyed: Mar 21 1856 - ISAAC O. HEADLEY Dept. Surv. D. L. D.
Chain Carriers: JOHN TRIMBLE, WM. TRIMBLE
Recorded: Apr 14 1856 - R. W. ALLEN, Dist. Surv. Denton L. D.

[64]   "P B E P 287" [left margin]
Denton Land Dist. TX - Z. P. SHIRLEY before ISAAC O. HEADLEY - took oath - believe land settled on is vacant - settled on or about May 31 1855
Signed: Z. P. SHIRLEY
Sworn to & subscribed Nov 24 1855 before ISAAC O. HEADLEY
Dept. Surv. Denton L. D.

Denton Land Dist. TX - Field notes of survey of 160 acs. for Z. P. SHIRLEY by virtue above affidavit - Situate in Tarrant Co. on Patrick's Cr., tributary of Brazos Riv. - Beg. SW & S from SE cor. WESLEY WHITE 160 ac. survey -
Surveyed: Nov 24 1855 - ISAAC O. HEADLEY Dept. Surv. D. L. D.
Chain Carriers: W. V. D. SHIRLEY, J. T. WEBB
Recorded: Apr 18 1856 - R. W. ALLEN, Dist. Surv. Denton L. D.

[65]   "P B E P 304" [left margin]
Denton Land Dist. TX - W. V. D. SHIRLEY before ISAAC O. HEADLEY took oath - believe land settled is vacant - settled on or about May 30 1855
Signed: W. V. D. SHIRLEY
Sworn to & subscribed Nov 24 1855 before ISAAC O. HEADLEY
Dept. Surv. Denton L. D.

Denton Land Dist. TX - Field notes of survey of 160 acs. for W. V. D. SHIRLEY by virtue above affidavit - Situate in Tarrant Co. on Patrick's Creek, tributary of Brazos Riv.- Beg. S from NE cor. J. T. WEBB 160 ac. survey & E boundary of same - E Boundary of B. P. SHIRLEY 160 ac. survey -
Surveyed: Nov 24 1855 - ISAAC O. HEADLEY Dept. Surv. D. L. D.
Chain Carriers: B. P. SHIRLEY, J. T. WEBB
Recorded: Apr 21 1856 - R. W. ALLEN, Dist. Surv. Denton L. D.

[66]   "P B E P 294" [left margin]
Denton Land Dist. TX - ELI BROWN before ISAAC O. HEADLEY - took oath - believe land settled is vacant - settled on or about Sep 12 1855
Signed: ELI BROWN
Sworn to & subscribed Nov 29 1855 before ISAAC O. HEADLEY
Dept. Surv. Denton L. D.

Denton Land Dist. TX - Field notes of survey of 160 acs. for ELI BROWN by virtue above affidavit - Situate in Tarrant Co. on Patrick's Creek, tributary of Brazos Riv. - Beg. SW cor. Z. P. SHIRLEY 160 ac. survey -
Surveyed: Nov 29 1855 - ISAAC O. HEADLEY Dept. Surv. D. L. D.
Chain Carriers: ELI BROWN, PLEASANT PRICE
Recorded: Apr 18 1856 - R. W. ALLEN, Dist. Surv. Denton L. D.

[67] "P B E P 79" [left margin]
Denton Land Dist. - WILLIAM SILLIVANT swears land settled on, improved & now resides on is vacant - am entitled to same by virtue of Act passed by Legislature of State of Texas granting to settlers 160 acs.
Signed: WILLIAM SILLIVANT
Sworn to & Subscribed Aug 9 1855 before L. E. CAMP, Dept. Surv. Denton L. D.

Denton Land Dist. TX - Field notes of survey of 160 acs. for WILLIAM SILLIVANT by virtue his affidavit - Situate Denton Land Dist.& Tarrant Territory, West Tarrant Co. on Clear Fork, Tributary of West Fork Trinity Riv. - Beg. [torn]
Surveyed: Aug 9 1855 - L. E. CAMP Dept. Surv. Denton L. D.
Chain Carriers: E. N. CANNAFAX, N. BROWN
Recorded: Oct 24 1855 - R. W. ALLEN, Dist. Surv. Denton L. D.

[68] "P B E P 30" [left margin]
Denton Land Dist. TX - JOSEPH WALKER before LEWELLEN MURPHY - took oath - believe land settled to be vacant Public domain - settled on or about Sep 4 1855 - was citizen at date of enactment of present preemption Law.
Signed: JOSEPH WALKER, [his mark]
Sworn to & subscribed Sep 19 1855 before LEWELLEN MURPHY Dept. Surv. Denton Land Dist.

Denton Land Dist. TX - Field notes of survey of 160 acs. for JOSEPH WALKER by virtue foregoing affidavit - Situate in Tarrant Co. Territory on waters of Clear Fork Trinity Riv. - Beg. W of NE cor. JONATHAN H. WALKER 160 ac. preemption survey -
Surveyed: Sep 19 1855 - LEWELLEN MURPHY, Dept. Surv. D. L. D.
Chain Carriers: ISAAC P. DAVID, JAMES W. SILLIVANT
Recorded: OCT 19 1855 - R. W. ALLEN, Dist. Surv. Denton L. D.

[69] "P B E P 21" [left margin]
Denton Land Dist. TX - WILLIAM COPELAND before LEWELLEN MURPHY - took oath - believe land settled to be vacant Public domain - [nothing else in statement]
Signed: WILLIAM COPELAND
Sworn to & subscribed Feb 22 1855 before LEWELLEN MURPHY, Dept. Surv. Denton L. D.

Denton Land Dist. TX - Field notes of survey of 160 acs. for WILLIAM COPELAND by virtue foregoing affidavit - Situate in

Tarrant Co. Territory on waters Walnut Creek, tributary stream West Fork Trinity Riv. - Beg. N of NE cor. JAMES SPROULS 160 ac. preemption survey -
Surveyed: [no date] LEWELLEN MURPHY, Dept. Surv. Denton L. D.
Chain Carriers: JAMES SPROULS, JESSE W. FRANKLIN
Apr 7 1855 - LEWELLEN MURPHY certifies foregoing survey made Feb 22 1855
Recorded: Oct 18 1855 - R. W. ALLEN, Dist. Surv. Denton L. D.

[70]   "P B E P 28" [left margin]
Denton Land Dist. TX - ROBERT MILTON WALKER before LEWELLEN MURPHY - took oath - believe land settled to be vacant Public domain - settled on or about Jun 12 1855 - was citizen of State at date of enactment of present preemption Law -
Signed: ROBERT MILTON WALKER, [his mark]
Sworn to & subscribed Jun 19 1855 before LEWELLEN MURPHY, Dept. Surv. Denton L. D.

Denton Land Dist. TX - Field notes of survey of 160 acs. for ROBERT MILTON WALKER by virtue foregoing affidavit - Situate in TC on waters Walnut Creek, tributary West Fork Trinity Riv. - Beg. at NE cor. SAMUEL H. WALKER 160 ac. preemption survey -
Surveyed: Jun 19 1855 -LEWELLEN MURPHY, Dept. Surv. D. L. D.
Chain Carriers: JOHN MATLOCK, SAMUEL H. WALKER
Recorded: Oct 19 1855 - R. W. ALLEN, Dist. Surv. Denton L. D.

[71]   "P B E P 34" [left margin]
Denton Land Dist. TX - SAMUEL H. WALKER before LEWELLEN MURPHY - took oath - believe land settled to be vacant Public domain - settled on or about May 1 1855 - was citizen at date of enactment of present preemption Law
Signed: SAMUEL H. WALKER
Sworn to & subscribed Jun 8 1855 before LEWELLEN MURPHY, Dept. Surv. Denton L. D.

Denton Land Dist. TX - Field notes of survey of 160 acs. for SAMUEL H. WALKER by virtue foregoing affidavit - Situate in Tarrant Co. Territory waters of Walnut Creek, tributary West Fork Trinity Riv. - Beg. W of NW cor. JOHN SHIRLEY 160 ac. preemption survey
Surveyed: Jun 9 1855 - LEWELLEN MURPHY, Dept. Surv. D. L. D.
Chain Carriers: JOHN MATLOCK, ROBERT MILTON WALKER
Recorded: Oct 19 1855 - R. W. ALLEN, Dist. Surv. Denton L. D.

[CHANGE OF FORM]

[72]   "P B E P 120" [left margin]
Denton Land Dist. TX - I, JOHN MATLOCK do Solemnly swear that on the 11th day of August A. D. 1854, I settled upon and sill [sic] reside on land which I believe to be vacant & unappropriated Public domain & claim 160 acs. under the preemption

law passed 13th Feb 1854 as follows In Denton Land Dist. on a branch of Walnut Creek, in the valley of the West Fork of Trinity & better described by my map & field notes.
Signed: JOHN MATLOCK
Sworn to & subscribed Oct 26 1854 before A. M. KEEN, Dept. Surv. Denton L. D.

Survey of 160 acs. lying on Walnut Creek, tributary of West Fork Trinity Riv. by virtue of his preemption affidavit - Beg. S of NW cor. WILLIAM WOODY
Surveyed: Oct 26 1854 - A. M. KEEN, Dept. Surv. Denton L. D.
[Chain Carriers ?] CHARLES L. WALKER, JAMES WHITE
Recorded: Oct 31 1855 - R. W. ALLEN, Dist. Surv. Denton L. D.

[73]   "P B E P 24" [left margin]
Denton Land Dist. TX - JOHN G. LANTZ before LEWELLEN MURPHY - took oath - believe land settled to be vacant Public domain - settled on or about Apr 16 1855 - was citizen at enactment of present preemption Law
Signed: JOHN G. LANTZ
Sworn to & subscribed Oct 5 1855 before LEWELLEN MURPHY, Dept. Surv. Denton L. D.

Denton Land Dist. TX - Field notes of survey of 160 acs. for JOHN G. LANTZ by virtue foregoing affidavit - Situate in Tarrant Co. Territory waters of Walnut Creek, tributary stream West Fork Trinity Riv. - Beg. S of SW cor. WILLIAM WOODY 320 ac. preemption survey -
Surveyed: Oct 6 1855 - LEWELLEN MURPHY, Dept. Surv. D. L. D.
Chain Carriers: RUSSELL H. DOYLE, MILTON MURPHY
Recorded: Oct 19 1855 - R. W. ALLEN, Dist. Surv. Denton L. D.

[74]   "P B E P 17" [left margin]
Denton Land Dist. TX - WILLIAM COFFY before LEWELLEN MURPHY - took oath - believe land settled to be vacant Public domain - settled on or about Jul 25 1855 - was citizen on date of enactment present preemption Law
Signed: WILLIAM COFFY
Sworn to & subscribed Jul 31 1855 before LEWELLEN MURPHY, Dept. Surv. Denton L. D.

Denton Land Dist. - Field notes of survey of 160 acs. for WILLIAM COFFY by virtue foregoing affidavit - Situate in Tarrant Co Territory on waters of Ash Creek, tributary West Fork Trinity Riv. - Beg. at SW cor. JESSE R. CLIFTON 160 ac. preemption survey - along W. boundary ISAAC H. MEEK 160 ac. preemption survey - SE cor. WILLIAM PENNINGTON 160 ac. preemption survey -
Surveyed: Jul 31 1855 - LEWELLEN MURPHY, Dept. Surv. D. L. D.
Chain Carriers: WILLIAM PENNINGTON, JOHN A. NEWSOM
Recorded: Oct 18 1855 - R. W. ALLEN, Dist. Surv. Denton L. D.

[75]   "P B E P 14" [left margin]
Denton Land Dist. TX - JOHN N. RASH before LEWELLEN MURPHY - took oath - believe land settled to be vacant Public domain - settled on or about Jun 18 1855 - was citizen date of enactment present preemption Law
Signed: JOHN N. RASH
Sworn to & subscribed Aug 1 1855 before LEWELLEN MURPHY, Dept. Surv. Denton Land Dist.

Denton Land Dist. TX - Field notes of survey of 160 acs. for JOHN N. RASH by virtue foregoing affidavit - Situate in Tarrant Co. Territory waters Ash Creek, tributary Stream West Fork Trinity Riv.- Beg. E of SE cor. CHRISTOPHER BEDWELL 160 ac. preemption survey -
Surveyed: Aug 1 1855 - LEWELLEN MURPHY, Dept. Surv. D. L. D.
Chain Carriers: BENJAMIN EVANS, ISAAC H. MEEK
Recorded: Oct 18 1855 - R. W. ALLEN, Dist. Surv. Denton L. D.

[76]   "P B E P 153" [left margin]
Denton Land Dist. TX - THOMAS HUDSON before ISAAC O. HEADLEY - took oath - believe land settled is vacant - settled on or about Mar 1 1855
Signed: THOMAS HUDSON
Sworn to & subscribed Sep 20 1855 before ISAAC O. HEADLEY, Dept. Surv. Denton L. D.

Denton Land Dist. TX - Field notes of survey of 160 acs. for THOMAS HUDSON by virtue his affidavit - Situate in Tarrant Co. on West Fork Trinity Riv.- Beg. SE from SE cor. JOHN NEWSOM 160 ac. survey -
Surveyed: Sep 20 1855 - ISAAC O. HEADLEY, Dept. Surv. D. L. D.
Chain Carriers: D. H. SISK, JAMES HOFFORD (?)
Recorded: OCT 31 1855 - R. W. ALLEN, Dist. Surv. Denton L. D.

[77]   "P B E P 147" [left margin]
Denton Land Dist. TX - J. R. CAMPBELL before ISAAC O. HEADLEY - took oath - believe land settled is vacant - settled on or about Aug 21 1855
Signed: J. R. CAMPBELL
Sworn to & subscribed Aug 29 1855 before ISAAC O. HEADLEY, Dept. Surv. Denton Land Dist.

Denton Land Dist. TX - Field notes of survey of 160 acs. for J. R. CAMPBELL by virtue his affidavit - Situate in Tarrant Co. on Clear Fork Trinity Riv.- Beg. N from NW cor. ELIJAH GILLILAND 160 ac. survey -
Surveyed: Aug 29 1855 - ISAAC O. HEADLEY, Dept. Surv. D. L. D.
Chain Carriers: W. B. GILLILAND, JOSEPH C. GILLILAND
Recorded: Oct 31 1855 - R. W.ALLEN, Dist. Surv. Denton L. D.

[78]   "P B E P 103" [left margin]
Denton Land Dist. TX - JAMES JOHNSON before LEWELLEN MURPHY -

took oath - believe land settled to be vacant Public domain -
settled on or about on May 1 1855 - was citizen at date enact-
ment present preemption Law
Signed: JAMES JOHNSON
Sworn to & subscribed Sep 1 1855 before LEWELLEN MURPHY, Dept.
Surv. Denton L. D.

Denton Land Dist. TX - Field notes of survey of 160 acs. for
JAMES JOHNSON by virtue foregoing affidavit - Situate in
Denton Land Dist. in Territory of Tarrant Co. on waters Clear
Fork Trinity Riv.- Beg. E of SE cor. JAMES J. BEEMAN 160 ac.
preemption survey -
Surveyed: Sep 17 1855 - LEWELLEN MURPHY, Dept. Surv. D. L. D.
Chain Carriers: WILLIAM B. GILLILAND, JAMES JOHNSON
Recorded: Oct 30 1855 - R. W. ALLEN, Dist. Surv. Denton L. D.

[79] "P B E P 95" [left margin]
Denton Land Dist. TX - OLIVER CHILDERS before ISAAC O. HEADLEY
- took oath - believe land settled is vacant - settled on or
about Dec 2 1854
Signed: OLIVER CHILDERS
Sworn to & subscribed Dec 7 1855 before ISAAC O. HEADLEY,
Dept. Surv. Denton L. D.

Denton Land Dist. TX - Field notes of survey of 160 acs. for
OLIVER CHILDERS by virtue his affidavit - Situate in Tarrant
Co. on Clear Fork Trinity Riv.- Beg. E from NE cor. JOHN ADAMS
320 ac. survey -
Surveyed: Dec 7 1855 - ISAAC O. HEADLEY, Dept. Surv. D. L. D.
Chain Carriers: IRA R. WOOD (?), ELI LEE
Recorded: Oct 27 1855 - R. W. ALLEN, Dist. Surv. Denton L. D.

[80] "P B E P 93" [left margin]
Denton Land Dist. TX - CALVIN LYNCH before ISAAC O. HEADLEY -
took oath - believe land settled is vacant - settled on or
about Jan 15 1855
Signed: CALVIN LYNCH
Sworn to & subscribed Mar 25 1855 before ISAAC O. HEADLEY,
Dept. Surv. Denton L. D.

Denton Land Dist. TX - Field notes of survey of 160 acs. for
CALVIN LYNCH by virtue his affidavit - Situate in Tarrant Co.
on Clear Fork Trinity Riv. - Beg. - W from NW cor. ISAAC GLASS
160 ac. survey in N. boundary of same - passing NE cor. L. P.
MC DONALD 320 ac. survey -
Surveyed: Mar 25 1855 - ISAAC O. HEADLEY, Dept. Surv. D. L. D.
Chain Carriers: ISAAC GLASS, ROBERT THOMPSON
Recorded: Oct 29 1855 - R. W. ALLEN, Dist. Surv. Denton L. D.

[81] "P B E P 96" [left margin]
Denton Land Dist. TX - ISAAC GLASS before ISAAC O. HEADLEY -
took oath - believe land settled is vacant - settled on or

about Dec 25 1854
Signed: ISAAC GLASS
Sworn to & subscribed Mar 25 1855 before ISAAC O. HEADLEY, Dept. Surv. Denton L. D.

Denton Land Dist. TX - Field notes of survey of 160 acs. for ISAAC GLASS by virtue his affidavit - Situate in Tarrant Co. Territory on Clear Fork Trinity Riv. - Beg. at SE cor. L. P. MC DONALD 320 ac. survey -
Surveyed: Mar 25 1855 - ISAAC O. HEADLEY, Dept. Surv. D. L. D.
Chain Carriers: CALVIN LYNCH, ROBERT THOMPSON
Recorded: Oct 29 1855 - R. W. ALLEN, Dist. Surv. Denton L. D.

[82] "E 123" [left margin]
Denton Land Dist. TX - STEPHEN KIDWELL before ISAAC O. HEADLEY - took oath - believe land settled is vacant - settled on or about Dec 30 1854
Signed: STEPHEN KIDWELL
Sworn to & subscribed Feb 25 1855 before ISAAC O. HEADLEY, Dept. Surv. Denton L. D.

Denton Land Dist. TX - Field notes of survey of 160 acs. for STEPHEN KIDWELL by virtue his affidavit - Situate in Tarrant Co. in upper Cross Timbers - Beg. W & N from SW cor. J. R. MITCHELL 160 ac. survey -
Surveyed: Feb 25 1855 - ISAAC O. HEADLEY, Dept. Surv. D. L. D.
Chain Carriers: MOSES ROLY (?), THOMAS WHITE
Recorded: OCT 31 1855 - R. W. ALLEN, Dist. Surv. Denton L. D.

[83] "E-92" [in ink left margin]
Denton Land Dist. TX - WILLIAM TRIMBLE before ISAAC O. HEADLEY - took oath - believe land settled is vacant - settled on or about Jan 1 1855
Signed: WM. TRIMBLE
Sworn to & subscribed Sep 13 1855 before ISAAC O. HEADLEY, Dept. Surv. Denton L. D.

Denton Land Dist. TX - Field notes of survey of 160 acs. for WILLIAM TRIMBLE by virtue above affidavit - Situate in Tarrant Co. on Clear Fork Trinity Riv. - Beg. at SE cor. G. W. SKIDMORE 160 ac. survey -
Surveyed: Sep 13 1855 - ISAAC O. HEADLEY, Dept. Surv. D. L. D.
Chain Carriers: J. H. MAYS, SILAS BARNS
Recorded: Oct 29 1855 - R. W. ALLEN, Dist. Surv. Denton L. D.

[84]

The State of Texas | I, Chas. C. LACY, Dist. Surveyor
Denton Land Dist. | of Denton Land Dist. do hereby
certify that the foregoing 83 pages is a true and correct coppy [sic] of the original records of the surveys of my office.
Given under my hand at Alton this the 21st day of March 1857
CHAS. C. LACY Dist.
Surveyor Denton Land District

The State of Texas | I, A. P. LLOYD, Clerk of the
County of Denton | County Court for the County
aforesaid, hereby certify that I assisted in comparing foregoing 83 pages of transcript with the original record of field notes in the office of the District Surveyor of the Denton Land District and that I believe the same to be a true and correct copy of said original records.
Given under my hand and seal of office at Alton this 21st day of March 1857.
A. P. LLOYD,
Clerk County Court D. C. T.

[Large round orange seal affixed]

PRE-EMPTION RECORD "D"
1854 - 1857
DENTON LAND DISTRICT

L22/100

am AMBOSICE [?]

TRANSCRIPT BOOK D
96 pages

[ALL THE FOLLOWING ENTRIES ARE IN PENCIL AND VERY FADED]

ALLEN, JAS.	8	DAVIS [?], WM.	76
ALLEN, J. P.	42	DAVIS, WILLIAM	7_
AND, ?. L.	78	DAVIS [?], ?. P.	??
		DENNISON, WILLIAM [?]	17?
BURRIP [SS ?] E.	26		
BROWN, R. W.	65	ENSEY, I. C.	??
BROWN, R. W., Jnr.	67	ENSEY, S. A.	28
BULLION, THOS.	62		
BEEDLE, HENRY	53	FRANCES, JNO.	5_
BAGLEY, WM. H.	96	FRANCES, H. E.	5_
		FRANCES, RAMY [?] L.	[torn]
CALDWELL, JOSHUA	4	F__?__, W. B.	[torn]
CAPPS, J.	94		
CALDWELL, JOHN [JOSHUA ?]	44	JACKSON, ?	[torn]
CALDWELL, JAMES	45	LEE, L. D.	[torn]
CALDWELL, HEZEKIAH	47	LEONARD, G. L [?]	[torn]
CALDWELL, THOS.	??		
CA__ELL, H. S.	49	MC MAHAN, J. L.	[torn]
___?___, ___?___	55	MILLER, __?__	[torn]
___?___, ___?___	58	MORRIS, JAS.	[torn]
[TORN]	69		

[Reverse side of 1st page – right hand column blank]

PASCHAL, J. C.   32
PARKER, CINNT__ [?]   69
REYNOLDS, M. A.   36
REYNOLDS, [no given name] 79
RIPPEY, E. M.   83

SNOW, J.   81
SILLIVANT [?], M. J.   41
STAGGS, MILLER   56

TAYLOR, WILLIAM   19
THOMAS, J. W.   7
TEETERS, G. G.   87
TEETERS, ISAAC   88
THORNHILL, A.   90

WARD, JOSEPH   59
WAUGH, T. G.   40
WHITE, JAMES   37
WALKER, C. [?] P.   29
WOMACK, T. J.   22
WOOD, C. [?] C.   5

[Next page]

Mt GOMERY, J. P.   160   1
Mt GOMERY [?], JOHN   "   2
CALDWELL, JOSHUA   "   4
WOOD, C. C.   5
THOMAS, J. T.   9
ALLEN, JAS. A.   8
MC MAHAN, J. L.   9
ENSEY, D. C.   11
MEEK, J. H.   13
MAJORS, J. B.   15
DENNISON, WM.   17
DAVIS, J. P.   18

[1]

The State of Texas | I, JOHN P MONTGOMRY, do solemnly swear
Denton Land District | that on or about the 14th of Oct 1854
                         I settled upon the land I now claim as
a preemption and believe the same to be vacant and unappropriated and claim the same by virtue of the Donation Law this
Dec 13th 1854

                        JOHN P. "X" MONTGOMRY (his mark)
Sworn to and subscribed before me this Dec 13th 1854
                              J. E. JENKINS, Dept.
                              Surveyor Denton L. D.

"Book C page 86" [left margin]
Dec 13th 1854 - Denton Land Dist. TX - Surveyed for JOHN P. MONTGOMRY 160 acs. of Land lying on the waters of Walnut Creek, the waters of the Trinity, by virtue of his Donation claim - Beg. E of NW cor. J. GARRISON - pass NE cor. J. HARRIS - containing in all 950 vrs.
Signed: J. E. JINKINS, Dept. Surv. Denton L. D.
Chain Carriers: J. L. LEONARD, THOS. WHITE

[2]   Recorded: Jun 30 1855

"BOOK F P 158" [left margin]
Denton Dist. TX - JOHN MONTGOMRY before LEWELLEN MURPHY - took oath - believe land settled to be vacant Public domain
Signed: JOHN MONTGOMRY
Sworn to & subscribed Feb 24 1855 before LEWELLEN MURPHY, Dept. Surv. Denton Land Dist.

Denton Land Dist. TX - Survey of 160 acs. for JOHN MONTGOMRY by virtue of foregoing affidavit - Situate Tarrant Co. Territory on waters of Walnut Creek, tributary stream West Fork Trinity Riv. Beg. NE cor. THOMAS J. LEWIS 160 ac. preemption survey -

[3]   Surveyed Feb 24 1855 - LEWELLEN MURPHY, Dept. Surv. D. L. D.
Chain Carriers: JESSE FRANKLIN MONTGOMRY, THOMAS JOHN LEWIS
Recorded: Aug 15 185? - R. W. ALLEN, Dist. Surv. Denton L. D.

[PAGES MISSING]

[6]   Denton Land Dist. TX - Surveyed 160 acs. for CHRISTOPHER C. W_?_D [tear middle of name] by virtue of foregoing affidavit Situate in Tarrant Co. Territory on waters of __?__ Creek, tributary of West Fork Trinity Riv. - Beg. S? from NW cor. CHARLES WESLEY BLANTON preemption survey - NW cor. NANCY MULLERS
Surveyed: Feb 15 1855 - LEWELLEN MURPHY, Dept. Surv. D. L. D.
Chain Carriers: CHARLES WESLEY BLANTON, ROBERT GEORGE
[bottom of page torn]

[7]   Denton Land Dist. TX - JOHN W. THOMAS took oath before LEWELLEN MURPHY, Dept. Surv. Denton L. D. - believe land settled to be vacant Public domain - settled on Apr 4 1855 - was citizen of state
Signed: JOHN W. THOMAS
Sworn to & subscribed Jul 26 1855 before LEWELLEN MURPHY, Dept. Surv. Denton L. D.

Denton Land Dist. TX - Field notes of survey of 160 acs. for JOHN W. THOMAS by virtue of foregoing affidavit - Situate Tarrant Co. Territory on waters of Salt Creek, tributary West

Fork Trinity Riv. - Beg. NW from NE cor. ISAAC BRISCO 160 ac. preemption survey -[bottom of page torn]

[PAGES MISSING]

[10] was citizen at enactment of present preemption Law
Signed: JOHN L. MC MAHAN
Sworn to & subscribed Mar 15 1856 before LEWELLEN MURPHY, Dept. Surv. Denton L. D.

Denton Land Dist. - Field notes of survey of 160 acs. for JOHN L. MC MAHAN by virtue of foregoing affidavit - Situate in Parker Co. on waters of Clear Fork Trinity Riv. - Beg. NW from NW cor. EDWARD HARRIS 160 ac. preemption survey -
Surveyed: Mar 15 1856 - LEWELLEN MURPHY, Dept. Surv. D. L. D.
Chain Carriers: JAMES A. MILLER, SAMUEL W. COWAN

[11 ?] "Book T [or F] p 72" [left margin]
Recorded: Jun 3 1856 - R. W. ALLEN, Dist. Surv. Denton L. D.

Denton Land Dist. TX - DENNIS C. ENSEY appeared before LEWELLEN MURPHY, Dept. Surv. Denton L. D. - took oath - believe land settled on to be vacant Public domain - settled on Mar 13 1856 - was citizen of state
Signed: DENNIS C. ENSEY
Sworn to & subscribed Mar 13 1856 - LEWELLEN MURPHY, Dept. Surv. Denton L. D.

Denton Land Dist. TX - Field notes of survey of 150 64/100 acs. for DENNIS C. ENSEY by virtue of foregoing affidavit - Situate in Parker Co. on waters of Walnut Creek, tributary stream West Fork Trinity Riv. - Beg. at NE cor. SALLY ASBERRY [?] 160 ac. preemption sur - W boundary line of FRANCIS LIDDY 320 ac. survey

[12] NW cor. SALLY ASBERRY ENSEY's 160 ac. preemption survey - E Boundary line of L. J. WOMACK 160 ac. preemption survey -
Surveyed: Mar 13 1856 - LEWELLEN MURPHY, Dept. Surv. Denton L. D.
Chain Carriers: EZEKIEL S. A. ENSEY, T. J. WOMACK
Recorded: Jun 3 1856 - R. W. ALLEN, Dist. Surv. Denton L. D.

[13] "Book F p 193" [left margin]

State of Texas   :   Personally appeared before LEWELLEN
Denton Land Dist.:   MURPHY, a Dept. Surveyor of Denton
                            Land District, ISAAC H. MEEK, who took and subscribed the following oath to wit: I do solemnly swear that I believe the land on which I am settled, was vacant Public domain at the date of my settlement thereon and that I settled on said land sometime in the autumn of the year 1854 and that I applied to Mr. JENKINS, legally authorized surveyor

of Denton Land District, who surveyed my preemption within the time prescribed by Law but as he has never succeeded in getting my preemption recorded I am therefore under the necessity of having it resurveyed at this date date [sic] and furthermore that I was a citizen of the state at the date of enactment of the present preemption Law. So help me God.
Signed: ISAAC H. MEEK
Sworn to and subscribed Aug 1 1855 before LEWELLEN MURPHY, Dept. Surv. Denton Land Dist.

Denton Land Dist. TX - Field notes of survey of 160 acs. for ISAAC H. MEEK by virtue of foregoing affidavit - Situate in Tarrant Co. Territory on waters of Ash Creek, tributary of W Fork Trinity Riv.-Beg at S cor of JESSE R. CLIFTON 160 ac survey

[14] SW cor WILLIAM R. FLECTCHER 160 ac. preemption survey
Surveyed: Aug 1 1855 - LEWELLEN MURPHY, Dept. Surv. D. L. D.
Chain Carriers: JOHN N. RASH, BENJAMIN EVANS
Recorded: Aug 22 1856 - R. W. ALLEN, Dist. Surv. Denton L. D.

[15] "Bk F P 168" [left margin]
Denton Land Dist. TX - ISAAC BARTON MAJORS appeared before LEWELLEN MURPHY Dept. Surv. Denton L. D. - took oath - believe land settled on to be vacant Public domain - settled on as preemptioner on or about Jul 23 1855 - was citizen at date of enactment of present preemption Law
Signed: ISAAC BARTON MAJORS
Sworn to & subscribed Apr 23 1856 before LEWELLEN MURPHY, Dept. Surv. Denton L. D.

Denton Land Dist. TX - Field notes of survey of 160 acs. in name of ISAAC BENTON MAJORS by virtue of foregoing affidavit - Situate in Parker Co. on Brazos Riv. - Beg. on Bank of Brazos & the SW cor. DAVID HERRIN 160 ac. preemption survey - S cor. PLEASANT H. MAJORS preemption survey -

[16] SE boundary line PLEASANT H. MAJORS - NW boundary line DAVID HERRINGs preemption - "This survey lies between 2 surveys of older date so that I couldn't front half the square without leaving a vacant slip so narrow or to be of little or no value so I conceived it to be in accordance with the spirit of the Law to embrace the entire space lying between the 2 older surveys"
Signed: LEWELLEN MURPHY, Dept. Surv. Denton L. D.
Chain Carriers: WILLIAM S. HERREN, PLEASANT H. MAJORS
Recorded: Aug 14 1856 - R. W. ALLEN, Dist. Surv. Denton L. D.

[17] "Bk F P 100" [left margin]
Denton Land Dist. TX - WILLIAM DENNISON appeared before L. E. CAMP, Dept. Surv. Denton L. D. - took oath - believe land settled, improved and now reside is vacant I commenced my set-

tlement 18th day of Dec 1855.
Signed: WILLIAM DENNISON
Sworn to & subscribed Jan 17 1856

Denton Land Dist. TX - Field notes of survey of 160 acs. for WILLIAM DENNISON by virtue his affidavit - Situate on headwaters of Rock Creek, tributary of Trinity - Beg. NE from NE cor. J. W. LITTLETON 160 ac. preemption survey -
Surveyed: Feb 21 1856 - L. E. CAMP, Dept. Surv. Denton L. D.
Chain Men: CHAS. LITTLETON, C. W. COOPER

[18]   "Bk D P 295" [left margin]
Denton Land Dist. TX - ISAAC P. DAVIS appeared before LEWELLEN MURPHY, Dept. Surv. Denton Land Dist. - took oath - believe land settled on to be vacant Public domain - settled on as preemptioner on or about Oct 14 1855 - was citizen at date of enactment of present preemption Law
Signed: ISAAC P. DAVIS
Sworn to & subscribed Nov 14 1855 before LEWELLEN MURPHY, Dept. Surv. Denton L. D.

Denton Land Dist. TX - Field notes of survey of 160 acs. in name of ISAAC P. DAVIS by virtue of foregoing affidavit - Situate in Denton Land Dist. on waters of Clear Fork Trinity Riv. - Beg. S boundary line & W of SE cor. GEORGE TAYLOR 160 ac. preemption survey -

[19] Surveyed: Nov 14 1855 - LEWELLEN MURPHY, Dept Surv D L D
Chain Carriers: WILLIAM BONDS, JONATHAN H. MULKEN [?]
Recorded: Mar [no day] 1856 - R. W. ALLEN, Dist. Surv. D.L.D.

"Bk D P 287" [left margin]
Denton Land Dist. TX - WILLIAM TAYLOR appeared before LEWELLEN MURPHY, Dept. Surv. Denton Land Dist. - took oath - believe land settled on to be vacant Public domain - settled on or about May 11 1855 as preemptioner - was citizen at date of enactment present preemption Law

[20]   Signed: WILLIAM "X" TAYLOR [his mark]
Sworn to & subscribed Dec 3 1855 before LEWELLEN MURPHY, Dept. Surv. Denton L. D.

Denton Land Dist. TX - Field notes of survey of 160 acs. in name of WILLIAM TAYLOR by virtue of foregoing affidavit - Situate in Denton Land Dist. in Tarrant Co. Territory on waters of Clear Fork of Trinity Riv. - Beg. NE from NE cor. EZRA JASPER CANAFAX 160 ac. preemption survey -
Surveyed: Dec 3 1855 - [no surveyors name]
Chain Carriers: JOSEPH WALKER, SAMUEL L. [S ?] WALKER

[21]   Recorded: Mar [no day] 1856 - R. W. ALLEN, Dist. Surv. Denton L. D.

"BK D P 275" [left margin]
Denton Land Dist. TX - THOMAS JEFFERSON WOMACK appeared before
LEWELLEN MURPHY, Dept. Surveyor Denton Land Dist. - took oath
- believe land settled on to be vacant Public domain - settled
on as preemptioner on or about Sep 20 1855 -

[22]   was citizen at date of enactment present preemption Law
Signed: THOMAS JEFFERSON "X" WOMACK [his mark]
Sworn to & subscribed Jan 17 1856 before LEWELLEN MURPHY,
Dept. Surv. Denton L. D.

Denton Land Dist. TX - Field notes of survey of 160 acs. in
name of THOMAS J. WOMACK

[23]   by virtue of foregoing affidavit - Situate in Denton
Land Dist. on waters Walnut Creek, tributary   stream West Fork
Trinity Riv. - Beg. on SE cor. RUBIN   ALLEN 160 ac. preemption
survey -

[24] Surveyed: Jan 17 1856 - LEWELLEN MURPHY, Dept Surv D L D
Chain Carriers: DENES [?] C. ENSEY, EZEKIEL L. A. ENSEY
Recorded: Mar 3 1856 - R. W. ALLEN, Dist. Surv. Denton L. D.

"Bk D P 195" [left margin]
Denton Land Dist. TX - I, L. D. LEE, solemnly swear the land
on which I made my preemption improvement is vacant land and I
am improving the same for my residence this 9th day Nov 1855
Signed: L. D. LEE
Sworn to & subscribed Nov 9 1855 before L. E. CAMP, Dept.
Surv. Denton L. D.

Denton Land Dist. TX - Survey of 160 acs. for L. D.   LEE by
virtue of his affidavit - Situate on waters of Walnut Creek in
Denton Land Dist. - Beg. at SW cor. THOMAS CALDWELL survey -

[25]   NW cor WM. ALLENs preemption - S boundary line JOHN
CALDWELL survey -
Surveyed: Nov 9 1855 - L. E. CAMP, Dept. Surv. Denton L. D.
Chain Men: W. W. ALLEN, SAMUEL S. LEONARD
Recorded: Nov 30 1855 - R. W. ALLEN, Dist. Surv. Denton L. D.

[26]   "Bk D P 208" [left margin]
Denton Land Dist. TX - I, ELIAS BURRIS, solemnly swear I believe land on which I have settled, improved and now reside is
vacant and I am entitled to same by virtue of Act of the Legislature of the State of Texas granting to settlers 160 acs.
of land This Nov 10th 1855
Signed: ELIAS BURRIS
Sworn to & subscribed Nov 10 1855 before L. E. CAMP, Dept.
Surv. Denton L. D.

Denton Land Dist. TX - Survey of 44 acs. made for ELIAS BURIS by virtue of his affidavit - Situate in Tarrant Co. on Walnut Creek, tributary of West Fork Trinity Riv. in Denton Land Dist. - Beg. at SE cor. of THOMAS BURRIS preemption survey in N boundary line of H. R. MORRIS preemption survey -

[27]   Surveyed: Nov 9 1855 - L. E. CAMP, Dept. Surv. D. L. D.
[Chain Men ?] THOMAS BURRIS, JAMES L. BURRIS
Recorded: Nov 30 1855 - R. W. ALLEN, Dist. Surv. Denton L. D.

Denton Land Dist. TX - SALLY ASBERRY ENSEY appeared before LEWELLEN MURPHY, Dept. Surveyor Denton Land Dist. - took oath - believe land settled on to be vacant Public domain - settled on as preemptioner on or about Dec 8 1855 - was citizen at date of enactment of Donation Law granting land to settlers approved Feb 13 1854
Signed: SALLY ASBERRY "X" ENSEY [her mark]
Sworn to & subscribed Jan 17 1856 before LEWELLEN MURPHY, Dept. Surv. Denton L. D.

[28]   "Bk D P 240" [left margin]
Denton Land Dist. TX - Field notes of survey of 160 acs. in name of SALLY ASBERRY ENSEY by virtue of foregoing affidavit - Situate in Denton Land Dist. on waters of Walnut Creek, tributary of West Fork Trinity Riv. - Beg. on SE cor. THOMAS JEFFERSON WOMACKs 160 ac. preemption survey - W boundary line of FRANCIS LIDDY 320 ac. survey - NW cor. JAMES HERNDON survey - N boundary line L. D. LEE 160 ac. preemption survey

[29]   SE cor. of EDDER BOXION [?] MILRONS [?] preemption - SE cor. RUBIN ALLEN preemption -
Surveyed: Feb 17 1856 [no surveyor's name]
Chain Carriers: DENNIS [?] C. ENSEY, EZEKIEL L. A. ENSEY
Recorded: Mar 3 1856 - R. W. ALLEN, Dist. Surv. Denton L. D.

"Bk D P 142" [left margin]
Denton Land Dist. TX - I, CHAS. P. WALKER, solemnly swear that on the 11th day of Aug 1854 I settled and still reside on land which I believe to be vacant and unappropriated Public domain and claim 160 acs. under the preemption Law passed 13th Feb 185[torn] as follows in Denton Land Dist. on [blank] branch Walnut Creek in the valley of the West Fork of the Trinity Riv. and better described by my map and field notes
Signed: CHAS. P. WAL[torn]
Sworn to & subscribed Oct 28 [remainder of sheet torn]

[30]   Denton Land Dist. TX - Survey for CHARLES WALKER 160 acs. lying on S prong Walnut Creek by virtue his preemption affidavit Beg. at SW cor. of JOHN MATLOCKs survey -
Surveyed: Oct 26 1854 - A. M. KEEN, Dept. Surv. D. L. D.
Chain Carriers: JOHN MATLOCK, JAMES WHITE
Recorded: Oct 31 1855 - R. W. ALLEN, Dist. Surv. Denton L. D.

[31]   Tarrant Co. TX - I, MARY A. MILLER, solemnly swear that I was on the land I have settled on or about Mar 15 1854 and claim 160 acs. by virtue of the preemption Law and believe it to be vacant land June 3rd 1854
Signed: MARY "X" A. MILLER [her mark]
Sworn to & subscribed June 3 1854 before J. E. JENKINS, Dept. Surv. Robertson Land Dist.

"Bk D P 76" [left margin]
Denton Land Dist. TX - Jun 3 1854 - Survey for MARY A. MILLER of the Dist. of Tarrant Co. 160 acs. lying on waters of Walnut Creek, the waters of the Trinity Riv. by virtue of her preemption claim - Beg. at SW cor. SAMUEL WOODY & E cor. __?__ 320 ac. survey -
Signed: J. E. JENKINS
Chain Carriers: JAMES REYNOLDS, B. WOODY

[32]   Recorded: Sep 9 1855 - R. W. ALLEN, Dist. Surv. D. L. D.

"Bk D P 384 [?]" [left margin]
Denton Land Dist. TX - JAMES C. PASCHALL solemnly swears I believe land on which I have settled, improved and now reside is otherwise vacant and I commenced my improvements on same about Aug 1 1855   - This 2nd day Feb 1856
Signed: JAMES C. PASCHALL
Sworn to & subscribed Feb 2 1856 before L. E. CAMP, Dept. Surv. Denton L. D.

Denton Land Dist. TX - Survey of 160 acs. for JAMES C. PASCHALL by virtue his affidavit - Situate in Denton Land Dist. and on waters of Walnut Creek, tributary of Trinity Riv. - Beg. at NE cor. MRS. MILLER preemption survey - W boundary line A. G. CANTRIL -

[33]   Surveyed: Feb 2 1856 - L. E. CAMP, Dept. Surv. D. L. D.
Chain Men: J. W. ERAIN [?], THOMAS BULLION
Recorded: Mar 28 1856 - R. W. ALLEN, Dist. Surv. Denton L. D.

"Bk D P 1" [left margin]
Denton Land Dist. TX - I, GEORGE L. LEONARD, solemnly swear that on or about Sep 15 1854 I settled upon land I now claim as a preemptionist - believe same to be vacant and unappropriated - claim same by virtue of the Donation Law this Dec 14 1854
Signed: GEORGE L. LEONARD
Sworn to & subscribed Dec 11 1854 before J. E. JENKINS, Dist. Surv. Denton L. D.

Denton Land Dist. TX - Dec 14 1854 - Survey for GEORGE L. LEONARD of 160 acs.- lying on Walnut Creek, waters of Trinity Riv. by virtue of his preemption claim -

[34]   Beg. W of SE cor. H. R. MORRIS 160 ac. survey -
Signed: J. E. JENKINS
Chain Carriers: A. MORRIS, M. E. MORRIS
Recorded: Aug 22 1855- R. W. ALLEN, Dist. Surv. Denton L. D.

[THE FOLLOWING ENTRY AND NEXT SHEET ARE SCRATCHED OUT]

* *
* "Bk D P 100" [left margin]   *
* Denton Land Dist. TX - WILLIAM H BAYLEY Solemnly swears   *
* that about Sep 23 1854 settled on land now claimed as   *
* preemptionist - believe to be vacant and unappropriated   *
* claims same by virtue -   *
*   *
* [35] Donation Law this 2nd Jan 1855   *
* Signed: WILLIAM H. BAYLEY   *
* Sworn to & subscribed Jan 2 1855 before J. E. JENKINS,   *
* Dept. Surv. Denton Land Dist.   *
*   *
* "THIS SURVEY MUST BE TRANSCRIBED AGAIN" [left margin]   *
* Denton Land Dist. TX - Field notes of survey of 160 acs.   *
* for WILLIAM H. BAYLEY by virtue his affidavit - Situate   *
* in Territory West of Tarrant Co. on Ash Creek tributary   *
* West Fork Trinity Riv. - Beg. S from SE cor. J. PRINCE   *
* 160 ac. survey -   *
* Surveyed: Jan 2 1855 - J. E. JENKINS, Dept. Surv. D.L.D.   *
* Chain Carriers: JAMES PIERCE, WM. BURROW   *
* I, R. W. ALLEN, Dist. Surv. Denton Land Dist.,hereby   *
* certify that I have examined foregoing plat and field   *
* notes and find them correct and the field notes are   *
* recorded in my office in Book D Preemption Record p 101   *
* Signed: R. W. ALLEN, Dist. Surv. Denton Land Dist.   *
*   *
* *

[36]   "Bk D P 78" [left margin]
Denton Land Dist. TX - MARK A REYNOLD, Solemnly swears - settled on land Jan 20 1854 - believe to be vacant & claim 320 acs. by virtue of preemption Law this May 30 1854
Signed: M. A. REYNOLD
Sworn to & subscribed May 30 1854 before J. E. JENKINS, Dept. Surv. Denton Land Dist.

Robertson Land Dist. TX - May 20 1854 - Survey for MARK A. REYNOLD of the Dist. of Tarrant Co. 320 acs. lying on Ash Creek, waters of West Trinity by virtue of his preemption claim - Beg. NW cor. W. H. BURROWS - J. WITCHERS West Boundary line - N with J. A. TINDAUS [?] W boundary line - S to W. J. REYNOLDS NE cor.
Signed: J. E. JENKINS, Dept. Surv. Robertson Land Dist.
Chain Carriers: BRICE WOODY, JAMES REYNOLD

[37] Recorded: Sep 9 1855 - R. W. ALLEN, Dist Surv Denton L.D.

"Bk D P 268" [left margin]
Denton Land Dist. TX - JAMES WHITE appeared before LEWELLEN MURPHY, Dept. Surv. Denton L. D. - took oath - believe land settled on to be vacant Public domain - settled on as pre-emptioner on or about Oct 12 1855 - was citizen at date of enactment of present preemption Law
Signed: JAMES "X" WHITE [his mark]
Sworn to & subscribed Nov 13 1855 before LEWELLEN MURPHY, Dept. Surv. Denton L. D.

Denton Land Dist. TX - Field notes of survey of 160 acs. in name of JAMES WHITE by virtue of foregoing affidavit - Situate in Tarrant Co. Territory on waters of Ash Creek, tributary of West Fork Trinity Riv. - Beg. E of SW cor. WILLIAM THOMAS REYNOLDS 320 ac. survey -

[38] Surveyed: Nov 13 1855 - LEWELLEN MURPHY, Dept Surv D.L.D.
Chain Carriers: JAMES WOODY, THOMAS GOLLIHER
Recorded: Mar 3 1856 - R. W. ALLEN, Dist. Surv. Denton L. D.

[WRITTEN ACROSS THE NEXT PAGE IN INK "NOT A CORRECT TRANSCRIPT - ERROR - TRANSCRIBE AGAIN "]

```
* * * * * * * * * * * * * * * * * * * * * * * * * * * * * *
*  "BK D P 50" [left margin]                                *
*  [39] Denton Land Dist. TX - EDWARD M. HORRIS [?]         *
*  appeared before LEWELLEN MURPHY, Dept Surv. Denton L. D. *
*  took oath - believe land settled on to be vacant Public  *
*  domain                                                   *
*  Signed: EDWARD M. HORRIS                                 *
*  Sworn to & subscribed Mar 6 1855 before LEWELLEN MURPHY  *
*  Dept. Surv. Denton Land Dist.                            *
*                                                           *
*  Denton Land Dist. TX - Survey of 160 acs. for EDWARD M.  *
*  HORRIS by virtue foregoing affidavit - Situate in Tarrant*
*  Co. Territory on waters of Clear Fork Trinity Riv.- Beg. *
*  at SW cor. CHARLES J. STANLEY preemption survey -        *
*  Surveyed: Mar 7 1855 - LEWELLEN MURPHY, Dept. Surv.      *
*  Denton Land Dist.                                        *
*  Chain Carriers: CLEMENT BLACKWELL, THOMAS G. WAUGH       *
*  Recorded: May 14 1855                                    *
*                                                           *
* * * * * * * * * * * * * * * * * * * * * * * * * * * * * *
```

[40] "Bk D P 58" [left margin]
Denton Land Dist. TX - THOMAS GEORGE WAUGH appeared before LEWELLEN MURPHY, Dept. Surv. Denton Land Dist. - took oath - believe land settled on to be vacant Public domain

Signed: T. G. WAUGH
Sworn to & subscribed Mar 7 1855 before LEWELLEN MURPHY, Dept. Surv. Denton L. D.

Denton Land Dist. TX - Survey of 160 acs. for THOMAS G. WAUGH by virtue foregoing affidavit - Situate in Tarrant Co. Territory on waters of Clear Fork Trinity - Beg. at SE cor. EDWARD M. HARRIS 160 ac. preemption survey -
Surveyed: Mar 7 1855 - LEWELLEN MURPHY, Dept. Surv. D. L. D.
Chain Carriers: CLEMENT BLACKWELL, EDWARD M. HARRIS

[41]   Recorded: Mar 14 1855 - R. W. ALLEN, Dist Surv D L D

"Bk D P 34" [left margin]
Denton Land Dist. TX - WILLIAM JAMES SILIVANT appeared before LEWELLEN MURPHY, Dept. Surveyor Denton Land Dist. - took oath - believe land settled on to be vacant Public domain
Signed: W. J. SILIVANT
Sworn to & subscribed Feb 9 1855 before LEWELLEN MURPHY, Dept. Surv. Denton Land Dist.

Denton Land Dist. TX - Survey of 160 acs. for WILLIAM JAMES SILIVANT by virtue foregoing affidavit - Situate in Tarrant Co. Territory on waters of Walnut Creek, tributary of West Fork Trinity Riv. - Beg. S & E from SW cor. JOHN PERRY ALLEN 160 ac. survey -

[42] Surveyed: Feb 12 1855 - LEWELLEN MURPHY, Dept Surv D L D
Chain Carriers: JAMES CALDWELL, F. M. HARRIS
Recorded: May 11 1855

"Bk D P 92" [left margin]
Denton Land Dist. TX - JOHN PERRY ALLEN appeared before LEWELLEN MURPHY, Dept. Surv. Denton Land Dist. - took oath - believe land settled on to be vacant Public domain
Signed: JOHN PERRY ALLEN
Sworn to & subscribed Feb 9 1855 before LEWELLEN MURPHY, Dept. Surv. Denton L. D.

[43]   Denton Land Dist. TX - Survey of 160 acs. for JOHN PERRY ALLEN by virtue foregoing affidavit - Situate in Tarrant Co. Territory on waters of Walnut Creek, tributary stream of West Fork Trinity Riv. - Beg. S of SW cor. JAMES CALDWELL 160 ac. preemption survey -
Surveyed: Feb 12 1855 - LEWELLEN MURPHY, Dept. Surv. D. L. D.
Chain Carriers: MERRICK BARTLETT, W. J. SILIVANT
Recorded: May 19 1855 - R. W. ALLEN, Dist. Surv. Denton L. D.

[44]   Denton Land Dist. TX - JOSHUA CALDWELL appeared before LEWELLEN MURPHY, Dept. Surv. Denton Land Dist. - took oath - believe land settled on to be vacant Public domain
Signed: JOSHUA CALDWELL

Sworn to & subscribed Feb 19 1855 before LEWELLEN MURPHY, Dept. Surv. Denton Land Dist.

"Bk D P 89" [left margin]
Denton Land Dist. TX - Survey of 126 acs. for JOSHUA CALDWELL by virtue foregoing affidavit - Situate in Tarrant Co. Territory on waters of Walnut Creek, tributary of West Fork Trinity Riv. - Beg. at SE cor. JOHN PERRY ALLEN 160 ac. preemption survey -

[45] SW cor. HEZEKIAH CALDWELL 160 ac. preemption survey -
Surveyed: Feb 12 1855 - LEWELLEN MURPHY, Dept Surv Denton L D
Chain Carriers: MERRICK BARTLETT, JAMES CALDWELL
Recorded: May 18 1855 - R. W. ALLEN, Dist. Surv. Denton L. D.

"Bk D P 44"
Denton Land Dist. TX - JAMES CALDWELL appeared before LEWELLEN MURPHY, Dept. Surv. Denton Land Dist. - took oath - believe land settled on to be vacant Public domain
Signed: JAMES CALDWELL
Sworn to & subscribed Feb 9 1855 before LEWELLEN MURPHY, Dept. Surv. Denton L. D.

Denton Land Dist. TX - Survey of 160 acs. for JAMES CALDWELL by virtue foregoing affidavit - Situate in Tarrant Co. Territory on waters of Walnut Creek, tributary of West Fork Trinity Riv. -

[46] Beg. at NW cor. HEZEKIAH CALDWELL 160 ac. preemption survey -
Surveyed: Feb 10 1855 - LEWELLEN MURPHY, Dept. Surv. D. L. D.
Chain Carriers: JOHN PERRY ALLEN, MERRICK BARTLETT
Recorded: May 12 1855

[47] Denton Land Dist. TX - HEZEKIAH CALDWELL appeared before LEWELLEN MURPHY, Dept. Surv. Denton Land Dist. - took oath - believe land settled on to be vacant Public domain
Signed: HEZEKIAH "X" CALDWELL [his mark]
Sworn to & subscribed Feb 8 1855 before LEWELLEN MURPHY, Dept. Surv. Denton L. D.

"Bk B P 155"
Denton Land Dist. TX - Survey of 160 acs. for HEZEKIAH CALDWELL by virtue foregoing affidavit - Situate in Tarrant Co. on waters of Walnut Creek, tributary of West Fork Trinity Riv. - Beg. NW from SW cor. THOMAS CALDWLELL 160 ac. survey -
Surveyed: Feb 10 1855 - LEWELLEN MURPHY, Dept. Surv. D. L. D.
Chain Carriers: JOHN PERRY ALLEN, MERICK BARTLETT

[48] Denton Land Dist. TX - THOMAS CALDWELL appeared before LEWELLEN MURPHY, Dept. Surv. Denton Land Dist. - took oath - believe land settled on to be vacant Public domain

Signed: THOMAS "X" CALDWELL [his mark]
Sworn to & subscribed Mar 10 1855 before LEWELLEN MURPHY,
Dept. Surv. Denton Land Dist.

"Bk B P 153" [left margin]
Denton Land Dist. TX - Survey of 160 acs. for THOMAS CALDWELL
by virtue foregoing affidavit - Situate in Tarrant Co. Territory on waters of Walnut Creek, tributary of West Fork Trinity
Riv. - Beg. S of SE cor. HEZEKIAH CALWELL 160 ac. preemption
survey -

[49] Surveyed: Mar 10 1855 - LEWELLEN MURPHY, Dept Surv D L D
Chain Carriers: WILLIAM ALLEN, JAMES CALDWELL
Recorded: May 28 1855 - R. W. ALLEN, Dist. Surv. Denton L. D.

."Bk B P 39" [left margin]
Denton Land Dist. TX - HEZAEL G. [?] CANTRELL appeared before LEWELLEN MURPHY, Dept. Surv. Denton Land Dist. - took
oath - believe land settled on to be vacant Public domain
Signed: H. G. CANTRELL
Sworn to & subscribed Jan 21 1855 before LEWELLEN MURPHY,
Dept. Surv. Denton L. D.

[50] Denton Land Dist. TX - Survey of 160 acs. for HAZAEL
CANTRELL by virtue foregoing affidavit - Situate in Tarrant
Co. Territory on waters of Ash Creek, tributary of West Fork
Trinity Riv. - Beg. W of NE cor. THOMAS BULLION 160 ac. preemption surv.
Surveyed: Feb 5 1855 - LEWELLEN MURPHY, Dept. Surv. D. L. D.
Chain Carriers: JERMIAH COCKBERN [?], RICHARD D. GODLYHENE [?]

[51] Recorded: May 11 1855

Denton Land Dist. TX - JOHN FRANCIS appeared before LEWELLEN
MURPHY, Dept. Surv. Denton Land Dist. - took oath - believe
land settled on to be vacant Public domain
Signed: JOHN FRANCIS
Sworn to & subscribed Jan 19 1855 before LEWELLEN MURPHY,
Dept. Surv. Denton L. D.

"BK B P 37" [Left margin]
Denton Land Dist. TX - Survey of 160 acs. for JOHN FRANCIS by
virtue foregoing affidavit - Situate in Tarrant Co. Territory
on waters of Ash Creek, tributary stream of West Fork Trinity
Riv. - Beg. W of SW cor. HENRY E. FRANCIS 160 ac. preemption
survey -
Surveyed: Jan 19 1855 - LEWELLEN MURPHY, Dept. Surv. D. L. D.
Chain Carriers: JOHN MATLOCK, JAMES WHITE

[52] Recorded: May 11 1855

"Bk B P 36"
Denton Land Dist. TX - HENRY E. FRANCES appeared before
LEWELLEN MURPHY, Dept. Surv. Denton Land Dist. - took oath -
believe land settled on to be vacant Public domain
Signed: HENRY E. FRANCES
Sworn to & subscribed Jan 19 1855 before LEWELLEN MURPHY,
Dept. Surv. Denton L. D.

Denton Land Dist. TX - Survey of 160 acs. for HENRY E. FRANCES
by virtue foregoing affidavit - Situate in Tarrant Co. Territory on waters of Ash Creek, tributary stream West Fork Trinity Riv. Beg. NW on SW cor. THOMAS BUTTON 160 ac. preemption
survey -

[53] Surveyed: Jan 19 1855 - LEWELLEN MURPHY, Dept Surv D L D
Chain Carriers: JOHN MATLOCK, JAMES WHITE
Recorded: May 15 1855 - R. W. ALLEN, Dist. Surv. Denton L. D.

Denton Land Dist. TX - HENRY BEADLE appeared before LEWELLEN
MURPHY, Dept. Surv. Denton Land Dist. - took oath - believe
land settled on to be vacant Public domain
Signed: HENRY BEADLE
Sworn to & subscribed Jan 29 1855 before LEWELLEN MURPHY,
Dept. Surv. Denton L. D.

[54] Denton Land Dist. TX - Survey of 160 acs. for HENRY
BEADLE by virtue foregoing affidavit - Situate in Tarrant Co.
Territory on waters of Ash Creek, tributary West Fork Trinity
Riv. - Beg. at NW cor. LURANS [?] CLIFTON 160 ac. preemption
survey -
Surveyed: Jan 31 1855 - LEWELLEN MURPHY, Dept. Surv. D. L. D.
Chain Carriers: WILLIAM PENNINGTON, L. M. MC CULLEY

[PAGES MISSING]

[57] Denton Land Dist. TX - Field notes survey of 160 acs.
for NOAH STERGGS [?] by virtue foregoing affidavit - Situate
on waters of Little Red Bear Creek, tributary Brazos Riv.,
County of Parker - Beg. E of NE cor. J. LOGSDON 320 ac. survey
[no survey date]
Chain Carriers: A. F. OBENCHAIN [?], A. F. STAGGS
Jan 9 1856 - J. E. JENKINS, Dept. Surveyor, certifies above
survey made by him
Recorded: - Jun 21 1856 - R. W. ALLEN, Dist Surv Denton L D

[58] Denton Land Dist. TX - JOHN C. CHAPMAN swears on or
about Mar 10 1856 settled on land now claimed as preemptionist
- believe same to be vacant and unappropriated
Signed: JOHN C. CHAPMAN
Sworn to and subscribed Apr 21 1856 before J. E. JENKINS,
Dept. Surv. Denton L. D.

"B F 115" [left margin]
Denton Land Dist. TX - Field notes of survey of 160 acs. for JOHN C. CHAPMAN by virtue his affidavit - Situate in Parker Co. S Fork Clear Fork Trinity Riv. - Beg. N of NW cor. G. K. ELKINS
Surveyed Apr 21 1856 - J. E. JENKINS, Dept. Surv. D. L. D.

[59] Chain Men: JOHN TRIMBLE, G. K. ELKINS
Recorded: Jun 21 1856 - R. W. ALLEN, Dist. Surv. Denton L. D.

"C 83" [left margin]
Denton Land Dist. TX - I, JOSEPH WARD, Do solemnly swear that on or about the 27th Nov 1854 I settled upon the land I now claim as a preemptionist and believe same to be vacant and unappropriated and claim 160 ac. by virtue of Donation Law this Dec 16th 1854
Signed: JOSEPH WARD
Sworn to and subscribed Dec 16 1854 before J. E. JENKINS, Dept. Surv. Denton L. D.

Denton Land Dist. TX - Dec 16 1854 - Survey of 160 acs. for

[60] JOSEPH WARD - lying on Walnut Creek, waters of Trinity Riv. by virtue his preemption claim - Beg. at NE cor. ___?___ BURRIS 160 ac. preemption survey -
Signed J. E. JENKINS, Dept. Surv. Denton Land. Dist.
Chain Carriers: J. _?_ LITTLTON, C. GEORGE [?]
Recorded: Jun 30 1855

[61] "C 98" [left margin]
Denton Land Dist. TX - RAMEY L. FRANCIS appeared before LEWELLEN MURPHY, Dept. Surv. Denton Land Dist. - took oath - believe land settled on to be vacant public domain
Signed: RAMEY L. "X" FRANCIS, signed by mark
Sworn to and subscribed Feb 19 1855 before LEWELLEN MURPHY, Dept. Surv. Denton L. D.

Denton Land Dist. TX - Survey of 160 acs. for RARNEY [?] L. FRANCIS by virtue foregoing affidavit - Situate in Tarrant Co. Territory on waters Walnut Creek, tributary of West Fork Trinity Riv. - Beg. N of NW cor. JOHN FRANCIS 160 ac. survey

[62] Surveyed Jan 20 1855 - LEWELLEN MURPHY, Dept Surv D L D
Chain Men: JOHN FRANCIS, [blank] COGBURN
Recorded: Jul 12 1855 - R. W. ALLEN, Dist. Surv. Denton L. D.

Denton Land Dist. TX - Before the undersigned authority personally appeared THOMAS BULLION who took and subscribed the following oath to wit: I, THOMAS BULLION do solemnly

[63] swear that I believe that the land upon which I am settled is vacant and unappropriated and that I am entitled to

the same by virtue of an Act of the Legislature of the State of Texas approved Feb 13th 1855
Signed: THOMAS BULLIONS
Sworn to & subscribed before me this the 29th day of Dec 1854
Signed: R. W. ALLEN, Dist. Surv. D. L. D.

" ? B C 77" [left margin]
Denton Land Dist. TX - Survey of 160 acs. for THOMAS BULLIONS by virtue foregoing affidavit - Situate in Tarrant Co. Territory on waters of Ash Creek, tributary West Fork Trinity Riv. - Beg. N from NW [?] cor. HENRY BEADLE 160 ac. preemption survey -

[64] Surveyed Feb 5 1855 - LEWELLEN MURPHY, Dept Surv D L D
Chain Men: JOHN C. RAMSEY, GEORGE MILLER
Recorded: Jun 27 1855 - R. W. ALLEN, Dist. Surv. Denton L. D.

[65] "Loc. Bk B 77" [left margin]
Denton Land Dist. TX - Field notes of survey of 63 [sic] acs. by virtue headright certificate of JOHN BROWN ? No. 2329/2430 issued by GEORGE [blank] Commissioner of the General Land Office on 18th Feb 1852 for 640 acs. of Land Situated in Denton Land Dist. in Tarrant Co. Territory on waters of Brazos Riv. - Beg. on NE cor. JOSEPH H. HEWETT 160 acs. preemption survey - S boundary line MONROE UPTION preemption survey -

[66] W boundary line ROBERT P. BAKERs preemption -
Surveyed: Dec 14 1855 - LEWELLEN MURPHY, Dept. Surv. D. L. D.
Chain Carriers: JOSEPH H. HEWETT, MILTON IKARD
Recorded: Aug 14 1856 - R. W. ALLEN, Dist. Surv. Denton L. D.

[67] Denton Land Dist. TX - Field notes of survey of 577 acs. by virtue of headright certificate of JOHN BROWN Rcd [?] No. 2329/2430 issued by GEORGE W. SMYTH Commissioner of the General Land Office on the 18th Feb 1832 [1852 ?] for 640 acs. land - Situate in Denton Land Dist. in Tarrant Co. Territory on waters of Brazos Riv. - Beg. NE from NE cor. WILLIAM C. BAKER 160 ac. preemption survey - SW cor. A. DODIONS [?] preemption - S boundary line of JOHN J. HAMILTONS preemption -

[68] Surveyed Dec 22 1855 - LEWELLEN MURPHY, Dept Surv D L D
Chain Carriers: WILLIAM C. BAKER, JAMES M. UPTON
Recorded: Aug 14 1856 - R. W. ALLEN, Dist. Surv. Denton L. D.

[69] "Loc. Bk E 155" [left margin]
Denton Land Dist. TX - Have surveyed for Parker Co. 320 ac. of land by order of the County Court and by virtue of the 4th section of an act by the Legislature of the State of Texas approved the 12th day Dec A. D. 1855 donating to said Parker Co. 320 acs. of the Public domain of the State aforesaid - Situated in Parker Co. on S prong of Clear Fork waters of the Trinity Riv. - Beg. W & N from NE cor. Leon Co. survey -

[70]   Surveyed May 28 1856 - ISAAC O. HEADLEY, Dept Surv Denton Land Dist.
Chain Carriers: JOHN PARKER, JOHN H. PRINCE
Recorded: Aug 22 1856 - R. W. ALLEN, Dist. Surv. Denton L. D.

[WRITTEN IN LARGE LETTERS AT BOTTOM OF THIS SHEET AND CIRCLED]
"THE STATE OF TEXAS, DENTON LAND DIST. SURVEY NO. ? I HAVE SURVEYED FOR THOMAS [?] J. ROBINSON"

[71]   "Loc. Bk C 310" [left margin]
Denton Land Dist. TX - Field notes of survey of 7,430,023 sq. vrs. by virtue of Headright Certificate No. 2710/2811 issued to JAMES MORRIS by the Commissioners of the General Land Office at Austin Feb 9 1853 for 1/3 League of Land Situate in Denton Land Dist. on waters of Clear Fork of Trinity Riv. - Beg. on SE cor. EZRA JASPER CANNAFAX 160 ac. preemption survey - W boundary line GEORGE TAYLOR preemption survey -

[72]   NW cor. Issac P. DAVIS preemption survey - [long physical description - no names]

[73]   NE cor. WILLIAM GREENs preemption - E boundary JOHN A. [?] CANNAFAX preemption -

[74]   This survey was commenced on the 2nd of Oct 1855 and finished on the 14th day of Nov 1855
Signed: LEWELLEN MURPHY
Chain Carriers: DAVID [?] STINSON, GEORGE TAYLOR
Recorded: Mar [no day] 1856 - R. W. ALLEN, Dist Surv D L D

[75]   "Loc. B 308" [left margin]
Denton Land Dist. TX - Field notes of survey of 160 acs. by virtue of Bounty Land Warrant No. 1526 issued to WILLIAM DAVIS by WILLIAM Y. LACY & WILLIAM H. CANCLIFF [?] assignee by JAMES S. GILLETT Adjutant General Feb 22 1854 for 320 acs. Situate in Denton Land Dist. in Tarrant Co. Territory on waters of Brazos Riv. - Beg. NE from NW cor. WILLIAM UPTON 160 ac. preemption survey -
Surveyed: Dec 15 1855 - LEWELLEN MURPHY, Dept. Surv. D. L. D.

[76]   Chain Carriers: MILTON IKARD, JOSEPH H. HEWETT
Recorded: Mar [no day] 1856 - R. W. ALLEN, Dist Surv D L D

"Loc. C 267" [left margin]
Denton Land Dist. TX - Field notes of survey of 160 acs. by virtue of Bounty Land Warrant No. 1526 issued to WILLIAM DAVIS by WILLIAM Y. LACY & WILLIAM H. CUNCLIFF Assignee by JAMES S. GILLETT Adjutant General Feb 22 1854 for 320 acs. Situate in Denton Land Dist. in Tarrant Co. Territory on waters of Brazos Riv. - Beg. W from SW [?] cor. MONROE UPTON 160 ac. preemption

[77] Surveyed: Dec 21 1855 - LEWELLEN MURPHY, Dept Surv D L D
Chain Carriers: JOSEPH H. HEWETT, DAVID HERRING
Recorded: Mar 3 1856 - R. W. ALLEN, Dist. Surv. Denton L. D.

[78]   "Loc. D P 1" [left margin]
Denton Land Dist. TX - Have surveyed for IGNATIUS L. AND (AUEL ?) 6,520,960 sq. vrs. by virtue of Duplicate Certificate No. 812/911 issued by THOMAS WILLIAM WARD Commissioner of the General Land Office Feb 16 1848 Situate in Tarrant Co. on Clear Fork Trinity Riv. - Beg. at SW cor. THOMPSON MASON 320 ac. survey - passing SW cor. STEPHEN TRIMBLE 160 ac. survey -

[79]   4 labors areable - balance pasture land
Surveyed: Sep 14 1856 - ISAAC O. HEADLEY, Dept. Surv. D. L. D.
Chain Carriers: JAMES KIDWELL Sen, JAMES KIDWELL Jun
Recorded: Apr 21 1856 - R. W. ALLEN, Dist. Surv. Denton L. D.

"Loc. D P 2" [left margin]
Denton Land Dist TX - Have surveyed for REYNOLD REYNOLDS 100 acs by virtue of Certificate No 83 Class 2nd issued to him by the Board of Land Commissioners for Nacagdoches Co for 1280 acs Jul 5 1858 [sic] Situate W of Tarrant Co. on head of Red Bear Creek

[80]   Beg. E of NE cor. STEPH. F. JONES 160 ac. survey - to W boundary S. R. BARBER 160 ac. survey -
Surveyed: Dec 10 1855 - I. O. HEADLEY, Dept. Surv. D. L. D.
Chain Carriers: JOHN S. WHITE, S. P. BARBER
Recorded: Apr 21 1856 - R. W. ALLEN, Dist. Surv. Denton L. D.

[81]   "Loc. B D 143" [left margin]
Denton Land Dist. TX - Field notes of survey of 417 acs. for JOHN C. CHAPMAN by virtue of Cert. No. 86 issued by County Court of Dallas Co. to JEREMIAH SNOW for 640 acs. Sep 5 1855 - Situate in Parker Co. on S Fork Trinity Riv. - Beg. N & SE of SW [?] cor. Leon School Land survey -

[82]   NE cor. JO. TRIMBLES - E boundary line of G. K. ELKINS survey -
Surveyed: Apr 21 1856 - J. E. JENKINS, Dept. Surv. D. L. D.
Chain Carriers: G. K. ELKINS, JOHN TRIMBLE
Recorded: Jun 21 1856 - R. W. ALLEN, Dist. Surv. Denton L. D.

[83]   "Pre Bk D 311" [left margin]
Denton Land Dist. TX - Before undersigned authority personally appeared E. M. RIPPY and took and subscribed the following oath I, E. M. RIPPY, do Solemnly swear that I believe the land upon which I am settled is vacant and that I settled upon the same on or about Feb 1 1855 - So help me God
Signed: E. M. RIPPY
Sworn to & subscribed before me, ISAAC O. HEADLEY, Dept. Surv. Denton Land Dist., this 6th day of July A. D. 1855

Denton Land Dist. TX - Field notes of 160 ac. survey for E. M. RIPPY by virtue above affidavit - Situate in Tarrant Co. in the upper Cross Timbers - Beg. NW from NW cor. W. M. LOW [?] 160 ac. survey -

[84] Surveyed: Jul 6 1855 - ISAAC O. HEADLEY, Dept Surv D L D
Chain Men: W. D. GUYTON, D. A. LOW
Recorded: Mar 19 1856 - R. W. ALLEN, Dist. Surv. Denton L. D.

"Pre B D 329" [left margin]
Denton Land Dist. TX - Before undersigned authority personally appeared W. B. FONDERN [?] - took and subscribed the following oath -

[85] believe land on which settled is vacant with the exception of the exception [sic] of the Rail Road Reservation and that said settlement was made on or about 9th Dec 1855
Signed: W. B. FONDEN
Sworn to & subscribed Aug 20 1855 before ISAAC O. HEADLEY, Dept. Surv. Denton L. D.

Denton Land Dist. TX - Survey of 160 acs. for W. B. FONDERN by virtue above affidavit - Situate in Tarrant Co. on Rock Creek, tributary of Brazos Riv. - Beg. NW from SW cor. H. KINNEDE [?] 160 ac. survey -
Surveyed: Aug 20 1855

[86] Recorded: Mar 21 1856 - R. W. ALLEN, Dist Surv D L D

[87] "Pre B D 314" [left margin]
Denton Land Dist. TX - Before undersigned authority appeared GEORGE G. TEETERS took and subscribed following oath - believe land settled on is vacant & said settlement was made on or about Oct 30 1855
Signed: GEORGE G. TEETERS
Sworn to & subscribed Nov 15 1855 before ISAAC O. HEADLEY, Dept. Surv. Denton Land Dist.

Denton Land Dist. TX - Field notes of survey of 160 acs. for GEORGE G. TEETERS by virtue of his affidavit - Situate in Tarrant Co. in Upper Cross Timbers - Beg. SW & N from SW cor. E. M. RIPPY 160 ac. survey -
Surveyed: Nov 15 1855 - ISAAC O. HEADLEY, Dept Surv Denton L. D.

[88] Chain Men: J. H. [?] TATE, J. S. STEPHENS
Recorded: Mar 17 1856 - R. W. ALLEN, Dist. Surv. Denton L. D.

"Pre Bk D P 315" [left margin]
Denton Land Dist. TX - Before undersigned authority personally appeared ISAAC TEETERS who took and subscribed following oath - believe land settled on is vacant - said settlement made on

or about Oct 20 1855
Signed: ISAAC TEETERS
Sworn to & subscribed Nov 18 1855 before ISAAC O. HEADLEY,
Dept. Surv. Denton Land Dist.

[89]   Denton Land Dist. TX - Field notes of Survey of 160
acs. for ISAAC TEETERS by virtue of his affidavit - Situate in
Tarrant Co. in Upper Cross Timbers - Beg. at SW cor. GEORGE G.
TEETERS 160 ac. survey -
Surveyed: Nov 15 1855 - ISAAC O. HEADLEY, Dept. Surv. D. L. D.
[Chain Carriers ?] J. H. TATE, J. S. STEPHENS
Recorded: Mar 19 1856 - R. W. ALLEN, Dist. Surv. Denton L. D.

[90]   "Bk E P 116" [left margin]
Parker Co. TX, Denton Land Dist.- Survey of 480 acs. by virtue
of ACHILLES THORNHILL Headright Cert. No. [blank] issued to
him by Co. Clerk of Grayson Co. as a settler in the Colony
granted to WILLIAM S. PETERS & others & dated [blank] for 640
acs. Situate in Parker Co. - Beg. E of NW cor. JEREMIAH CAPPS
480 ac. survey -
Surveyed: Jul 18 1856 - JAMES W. LIVELY Dept. Surv. D. L. D.
Chain Men: T. STEEL, WM. RIDER

[91]   Sep 12 1856 - CHAS. C. LACY, Dist. Surveyor Denton Land
Dist., hereby certify foregoing described field notes are correctly recorded in "my" office in Book C p 116

"Bk E P 217" [left margin]
Parker Co. TX, Denton Land Dist. - Surveyed 320 acs. by virtue
of P. J. MC CARY's [?] Headright Cert. No. 88 issued to him
for 320 acs. as a settler in the Colony granted to WILLIAM S.
PETERS & others by the Co. Clerk of Collin Co. on Jul 1 1856 -
said land situate in Parker Co. on S prong Mary's Creek - Beg.
S of NW cor. C. JACKSONs 320 ac. survey -

[92]   Surveyed: Jul 19 1856 - JAS. W. LIVELY, Dept Surv D L D
Chain Men: T. STREET, WM. H. STREET
Sep 12 1856 - CHAS. C. LACY, Dist. Surveyor Denton Land Dist.,
certifies foregoing correctly recorded his office in Alton Bk
E p 217

[93]   "Located Bk E 218"
Parker Co. TX, Denton Land Dist. - Surveyed 320 acs. by virtue
of CALVIN JACKSON Headright Cert. No. 63 issued to him as a
settler in the Colony granted to W. S. PETERS & others for 320
acs. by Co. Clerk Grayson Co. Feb 19 1856 - said land situate
in Parker Co. on Mary's Creek, tributary Clear Fork of Trinity
Riv. Beg. N of NW cor. ACHILLES THORNHILLS 480 ac. survey -
Surveyed: Jul 19 1856
Chain Men: T. STREET, W. H. STREET

[94]   Signed: JAS. W. LIVELY, Dept. Surv. Denton Land Dist.

[no date] CHAS. C. LACY, Dist. Surveyor Denton Land Dist., certifies foregoing recorded his office in Alton Bk E p 218

"Location Bk E P 220" [left margin]
Tarrant Co. TX - Surveyed 480 ac. by virtue of JEREMIA [sic] CAPP's Headright Cert. No. 89 issued to him by the Co. Clerk of Collin Co. as a headright in the Colony granted to WM. PETERS & others dated Jul 1 1856 - Situate in Tarrant & Parker Counties on Mary's Creek, branch of Clear Fork Trinity Riv. - Beg. in E line of Parker & W line of Tarrant Co. 13 mi. N of SW cor. said Tarrant Co. -

[95] Surveyed: Jul 18 1856 JAMES. W. LIVELY
Chain Men: THOMAS STREET, WM. RIDER

[96] [no date] CHAS. C. LACY, Dist. Surveyor Denton Land Dist., certifies foregoing recorded his office in Alton Bk E p 220

Denton Land Dist. TX - WILLIAM H. BAYLEY solemnly swears that on or about Sep 23 1854 settled upon land now claim as preemptionist & believe same to be vacant & unappropriated & claim same by virtue of Donation Law this Jan 2 1855
Signed: WM. H. BAYLEY
Sworn to & subscribed Jan 2 1855 before J. E. JENKINS, Dept. Surv. Denton Land Dist.

Denton Land Dist. TX - Field notes survey of 160 acs. for WILLIAM H. BAYLEY by virtue his affidavit - Situate in Tarrant & Territory West of Tarrant Co. on Ash Creek, tributary of West Fork Trinity Riv. - Beg. S of SE cor. -

[97] J. PRICE 160 ac. survey -
Surveyed: Jan 2 1855 - J. E. JENKINS, Dept. Surv. Denton L. D.
Chain Carriers: JAMES PRICE, WM. BURROW
R. W. ALLEN, Dist. Surveyor Denton Land Dist., certifies he has examined foregoing field notes - finds them correct - recorded his office Bk D Preemption Record p 101

[new sheet - no number]

The State of Texas
Denton Land District | I, CHAS. C. LACY, District Surveyor of Denton Land District do hereby certify that the foregoing 97 pages is a true and correct coppy [sic] of the surveys herein transcribed from the original records of surveys in my office

    Given under my hand
    at Alton this March 21st 1857
     CHAS. C. LACY District
     Surveyor Denton Land District

The State of Texas
County of Denton | I, A. P. LLOYD, Clerk of the County
Court of Denton County, Texas, hereby
certify that the foregoing pages was examined by me with the
assistance of the District Surveyor of Denton Land District
and I believe the same to be a true copy of the original records in said District Surveyors office.
                      Given under my hand and seal of office
                      at Alton March 21st 1857
                      A. P. LLOYD
                      Clerk County Court D. C. T.

[Large Round Yellow Seal affixed]

INDEX TO PRE-EMPTION RECORDS A, C, D
DENTON LAND DISTRICT
23 pp

[NOTE: Pages are not numbered]

[1st sheet]

The State of Texas
Denton Land District | I, CHAS. C. [?] LACY District Surv [torn] of Denton Land District Do hereby certify that th[torn] 283 Pages is a true and correct Record of the origin[torn] d of Survey of my office.
Given under My Hand at Alton this the 21st day of March A. D. 1857
CHAS. C. LACY Distric[torn]
Survey of Denton La[torn] Dist.

The State of Texas
County of Denton | I, A. P. LLOYD Clerk of the County Court of Denton County Texas hereby certify that I assisted in Comparing foregoing 283 pages of Transcript with the Original Records in the office of the District Surveyors office at Alton in Denton Land Dist[torn] [obliterated]d believe the Same to be a Correct Copy of Sa[torn] Original Record
Given under My han[torn] and Seal of Office at Alt[torn] March 21st A. D. 1857
A. P. LLOYD Clerk Co. D. C. L.

[Large round yellow seal affixed]

[Page 2] B

	Acres	Book	Page
ALLEN, GEORGE			8
BALEMAN, JAMES	640	A	25
BIDIORNEL [?], L. M.	640	"	57
BARKER, JOSEPH	320	"	107
BANNER, MAHALA	320	"	145

[Page 3]

	Acres	Book	Page
BEDWELL, CHRISTOPHER			21
BILLINGSLEE, ROBT.			31
BARNES, SILAS			46
BAKER, WM.C.			57
BAKER, R. P.			61
BRISCO, ISAAC			67
BILLINGSLEY, JAMES	320	A	117
BERGES, ELIJAH	320	"	125
BOWMAN C. F.	160	"	224

[Page 4]
ADAMS, WILLIAM	320	A	38
ANDERSON, P. H.	640	"	15
ADAMS, JOHN	320	"	[torn]
ALLEN, GEORGE	320	C	8[torn]

[page 5 blank]

[Page 6]
	Acres	Book	Page
EDDLEMAN, R. C.	320	A	127
EVANS, ROBERT	1920	"	8
EARNEST, JAMES H.	320	"	124
EDDLEMAN, DAVID	320	"	133
" COLUMBUS J.	320	"	134
FRANKLIN, WESLEY	320	A	77
FROMAN, JOHN M.	320	"	79
FREEMAN, JOHN	160	"	182
FREEMAN, JOHN A.	160	"	194
FIELDS, NOAH	320	C	9

[Page 7]
FIELDS, NOAH			9
FLETCHER, WM.K			28
GREEN GEORGE	640	A	29
GOMER F	640	"	53
" "	"	"	54
GLENN, JAMES A. [?]	320	"	102
GONZALES DINNSEZ [?]		C	5
GLENN, WALTER B.	320	"	112

[page 8]
	League	Acres	Book	Page
GONZALES, DINNSES (?)				5
HODGES, HENRY		2302 1/2	A	20
HEAVEN [?] SMITH, L.		320	"	50
HALEY, W. D. dived [sic]		320	"	65 & 63
HUNT, M.		160	"	72
HIUSTAN [?], WALTER		398	"	73
HEADLEY ISAAC O		320	"	84
HEFFINGTON, STEPHEN		320	"	104
HOLDEN, PETER B.		320	"	109
HAYNES, BLEUFORD		320	"	111
HIBBERT, JOHN B.		320	"	153
HAWPE, JOHN W.		320	"	155
HIGANS, WILLIAM		160	"	178
HIGGINS, WILLIAM		480	"	204
" "		160	"	206
HALLER, FRANCIS		320	"	61

[page 9]
	Acres	Book	Page
HARRISON, WM.D		G [?]	24
HITTSON, JOHN			54

Name	League	Acres	Book	Page
HEWIT, JOSEPH				60
HALL, PETER S [in pencil]		160	A	214

[page 10]

Name	League	Acres	Book	Page
JONES, HEZEKIAH		640	A	5
" "		"	"	7
JONES, JAMES		320	"	123
JOHNSON, GEORGE M. P.		320	"	132
JENKIN, J. E.		320	"	143
JENKINS, JAMES M.		320	"	200
" " "		320	"	202
KIRK, WILLIAM		160	A	168
" "		"	"	169
KIRK, PETER		320	"	186

[page 11 - HEADINGS ONLY - NO NAMES]

[page 12]

Name	League	Acres	Book	Page
LANG, EDWARD			A	32
Leon County School Land	1 1/2		"	16
" " " "	"		"	17
LONG, WILLIAM		960	"	30
LOWDERS, ADAM L.		640	"	60
LEWIS, LINZY [?]		320	"	119
LEAK, SAMUEL		320	"	150
LYNCH, JOHN		320	"	165
LADGSDON, JOSEPH		320	"	171
LODGSDON, "		260	"	187
LODGSDON, JOSEPH		280	"	188
LEE, GEORGE [in pencil]		160	"	213
MILLS, WM. Junr		320	[blank]	33
MAYS, JAMES H.		320	A	35
MAYS, WILLIAM J.		320	"	36
MC [A?]NNEELY [?] PEASET [sic]		320	"	39
MOOR, JOHN H.		320	"	48
MC CARVER WILLIAM PITTS		320	"	79
" Adm.		320	"	87
McDonnal, LEWIS P.		320	"	88
MC CARVER, C. C.		320	"	90
MASON, THOMPSON		[blank]	"	100
MC CULLAH, JOHN		320	"	137
MONTRY, WILLIAM		442 1/?	"	175
MILES, JOHN H.		[blank]	C	13
MC EWIN, NANCY		640	C	2
MC CARTY LARKIN [in pencil]		160	A	220

[page 13]

Name	League	Acres	Book	Page
MILES, JOHN H.				13
MORRIS, ACHILLES				25
MC LAREN, JOHN				35

```
MILLER, A. O.                                    36
MATTHEWS, R. H.                                  40
MITCHELL, J. R.                                  48
MATTHEWS, R. H.                                  63

[page 14]
OXIER JAMES S.                 320       A      128
OXIER ELZA                     320       "      139

NELIWS, [?] C. C.              160       A      196
NELIWS, [?] C. C.              160       "      198

[page 15 - HEADINGS ONLY - NO NAMES]

[page 16]
PIERCE, JAMES                                    26
PINNELL, [?] HIRAM                               44
PORTER, J. F.                                    53
PORTER, C. C.                                    55
PASCHAL, J. T.                                   38
PATRICK, WILLIAM W.            320       A       32
PINKNEY, JOHN L.               177       "      177
Parker County                  320       D       69
POLK, B. K. [in pencil]        160       A      216

[page 17 - HEADINGS ONLY - NO NAMES]

[page 18 - upper right corner torn off]
[RE]YNOLDS, J. C.                       [torn]
RASH, JOSEPH                            [torn]
RIDDLE, SAMUEL                1858       A     [torn]
RIDDLE, SAMUEL                  62       "     [torn]
   "         "                1476       "       14
RIDDLE, SAMUEL                 640       A       28
BABINSON, WILLIAM M            320       "       96

STARR, RICHARD                1476       A       22
SMITH, A. B.                   320       "       85
S____ELL, JAMES H.             320       "       98
SA__AT, THOMPSON D.            320       "      141
SPEARMAN, JOHN W.              320       "      149
SNYDER, JOHN                   320       "      153
STWLTS, [?] JOHN               320       "      167
SMYMS, GEORGE                  160       "      184
SHELTON, J.                    320       C       10
SNOW, JEREMIAH                 417       D       81
SPARKS, A. [in pencil]         160       A      221

[page 19]
SHELTON, J                            [blank   blank   blank]

[page 20 - Tear in upper right corner - left edges torn]
```

	League	Acres	Book	Page
UPTON, WM.				43
UPTON, WM.				58
WHITE, JESSE	1000	177	A	19
WILSON, CRAIN		320	"	26
WALKER, JOSEPH L.		320	"	42
WHITE, BENJAMIN J.		320	"	45
WILCOX, JACOB		640	"	67
" "		[torn]	"	69
WILCOX, JACOB		[torn]	"	70
WYNN, JOSEPH B.		32[torn]	"	94
[W]OOSLEY, JOHNSON		"[torn]	"	101
WILLIAMs, JAMES		320	"	116
WOODEY, WILLIAM		320	[torn]	
WOODES, [?] WILLIAM		"	"	130
WOOSLEY, WILLIAM		320	"	138
WILBURN, F. C.		320	"	209
WALDREN, JOSEPH B.		[blank]	C	15
WILSON, W. T. [in pencil]		160	A	211
WRAY, J. G. [in pencil]		160	"	223

[page 21]

	League	Acres	Book	Page
TAYLOR, GEORGE				1
THOMASON, W. D.				6
TATE, J. H.				41
TRIMBLE, STEPHEN				65
TANKERSLEY SARAH		1476	A	23
TURNER, F. B.		320	"	41
THOMPSON JAMES		640	"	44
THURMEN, JOHN M.		640	"	5‾
THARP, WILLIAM		320	"	8‾
TARPLEY, GREEN H.		320	"	1‾
THOMAS, D. [?] C.		320	"	1‾
THROGM[torn]RTON, ROBERT M.		160	"	190‾
[torn] GEORGE		[blank]	G	1
THOMASON, WM. D.		"	"	6
UNDERWOOD, NORMAN		320	A	95

PRE-EMPTION RECORD "B" PARKER COUNTY
1856 - 1858

[1]   "Preemption Book B"

The State of Texas | No. 100
County of Parker | Before me, JOHN MATLOCK, Chief Justice of Parker County, this day personally came EZRA J. CANAFAX as applicant and WILLIAM TAYLOR and ELIJAH N. CANAFAX, two disinterested and respectable witnesses, to me known, All of them being by me duly sworn, saith on their oath, that the applicant EZRA CANAFAX was bonafide settled upon vacant land before and on the 26th day of August 1856 and that he claims the right of purchase on said settlement under an act to authorize the sale and settlement of the vacant public land within the limits of the Mississippi & Pacific Railroad Reservation passed August the 26th A D 1856.

EZRA J. CANAFAX
WILLIAM TAYLOR
ELIJAH N. CANAFAX

Sworn to & subscribed before me to certify which I have hereunto set my name and the seal of the County Court at Weatherford this the 22nd of September A. D. 1856
JOHN MATLOCK Chief Justice
of Parker County Texas

The State of Texas |
County of Parker | Survey of 160 acs. of Land made for EZRA J. CANAFAX by virtue of affidavit No. 100 issued to him by JOHN MATLOCK, Chief Justice, within and for said county on 22nd day of September 1856 under the provisions of an act to authorize the location, sale and settlement of the Mississippi & Pacific

[new sheet-page number torn] Railroad Reserve passed Aug 26th 1856 - Situate on the Clear Fork of Trinity River - Beg. N of SE cor. ELIZAH B. CANAFAX -
Surveyed: Oct 6 1857 - LEWELLEN MURPHY, Co Surv for Parker Co
Chain Carriers: JOHN A. CANAFAX, ELIZAH N. CANAFAX
Recorded in my office on page [blotted out] of Book B
Dated: Oct 27 1857 - LEWELLEN MURPHY, Co. Surv. P. C. [sic]

Parker Co. TX - 103 - Before JOHN MATLOCK, Chief Justice of Parker Co., personally came GEORGE W. DUNCAN, as applicant, and JOSEPH WARD and HENRY WARD, two disinterested and respectable witnesses - all duly sworn and saith that applicant (GEORGE W. DUNCAN) was bonafide settled upon vacant land on

[3]   26th Aug 1856, date of enactment Act authorizing settlement of vacant land within limits of Mississippi & Pacific

77

Railroad Reservation passed Aug 26 1856, and he continues to reside within the limits of said reserve and he claims the right of purchase on said settlement under said act.
Signed: G. W. DUNCAN, JOSEPH WARD, HENRY WARD
Sworn to & subscribed Oct 1 1857 - JOHN MATLOCK, Chief Justice Parker Co.

Parker Co. TX - Field notes of survey of 160 acs. in name of G. W. DUNCAN by virtue of affidavit No. 103 - Situate in Parker Co. on waters of Walnut Creek, tributary West Fork Trinity Riv. - Beg. on SE cor. JESSE FRANKLINS 160 ac. survey -

[4] Surveyed: Oct 15 1857 - R. J. BILLINGSLEA, Dept. Surv. Parker Co.
Chain Carriers: TARLETON BURRIS, JAMES SPROULS
Recorded: Oct 27 1857 - LEWELLEN MURPHY, Co. Surv. Parker Co.

Parker Co. TX - 101 - Before JOHN MATLOCK, Chief Justice Parker Co. TX - personally came HAZAEL E. CANTRELL, as applicant and JAMES LONG & WILLIAM WOODY, two disinterested and respectable witnesses - all duly sworn and saith that applicant (HAZAEL E. CANTRELL) was bonafide settled upon vacant land on Aug 26 1856, date of enactment of act authorizing settlement of vacant land within limits of Mississippi & Pacific R. R. - continues to reside within limits - claims right of purchase under said act.
Signed: H. E. CANTRELL, JAMES LONG, WILLIAM WOODY

[5] Sworn to & subscribed Sep 24 1857 - JOHN MATLOCK, Chief Justice Parker Co.

Parker Co. TX - Field notes of survey of 160 acs. for HAZAEL E. CANTRELL by virtue of his preemption affidavit No. 101 - Situate in Parker Co. on waters of Ash Creek, tributary of West Fork Trinity Riv. - Beg. SE of SE cor. JEREMIAH COCKBURN 160 ac. preemption survey - N boundary line of S. SKIDMORE 320 ac. survey -
Surveyed: Oct 27 1857 - LEWELLEN MURPHY, Co Surv Parker Co TX
Chain Carriers: JEREMIAH COCKBURN, RICHARD D. GODBEKERE [?]
Oct 27 1857 - LEWELLEN MURPHY, Co. Surv. Parker Co. TX, certifies field notes

[6] Parker Co. TX - 104 - Before JOHN MATLOCK, Chief Justice Parker Co., TX - personally came JOHN G. LANTZ, as applicant and WILLIAM WOODY and HENRY LANTZ two disinterested and respectable witnesses - all duly sworn and saith that applicant (JOHN G. LANTZ) was bonafide settled upon vacant land on Aug 26 1856, date of enactment of act authorizing settlement of vacant land within limits of Mississippi & Pacific R. R. - continues to reside within limits - claims right of purchase under said act.
Signed: JOHN G. LANTZ, WILLIAM "X" WOODY [his mark], H. LANTZ

Sworn to & subscribed Sep 2 1857 before JOHN MATLOCK, Chief Justice Parker Co. TX

[7] Parker Co. TX - Field notes of survey of 160 acs. made for JOHN G. LANTZ by virtue of his preemption affidavit No. 104 Situate in Parker Co. on waters of Walnut Creek, tributary of N West Fork Trinity Riv. - Beg. S of SW cor. JAMES M TUCKER 320 ac. survey -
Surveyed: Sep 25 1857 -
Chain Carriers: JOHN MATLOCK, HENRY LANTZ
Oct 27 1857 - LEWELLEN MURPHY, Co. Surv. Parker Co., certifies

[8] Parker Co. TX - 46 - Before undersigned authority came A. M. GARY, as applicant and W. G. MOORE and T. C. MOORE, two disinterested and respectable witnesses - all duly sworn and saith that A. M. GARY (applicant) was bonafide settled upon vacant land on Aug 26 1856, date of enactment of act authorizing settlement of vacant land within limits of Mississippi & Pacific R. R. - continues to reside within limits - claims right of purchase under said act.
Signed: A M GARY, W "X" G MOORE [mark], F "X" C MOORE [mark]
Sworn to & subscribed Feb 24 1857 before JOHN H. PRINCE, Co. Clerk Parker Co. TX by WM. M. GREEN, Dept.

Parker Co. TX - Field notes of survey of 160 acs. made for A. M. GARY by virtue of his preemption affidavit No. 4 -

[9] Situate in Parker Co. on waters of Dry Creek, triubutary of Brazos Riv. about 7 mi N 45° W from town of Weatherford - Beg. NW from NE cor. PETER WELDON 160 ac. preemption survey -
Surveyed: Sep 11 1857
Chain Carriers: Thomas C. MOORE, WILLIAM G. MOORE
Oct 28 1857 - LEWELLEN MURPHY, Co. Surv. Parker Co., certifies foregoing survey

[10] Parker Co. TX - 179 - Before undersigned authorized authority came JOHN BROWN as applicant and ROBERT J. BILLINGSLEA and HIRAM PINNEL two disinterested and respectable witnesses - all duly sworn and saith that applicant was bonafide settled upon vacant land on Aug 26 1856, date of enactment of act authorizing settlement of vacant land within limits of Mississippi & Pacific R. R. - continues to reside within limits claims right of purchase under said act.
Signed: JOHN BROWN, R. J. BILLINGSLEA, H. PINNEL
Sworn to & subscribed Jul 7 1857 before JOHN H. PRINCE, Co. Clerk Parker Co. by WILLIAM M. GREEN, Dept.

Parker Co. TX - Have surveyed for JOHN BROWN 160 acs. by virtue of affidavit No. 179 - Situate in Parker Co. in Upper Cross Timbers about 15 mi. N 45° W from town of Weatherford - Beg. NW from NE cor. D. A. LAW 160 ac. survey

[11]   Surveyed: Aug 21 1857 ISAAC O. HEADLEY, D _?_ P. C.
Chain Carriers: E. M. RIPPY, D. A. LAW
Recorded: Oct 28 1857 - LEWELLEN MURPHY, Co Surv Parker Co TX

Parker Co. TX - 44 - Before JOHN MATLOCK, Chief Justice Parker Co. TX - appeared JOHN M. HEFLEY as applicant and JESSE W. FRANKLIN and JOHN MONTGOMERY two disinterested and respectable witnesses - all duly sworn and saith that applicant was bonafide settled upon vacant land on Aug 26 1856, date of enactment of act authorizing settlement of vacant land within limits of Mississippi & Pacific R. R. - continues to reside within limits claims right of purchase under said act.

[12]   Signed: JOHN M. HEFLEY, J. W. FRANKLIN, JOHN MONTGOMERY
Sworn to & subscribed Feb 14 1857 before JOHN MATLOCK, Chief Justice Parker Co. TX

Parker Co. TX - Field notes of survey of 160 acs. for JOHN M. HEFLEY by virtue of his preemption affidavit No. 44 - Situate in Parker Co. on waters of Walnut Creek tributary West Fork Trinity Riv. - Beg. at SE cor. JOHN MONTGOMERY 160 ac. preemption survey

[13]   Surveyed: Oct 27 1857 - LEWELLEN MURPHY, Co. Surv. Parker Co. TX
Chain Carriers: JOHN MONTGOMERY, JESSE F. MONTGOMERY

Parker Co. TX - 211 - Personally came ISRAEL BURROWS as applicant and ROBERT S. PORTER and JOSEPH C. REEVES two disinterested and respectable witnesses - all duly sworn and saith that applicant was bonafide settled upon vacant land on Aug 26 1856, date of enactment of act authorizing settlement of vacant land within limits of Mississippi & Pacific R. R. - continues to reside within limits - claims right of purchase under said act.
Signed: ISRAEL BURROWS, ROBT. S. PORTER, JOSEPH REEVES

[14]   Sworn to & subscribed Nov 9 1857 before JOHN H. PRINCE, Clerk Co. Court Parker Co. TX, by B. F. WALKER, Dept.

Parker Co. TX - Field notes of survey of 160 acs. for ISRAEL BURROWS by virtue of his preemption affidavit No. 211 - Situate in Parker Co. on Grindstone Creek, tributary of Brazos Riv. - Beg. SW from SE cor. ROBERT S. PORTER 160 ac. preemption survey
Surveyed: Nov 12 1857 - LEWELLEN MURPHY, Co Surv Parker Co TX

[15]   Chain Carriers: WILLIAM C. HALL, JOSEPH REEVES
Nov 14 1857 - LEWELLEN MURPHY certifies foregoing survey

Parker Co. TX - 31 - Before me JAMES J. BEEMAN, Notary Public within & for the county aforesaid, personally came WILLIAM D.

GUYTON [?], as applicant and JOHN BROWN & NEWTON CANAFAX, two disinterested and respectable witnesses - all duly sworn and saith that applicant was bonafide settled upon vacant land on Aug 26 1856, date of enactment of act authorizing settlement of vacant land within limits of Mississippi & Pacific R. R. - continues to reside within limits - claims right of purchase under said act.
Signed: WM. D. GUYTON, JOHN BROWN, NEWTON CANAFAX
Sworn to & subscribed Oct 9 1857 before J. J. BEEMAN, Notary Public Parker Co. TX

[16] Parker Co. TX - Field notes of survey of 160 acs. for WILLIAM D. GUITON [?] by virtue of his preemption affidavit No. 31 - Situate in NW part of Parker Co. on waters of Rock Creek, tributary Brazos Riv. - Beg. W of NE cor. JOHN BROWN 160 ac. preemption survey - N. boundary line said survey -
Surveyed: Nov 2 1857 - LEWELLEN MURPHY, Co Surv Parker Co TX
Chain Carriers: WILLIAM B. FONDREN, JOSEPH H. LITTLETON
Nov 14 1857 - LEWELLEN MURPHY, Co. Surv. Parker Co. TX, certifies foregoing

[17] Parker Co. TX - 2 - Before undersigned authority personally came JEREMIAH POSEY as applicant and G. P. BARBER and ROBERT BROWN, two disinterested and respectable witnesses - all duly sworn and saith that applicant was bonafide settled upon vacant land on Aug 26 1856, date of enactment of act authorizing settlement of vacant land within limits of Mississippi & Pacific R. R. - continues to reside within limits - claims right of purchase under said act.
Signed: J. POSEY, G. P. BARBER, ROBERT BROWN
Sworn to & subscribed Feb 2 1857 before JOHN H. PRINCE, Co. Clerk Parker Co. TX

[18] Parker Co. TX - Field notes of survey of 160 acs. for JEREMIAH POSEY by virtue of his preemption affidavit No. 2 - Situate in Parker Co on waters Patrick's Creek, tributary Brazos Riv. about 4 1/2 mi. N 85° W from town of Weatherford - Beg. E of SE cor. JOHN JONAS 160 ac. preemption survey -
Surveyed: Nov 14 1857 -
Chain Carriers: EMRY A. HOWARD, STEPHEN KIDWELL

[19] Nov 16 1857 - LEWELLEN MURPHY, Co. Surveyor Parker Co. TX, certifies foregoing

Parker Co. TX - Before undersigned authority personally came JOHN JONES as applicant and AUGER PRICE and ROBERT BROWN two disinterested and respectable witnesses - all duly sworn and saith that applicant was bonafide settled upon vacant land on Aug 26 1856, date of enactment of act authorizing settlement of vacant land within limits of Mississippi & Pacific R. R. - continues to reside within limits - claims right of purchase under said act.

Signed: JOHN "X" JONES [mark], A. PRICE, ROBERT BROWN
Sworn to & subscribed Aug 29 1857 before JOHN H. PRINCE, Co.
Clerk Parker Co. TX

[20] Parker Co. TX - Field notes of survey of 160 acs. for
JOHN JONES by virtue of his preemption affidavit No. 191 -
Situate in Parker Co. on waters of Patrick's Creek, tributary
Brazos Riv. - Beg. SE from SE cor. AUGER PRICE 160 ac. preemption survey -
Surveyed: Nov 14 1857 -
Chain Carriers: LEVI KIDWELL, WILLIAM HOWARD

[21] Nov 16 1857 - LEWELLEN MURPHY, Co. Surveyor Parker Co.
TX, certifies foregoing

Parker Co. TX - 56 - Before me JOHN MATLOCK, Chief Justice
Parker Co., personally came ROBERT P. TEETERS as applicant and
JAMES WHITE and RANEY L. FRANCIS two disinterested and respectable witnesses - all duly sworn and saith that applicant
was bonafide settled upon vacant land on Aug 26 1856, date of
enactment of act authorizing settlement of vacant land within
limits of Mississippi & Pacific R. R. - continues to reside
within limits - claims right of purchase under said act.
Signed: ROBERT P. TEETERS, JAMES WHITE, RAMEY L. FRANCIS

[22] Sworn to & subscribed Feb 24 1857 before JOHN MATLOCK,
Chief Justice of Parker Co.

Parker Co. TX - Field notes of survey of 54 acs. in name of
ROBERT P. TEETERS by virtue of his preemption affidavit No. 56
- Situate in Parker Co. on waters of Ash Creek, tributary West
Fork Trinity Riv. - Beg. SE from SE cor. WILLIAM RIGGINS 480
ac. survey - SE cor. WILLIAM WOODY 320 ac. preemption survey
Surveyed: Feb 24 1857 -
Chain Carriers: WILLIAM G. VEAL, JOHN W. SWALLOW

[23] Nov 16 1857 - LEWELLEN MURPHY, Co. Surveyor Parker Co.,
certifies foregoing

Parker Co. TX - Before CHARLES GILDON, Notary Public of Parker
Co. TX personally came JAMES M. BURRIS as applicant and L. J.
FRANCIS and J. W. GODFREY two disinterested and respectable
witnesses - all duly sworn and saith that applicant was bonafide settled upon vacant land on Aug 26 1856, date of enactment of act authorizing settlement of vacant land within limits of Mississippi & Pacific R. R. -

[24] continues to reside within limits - claims right of
purchase under said act.
Signed: JAMES M "X" BURRIS [mark], L. D. "X" FRANCIS [mark],
JOHN W. GODFREY

Sworn to & subscribed Apr 8 1857 before CHARLES GILDON, Notary Public

Parker Co. TX, Denton Land Dist. - Field notes of survey of 160 acs. in name of JAMES M. BURRIS by virtue of affidavit No. 53 - Situate on waters of Clear Fork, tributary of West Fork Trinity Riv. - Beg. on NW cor. THOS. BURRIS 160 ac. survey - Surveyed: May 1 1857 - R. J. BILLINGSLEA, D. S. D. L. D. [sic] who certifies foregoing survey
Chain Carriers: W. G. VEAL, JOS. S. AMOS

[25] Recorded: Nov 16 1857 - LEWELLEN MURPHY, Co. Surv. Parker Co. TX

Parker Co. TX - 30 - Before CHARLES GILDON, Notary Public of Parker Co. TX personally came L. T. SHEPPARD as applicant and JOHN N. RASH and S. P. RASH two disinterested and respectable witnesses - all duly sworn and saith that applicant was bonafide settled upon vacant land on Aug 26 1856, date of enactment of act authorizing settlement of vacant land within limits of Mississippi & Pacific R. R. - continues to reside within limits claims right of purchase under said act.
Signed: L. T. SHEPPARD, J. N. RASH, S. P. "X" RASH [mark]

[26] Sworn to & subscribed Mar 5 1857 before CHARLES GILDON, Notary Pubic

Parker Co. TX, Denton Land Dist. - Field notes of survey of 160 acs. for L. P. SHEPPARD by virtue of affidavit No. 30 - Situate on waters of Ash Creek, tributary West Fork Trinity Riv. - Beg. W of SE cor. WM. D. FORD 160 ac. survey
Surveyed: Apr 27 1857 - R. J. BILLINGSLEA, D. S. D. L. D.
Chain Carriers: WILLIAM WILLSON, A. R. SENALDEUR [?]

[27] Recorded: Nov 16 1857 - LEWELLEN MURPHY, Co. Surv. Parker Co. TX

Parker Co. TX - 77 - Before JOHN MATLOCK, Chief Justice Parker Co. TX personally came WILLIAM J. ELLIS as applicant and JOSHUA BARKER and SAMUEL S. LEONARD two disinterested and respectable witnesses - all duly sworn and saith that applicant was bonafide settled upon vacant land on Aug 26 1856, date of enactment of act authorizing settlement of vacant land within limits of Mississippi & Pacific R. R. - continues to reside within limits claims right of purchase under said act.
Signed: WM. J. ELLIS, JOSHUA BARKER, SAMUEL S. LEONARD
Sworn to & subscribed Mar 3 1857 before JOHN MATLOCK, Chief Justice Parker Co. TX

[28] Parker Co. TX, Denton Land Dist. - Field notes of survey of 160 acs. for WILLIAM J. ELLIS by virtue of affidavit No. 77 - Situate in Parker Co. on waters Clear Fork, tributary

of West Fork Trinity Riv. - Beg. SE of SW cor. M. D. TACKITT 160 ac. survey -
Surveyed: Apr 3 1857 - R. J. BILLINGSLEA, D. S. D. L. D.
Chain Carriers: N. G. LEE [?], J. H. TACKITT

[29]   Recorded: Nov 16 1857 - LEWELLEN MURPHY, Co. Surv. Parker Co. TX

Parker Co. TX - Before CHARLES GILDON, Notary Public for Parker Co. TX personally came E. STIMMONS [?] as applicant and L. T. SHEPPARD and R. J. BILLINGSLEA two disinterested and respectable witnesses - all duly sworn and saith that applicant was bonafide settled upon vacant land on Aug 26 1856, date of enactment of act authorizing settlement of vacant land within limits of Mississippi & Pacific R. R. - continues to reside within limits claims right of purchase under said act.
[No Signatures]
Sworn to & subscribed Apr 29 1857 before CHARLES GILDON, Notary Public Parker Co. TX

[30]   Parker Co TX, Denton Land Dist - Field notes of survey of 160 acs. for E. SAMOND by virtue of affidavit No. 55 - Situate on waters Ash Creek, tributary West Fork Trinity Riv. - Beg. S of NE cor. L. T. SHEPPARD 160 ac. survey -
Surveyed: Apr 29 1857 - R. J. BILLINGSLEA, D. S. D. L. D.
Chain Carriers: WILLIAM WILSON, A. R. SWALLOW
Recorded: Nov 16 1857 - LEWELLEN MURPHY, Co Surv Parker Co TX

[31]   Parker Co. TX - 76 - Before JOHN MATLOCK, Chief Justice Parker Co. TX personally came CHARLES T. STANLY as applicant and EDWARD M. HARRIS and JOSEPH WALKER two disinterested and respectable witnesses - all duly sworn and saith that applicant was bonafide settled upon vacant land on Aug 26 1856, date of enactment of act authorizing settlement of vacant land within limits of Mississippi & Pacific R. R. - continues to reside within limits - claims right of purchase under said act.
Signed: CHARLES L. STANLEY, EDWARD M. HARRIS, JOSEPH WALKER
Sworn to & subscribed Feb 28 1857 before JOHN MATLOCK, Chief Justice Parker Co. TX

[32]   Parker Co. TX - Field notes of survey of 157 83/100 acs. for CHARLES T. STANLEY by virtue of preemption affidavit No. 76 Situate in Parker Co. on waters of Clear Fork Trinity Riv. - Beg. on NW cor. EDWARD M. HARRIS 160 ac. preemption survey - S. boundary of JAMES A. MILLER 160 ac. preemption survey -
Surveyed: Mar 30 1857 - LEWELLEN MURPHY, Co Surv Parker Co TX
Chain Carriers: EDWARD M. HARRIS, THOMAS G. WAUGH

[33]   Recorded: Nov 16 1857 - LEWELLEN MURPHY, Co Surv Parker Co TX

Parker Co. TX - 62 - Before JOHN MATLOCK, Chief Justice Parker Co. TX, personally came WOODSON D. HENRY as applicant and CALVIN M. CRISWELL and VOLENTINE YOAKUM two disinterested and respectable witnesses - all duly sworn and saith that applicant was bonafide settled upon vacant land on Aug 26 1856, date of enactment of act authorizing settlement of vacant land within limits of Mississippi & Pacific R. R. - continues to reside within limits - claims right of purchase under said act.
Signed: WOODSON D. HENRY, C. M. CRISWELL, VOLENTINE YOAKUM

[34]   Sworn to & subscribed Feb 25 1857 before JOHN MATLOCK, Chief Justice Parker Co. TX

Denton Land Dist. TX - Field notes of survey of 160 acs. for WOODSON D. HENRY by virtue of his preemption affidavit No. 62 - Situate in Parker Co. on waters of Walnut Creek, a stream of West Fork Trinity Riv. - Beg. SW of the 23 mi. post on N boundary Line of said Parker Co., which line was run and numbered from W to E
Surveyed: Feb 26 1857 - L. E. CAMP, Dept. Surv. Denton L. D.
Chain Carriers: C. M. CRISWELL, J. B. THOMAS

[35]   Recorded: Nov 16 1857 - LEWELLEN MURPHY, Co Surv Parker Co TX

Parker Co. TX - 26 - This is to certify that this day personally appeared EBENEZER MILLER as applicant and S. T. SHEPPARD and SAML. WOODY, two disinterested and respectable witnesses before me - all duly sworn and saith that applicant was bonafide settled upon vacant land on Aug 26 1856, date of enactment of act authorizing settlement of vacant land within limits of Mississippi & Pacific R. R. - continues to reside within limits claims right of purchase under said act.
Signed: EBENEZER MILLER, S. T. SHEPPARD, SAMUEL WOODY

[36]   Sworn to & subscribed Mar 7 1857 before CHARLES GILDON, Notary Public for Parker Co. TX

Parker Co. TX - Field notes of survey of 160 ac. for E. MILLER by virtue of affidavit No. 26 - Situate on waters of Walnut Creek, tributary West Fork Trinity Riv. - Beg. SE of SW cor. of S. T. THORP preemption survey -
Surveyed: Jul 31 1857 - J. R. BILLINGSLEA, D. S. D. L. D.
Chain Carriers: J. L. BYERS, J. A. MORRIS

[37]   Recorded: Nov 16 1857 - LEWELLEN MURPHY, Co Surv Parker Co TX

Parker Co. TX - 39 - Before JOHN MATLOCK, Chief Justice Parker Co. TX, personally came WILLIAM SILLIVANT applicant and JONATHAN H. WALKER and WILLIAM TAYLOR two disinterested and

respectable witnesses - all duly sworn and saith that applicant was bonafide settled upon vacant land on Aug 26 1856, date of enactment of act authorizing settlement of vacant land within limits of Mississippi & Pacific R. R. - continues to reside within limits claims right of purchase under said act.
Signed: WILLIAM SILLIVINT, JONATHAN H. WALKER, WILLIAM TAYLOR

[38]   Sworn to & subscribed Feb 14 1857 before JOHN MATLOCK, Chief Justice Parker Co. TX

Parker Co. TX - Field notes of survey of 160 acs. for WILLIAM SILLIVINT by virtue of his preemption affidavit No. 39 - Situate in Parker Co. on waters of Clear Fork Trinity Riv. about 11 mi. N of town of Weatherford - Beg. W of NW cor. ELIZAH NEWTON CANAFAX 160 ac. preemption survey -

[39]   Surveyed: Oct 7 1857 - LEWELLEN MURPHY, Co Surv Parker Co TX
Chain Carriers: JOSEPHUS H. TACKITT, FRANCIS M. SILLIVINT
Recorded: Nov 16 1857 - LEWELLEN MURPHY, Co Surv Parker Co TX

Parker Co. TX - 203 - Before JOHN H. PRINCE, Co. Clerk Parker Co. TX, personally came A. W. EMERSON as applicant and A. M. GARY and W. B. FONDREN two disinterested and respectable witnesses - all duly sworn and saith that applicant was bonafide settled upon vacant land on Aug 26 1856, date of enactment of act authorizing settlement of vacant land within limits of Mississippi & Pacific R. R. - continues to reside within limits claims right of purchase under said act.

[40]   Signed: A W "X" EMERSON [mark], W B FONDREN, A M GARY
Sworn to & subscribed Sep 30 1857 before JOHN H. PRINCE, Co. Clerk Parker Co. TX

Parker Co. TX - Field notes of survey of 160 acs. for E. A. W. EMERSON by virtue of preemption affidavit No. 203 - Situate in Parker Co. on Rock Creek, tributary Brazos Riv. about 18 mi. NW from town of Weatherford - Beg. W & N from NW cor. EDWARD RIPPEY 160 ac. preemption survey -

[41]   Surveyed: Nov 7 1857 - LEWELLEN MURPHY, Co Surv Parker Co TX
Chain Carriers: WILLIAM B. FONDREN, JOHN BROWN
Recorded: Nov 16 1857 - LEWELLEN MURPHY, Co Surv Parker Co TX

[42]   Parker Co. TX - 108 - Before undersigned Chief Justice of Parker Co. TX, personally came WILLIAM K. FLETCHER as applicant and JOHN N. RASH and JOSEPH RASH two disinterested and respectable witnesses - all duly sworn and saith that appli-cant was bonafide settled upon vacant land on Aug 26 1856, date of enactment of act authorizing settlement of vacant land within limits of Mississippi & Pacific R. R. - continues to

reside within limits - claims right of purchase under said act.
Signed: WILLIAM "X" K. FLETCHER [mark], JOHN N. RASH, JOSEPH RASH
Sworn to & subscribed Nov 12 1857 before JOHN MATLOCK, Chief Justice Parker Co. TX

[43]   Parker Co. TX - Field notes of survey of 160 acs. for WILLIAM K. FLETCHER by virtue of preemption affidavit No. 108 - Situate in Parker Co. on waters Ash Creek, tributary West Fork Trinity Riv. about 15 mi. N 50° E from town of Weatherford - Beg. E of SW cor. JOSEPH RASH 160 ac. preemption survey
Surveyed: Nov 16 1857 -

[44]   Chain Carriers: WILLIAM D CALLAWAY, CHRISTOPHER BEDWELL
Recorded: Nov 16 1857 - LEWELLEN MURPHY, Co Surv Parker Co TX

Parker Co. TX - 164 - Before undersigned authority personally came DAVID A. LOW as applicant and E. M. RIPPY and WM. M. LOW two disinterested and respectable witnesses - all duly sworn and saith that applicant was bonafide settled upon vacant land on Aug 26 1856, date of enactment of act authorizing settlement of vacant land within limits of Mississippi & Pacific R. R. - continues to reside within limits - claims right of purchase under said act.
Signed: D. A. LOW, E. M. RIPPY, WM. M. LOW

[45]   Sworn to & subscribed Jun 1 1857 before JOHN H. PRINCE, Clerk Co. Court Parker Co. TX

Parker Co. TX - Have surveyed 160 acs for DAVID A. LOW by virtue of his affidavit No. 164 - Situate in Parker Co. in Upper Cross Timbers about 14 mi. N 50° W from town of Weatherford - Beg. NW from SW cor. W. B. FONDREN 160 ac. survey -
Surveyed: Jul 2 1857 - ISAAC O. HEADLEY, D. S. P. C. [sic]
Chain Carriers: W. D. GUYTON, E. M. RIPPY

[46]   Recorded: Nov 16 1857 - LEWELLEN MURPHY, Co Surv Parker Co TX

Parker Co. TX - 162 - Before undersigned authority personally came WILLIAM M. LOW as applicant and DAVID A. LOW and E. M. RIPPY two disinterested and respectable witnesses - all duly sworn and saith that applicant was bonafide settled upon vacant land on Aug 26 1856, date of enactment of act authorizing settlement of vacant land within limits of Mississippi & Pacific R. R. - continues to reside within limits - claims right of purchase under said act.
Signed: W. M. LOW, D. A. LOW, E. M. RIPPEY
Sworn to & subscribed Jun 1 1857 before JOHN H. PRINCE, Co. Clerk Parker Co. TX

[47] Parker Co. TX - Have surveyed for WILLIAM M. LOW 160 acs. by virtue of affidavit No. 162 - Situate in Parker Co. in Upper Cross Timbers about 14 mi. N 50° W from town of Weatherford - Beg. W from SE cor. D. A. LOW 160 ac. survey -
Surveyed: Jul 2 1857 - ISAAC O. HEADLEY, D. S. P. C.
Chain Carriers: W. D. GUYTON, E. M. RIPPY
Recorded: Nov 16 1857 - LEWELLEN MURPHY, Co Surv Parker Co TX

[48] Parker Co. TX - 163 - This day came EDWARD M. RIPPY as applicant and WILLIAM M. LOW and DAVID A. LOW two disinterested and respectable witnesses - all duly sworn and saith that applicant was bonafide settled upon vacant land on Aug 26 1856, date of enactment of act authorizing settlement of vacant land within limits of Mississippi & Pacific R. R. - continues to reside within limits - claims right of purchase under said act.
Signed: E. M. RIPPY, D. A. LOW, WM. M. LOW
Sworn to & subscribed Jun 1 1857 before JOHN H. PRINCE, Co. Clerk Parker Co. TX

Parker Co. TX - Have surveyed for E. M. RIPPY 160 acs. by virtue of affidavit No. 163 - Situate in Parker Co. in Upper Cross Timbers about 15 mi. N 45° W from the town of Weatherford - Beg. NW from NW cor -

[49] WILLIAM M. LOW 160 ac. survey -
Surveyed: Jul 2 1857 - ISAAC O. HEADLEY, D. S. P. C.
Chain Carriers: W. D. GUYTON, D. A. LOW
Recorded: Nov 16 1857 - LEWELLEN MURPHY, Co Surv Parker Co TX

[50] Parker Co. TX - 111 - Before undersigned authority personally came DAVID W. PATTON as applicant and GEORGE FEATHERKILE and THOMAS B. MARTIN two disinterested and respectable witnesses - all duly sworn and saith that applicant was bonafide settled upon vacant land on Aug 26 1856, date of enactment of act authorizing settlement of vacant land within limits of Mississippi & Pacific R. R. - continues to reside within limits - claims right of purchase under said act.
Signed: DAVID W. PATTON, GEORGE "X" FEATHERKILE [mark], THOMAS B."X" MARTIN [mark]
Sworn to & subscribed Mar 14 1857 before JOHN H. PRINCE, Co. Clerk Parker Co. TX

Parker Co. TX - Field notes of survey of 160 acs. for DAVID W. PATTON by virtue of his preemption affidavit No. 111 - Situate in Parker Co. on waters of Rock Creek, tributary Brazos Riv. about 9 mi. N 68° W from Weatherford -

[51] Beg. NW from NW cor. JAMES H. PORTER 160 ac. preemption survey -
Surveyed: Oct 29 1857
Chain Carriers: GEORGE FEATHERKILE, THOMAS B. MARTIN

Recorded: Nov 16 1857 - LEWELLEN MURPHY, Co Surv Parker Co TX

[52] Parker Co. TX - 118 - Before undersigned authority came J. W. GUEST as applicant and F. M. ELLISON and SAMUEL LITTLEFIELD two disinterested and respectable witnesses - all duly sworn and saith that applicant was bonafide settled upon vacant land on Aug 26 1856, date of enactment of act authorizing settlement of vacant land within limits of Mississippi & Pacific R. R. - continues to reside within limits - claims right of purchase under said act.
Signed: J W "X" GUEST [mark], F M ELLISON, SAMUEL LITTLEFIELD
Sworn to & subscribed Mar 28 1857 before JOHN H. PRINCE, Co. Clerk Parker Co TX

Parker Co. TX - Field notes of survey of 160 acs for J. W. GUEST by virtue of his preemption affidavit No. 118 - Situate in Parker Co. on Waters of Brazos Riv. about 16 mi. S 63° W from Weatherford - Beg. SW of SW cor. E. A. S. L. IKARD 160 ac. preemption survey -

[53] Surveyed: Nov 7 1857 - LEWELLEN MURPHY, Co Surv Parker Co TX
Chain Carriers: BENJAMIN FELKISON, REUBEN B. BARTEM
Recorded: Nov 19 1857 - LEWELLEN MURPHY

[54] Parker Co. TX - 58 - Before JOHN MATLOCK, Chief Justice Parker Co. TX personally came ZACHERIAH BURRIS as applicant and AMBERS ANJELY and THOMAS BURRIS two disinterested and respectable witnesses - all duly sworn and saith that applicant was bonafide settled upon vacant land on Aug 26 1856, date of enactment of act authorizing settlement of vacant land within limits of Mississippi & Pacific R. R. - continues to reside within limits - claims right of purchase under said act.
Signed: Zacheraih BURRIS, AMBERS ANJELY, THOMAS BURRIS
Sworn to & subscribed Feb 25 1857 before JOHN MATLOCK, Chief Justice Parker Co. TX

Parker Co. TX - Field notes of survey of 63 3/10 for ZACHERIAH BURRIS by virtue of his preemption affidavit No. 58 -

[55] Situate in Parker Co. on waters of Walnut Creek, tributary of West Fork Trinity - Beg. W of NW cor. JESSE W. FRANKLIN, 160 ac. preemption survey -
Surveyed: Mar 18 1756 - LEWELLEN MURPHY, Co Surv Parker Co TX
Chain Carriers: JESSE WRIGHT FRANKLIN, JAMES SPROULS
Recorded: Nov 19 1857 - LEWELLEN MURPHY, Co Surv Parker Co TX

[56] Parker Co. TX - 170 - I, JOHN JEMASON do swear that my preemption affidavit No. 170 dated 4th Jun 1857 taken be- fore before [sic] J. H. PRINCE, Clerk of Co. Court of Parker Co. is lost or mislaid
Signed: JOHN "X" JEMASON

Sworn to & subscribed Nov 4 1857 before J. H. PRINCE, Co Clerk Parker Co

Parker Co. TX - I, JOHN H. PRINCE, Clk. Co. Court, hereby certify that on the 4th of June 1857 I issued to JOHN JEMASON pre aff [sic] No. 170 upon the evidence of Z. P. SHIRLEY and SPENCE M. WOODS, two disinterested and respectable witnesses Nov 4 1857 - JOHN H. PRINCE, Clerk Co. Court Parker Co. TX

Parker Co. TX - Have surveyed 160 acs. for JOHN JIMERSON by virtue of his affidavit No. 170 - Situate in Parker Co. on Patrick's Creek, tributary of Brazos Riv. - Beg. NW from N cor. WILLIAM LONG 640 ac. survey

[57] Surveyed: Aug 14 1857 - ISAAC O. HEADLEY, D. S. P. C.
Chain Carriers: J. B. PINKSTON, G. W. PORSEN
Recorded: Nov 19 1857 - LEWELLEN MURPHY, Co Surv Parker Co TX

Parker Co. TX - 201 - Before undersigned authority came DAVIS CRISSWELL as applicant and T. J. SHAW and TILMON BOYD, two disinterested and respectable witnesses - all duly sworn and saith that applicant was bonafide settled upon vacant land on Aug 26 1856, date of enactment of act authorizing settlement of vacant land within limits of Mississippi & Pacific R. R. - continues to reside within limits - claims right of purchase under said act.

[58] Signed: DAVIS "X" CRISWELL [mark], T. J. SHAW, TILMON BOYD
Sworn to & subscribed Sep 11 1857 before JOHN H. PRINCE, Co. Clerk Parker Co. TX

Parker Co. TX - Field notes of survey of 160 acs. for DAVIS CRISWELL by virtue of his preemption affidavit No. 201 - Situate in Parker Co. on waters Spring Creek, tributary of Brazos Riv. about 7 1/2 mi. S 11° E from Weatherford - Beg. SE of S or SW cor. JESSE THOMAS 320 ac. survey -

[59] Surveyed: Nov 18 1857 - LEWELLEN MURPHY, Co Surv Parker Co TX
Chain Carriers: JEFFERSON W. PETTILLO, WILLIAM CRISWELL
Recorded: Nov 25 1857 - LEWELLEN MURPHY, Co Surv Parker Co TX

Parker Co. TX - 49 - Before undersigned authority came T. C. MOORE as applicant and A. M. GARY and STEPHEN KIDWELL two disinterested and respectable witnesses - all duly sworn and saith that applicant was bonafide settled upon vacant land on Aug 26 1856, date of enactment of act authorizing settlement of vacant land within limits of Mississippi & Pacific R. R. - continues to reside within limits - claims right of purchase under said act.
Signed: T C "X" [mark] MORE [sic], A M GARY, STEPHEN KIDWELL

Sworn to & subscribed Feb 24 1857 before JOHN H. PRINCE, Clerk Co. Court Parker Co TX, by WM. M. GREEN, Dept.

Parker Co. TX - Field notes of survey of 160 acs. for T. C. MORE by virtue of his preemption affidavit No. 49 - Situate in on [sic] waters of Grindstone Creek, tributary of Brazos Riv. about 7 mi. N 68° W from Weatherford - Beg. W & S from SW cor. THOMAS B. MARTIN 160 ac. preemption survey - S boundary line JOHN LYNCH 320 ac. survey -

[61] Surveyed: Sep 10 1857 - LEWELLEN MURPHY, Co Surv Parker Co TX
Chain Carriers: WILLIAM G. MORE, THOMAS B. MARTIN
Recorded: Nov 25 1857 - LEWELLEN MURPHY, Co Surv Parker Co TX

[62] Parker Co. TX - 24 - Before J. J. BEEMAN, Notary Public in and for Co. aforesaid personally came WALDEN WALTERS as applicant and D. C. NORTON and JAMES B. GILLILAND two disinterested and respectable witnesses - all duly sworn and saith that applicant was bonafide settled upon vacant land on Aug 26 1856, date of enactment of act authorizing settlement of vacant land within limits of Mississippi & Pacific R. R. - continues to reside within limits - claims right of purchase under said act.
Signed: HALLDEN WALTERS, D. C. NORTON, JAMES B. GILLILAND,
Sworn to & subscribed Mar 7 1857 before J. J. BEEMAN, Notary Public Parker Co. TX

Parker Co. TX - Field notes of survey of 160 acs. for WALLDEN WALTERS by virtue of his preemption affidavit No. 24

[63] Situate in Parker Co. on Willow Branch, tributary Clear Fork Trinity Riv. about 3 mi. N of Weatherford - Beg. on S boundary line JOHN ADAMS 320 ac. preemption survey -
Surveyed: Jun 25 1857 - LEWELLEN MURPHY - Co Surv Parker Co TX
Chain Carriers: Eli LEE, DANIEL LEE

[64] Recorded: Nov 25 1857 - LEWELLEN MURPHY, Co Surv Parker Co TX

Parker Co. TX - 68 - Before undersigned authority came MICHEL SEE as applicant and JOHN GRISHAM and JOHN W. BASHERS two disinterested and respectable witnesses - all duly sworn and saith that applicant was bonafide settled upon vacant land on Aug 26 1856, date of enactment of act authorizing settlement of vacant land within limits of Mississippi & Pacific R. R. - continues to reside within limits - claims right of purchase under said act.
Signed: MICHEL SEE, JOHN GRISHAM, JOHN W. BRASHEARS
Sworn to & subscribed Feb 26 1857 before JOHN H. PRINCE, Clerk Co. Court Parker Co. TX by WM. M. GREEN, Dept.

Parker Co. TX - Field notes of survey of 160 acs. for MICHEL SEE by virtue of his preemption affidavit No. 68 -

[65]   Situate in Parker Co. on waters of Brazos Riv.- Beg. W & N of SW cor. GEORGE W. LIGHT 160 ac. preemption survey -
Surveyed: Mar 6 1857 - LEWELLEN MURPHY, Co Surv Parker Co TX
Chain Carriers: JEREMIAH POSEY, WILLIAM P. WILSON
Recorded: Nov 25 1857 - LEWELLEN MURPHY, Co Surv Parker Co TX

[66]   Parker Co. TX - 73 - Before undersigned authority came WYATT WILLIAMS as applicant and WM. N. BLAIR and JEREMIAH T. WILLIAMS two disinterested and respectable witnesses - all duly sworn and saith that applicant was bonafide settled upon vacant land on Aug 26 1856, date of enactment of act authorizing settlement of vacant land within limits of Mississippi & Pacific R. R. - continues to reside within limits - claims right of purchase under said act.
Signed: WYATT WILLIAMS, WM. N. BLAIR, J. T. WILLIAMS
Sworn to & subscribed Feb 27 1857 before JOHN H. PRINCE, Clerk Co. Court Parker Co. TX

Parker Co. TX - Have surveyed 160 acs. for WYATT WILLIAMS by virtue of his affidavit No. 73 - Situate in Parker Co. on Spring Cr. waters of Brazos Riv. about 8 mi. S 25° E from Weatherford - Beg. SW from S or SW cor -

[67]   DAVIS CRISWELL 160 ac. survey -
Surveyed: Sep 3 1857 - ISAAC O. HEADLEY, D. S. P. C.
Chain Carriers: DAVIS S. CRISWELL, WYATT WILLIAMS
Recorded: Nov 25 1857 - LEWELLEN MURPHY, Co Surv Parker Co TX

[68]   Parker Co. TX - 50 - Before CHARLES GILDON, Notary Public in and for Co. aforesaid personally appeared BAILEY HILL as applicant and A. M. GARY and D. STIMPSON two disinterested and respectable witnesses - all duly sworn and saith that applicant was bonafide settled upon vacant land on Aug 26 1856, date of enactment of act authorizing settlement of vacant land within limits of Mississippi & Pacific R. R. - continues to reside within limits - claims right of purchase under said act.
Signed: BALY HILL, DAVID STIMSON, A. M. GARY
Sworn to & subscribed Mar 28 1857 before CHARLES GILDON, Notary Public Parker Co. TX

[69]   Parker Co. TX, Denton Land Dist. - Field notes of survey of 160 acs. for BALY HILL by virtue of affidavit No 50 - Situate on waters of Grindstone, tributary of Brazos Riv. - Beg. N of NE cor. PETER WALKER [WALDEN ?] 160 ac. survey -
Surveyed: Mar 30 1857 - R. J. BILLINGSLEA, D. S. D. L. D.
Chain Carriers: WM. P. DULANEY, R. M. MEADOR
Recorded: Nov 25 1857 - LEWELLEN MURPHY, Co Surv Parker Co TX

[70] Parker Co. TX - 186 - Before undersigned authority personally came MARTHA HUNTER as applicant and P. H. BOYD and WILLIAM CRISWELL two disinterested and respectable witnesses - all duly sworn and saith that applicant was bonafide settled upon vacant land on Aug 26 1856, date of enactment of act authorizing settlement of vacant land within limits of Mississippi & Pacific R. R. - continues to reside within limits claims right of purchase under said act.
Signed: MARTHA "X" HUNTER [mark], P. H. BOYD, WILLIAM "X" CRISWELL [mark]
Sworn to & subscribed Aug 5 1857 before JOHN H. PRINCE, Clerk Co. Court Parker Co. TX

Parker Co. TX - Field notes of survey of 160 acs. for MARTHA HUNTER by virtue of her preemption affidavit No. 186 - Situate in Parker Co. on Little Red Bear Creek, tributary Brazos Riv. about 4 mi. S 40° W from Weatherford - Beg. SE of SE cor. STEPHEN F. JONES 160 ac. preemption survey -

[71] Surveyed: Nov 20 1857 - LEWELLEN MURPHY, Co Surv Parker Co TX
Chain Carriers: ABRAM M. HUNTER, SHADRACK V. HUNTER
Recorded: Nov 27 1857 - LEWELLEN MURPHY, Co Surv Parker Co TX

[72] Parker Co. TX - 179 - Before JOHN H. PRINCE personally came M. O. BARTON as applicant and G. W. MEEK and W. T. BARTEN two disinterested and respectable witnesses - all duly sworn and saith that applicant was bonafide settled upon vacant land on Aug 26 1856, date of enactment of act authorizing settlement of vacant land within limits of Mississippi & Pacific R. R. - continues to reside within limits - claims right of purchase under said act.
Signed: M. O. BARTON, W. T. BARTEN, G. W. "X" MEEK [mark]
Sworn to & subscribed Sep 8 1857 before JOHN H. PRINCE, Clerk Co. Court Parker Co. TX

Parker Co. TX - Field notes of survey of 160 acs. for MANELIES OLIVER BARTEN by virtue of his preemption affidavit No. 179 - Situate on Brazos Riv. about 16 mi. S. 60° W from Weatherford - Beg. at NW cor. -

[73] REUBEN P. BARTEN 160 ac. preemption survey -
Surveyed: Nov 7 1857 - LEWELLEN MURPHY, Co Surv Parker Co TX
Chain Carriers: R. P. BARTEN, G. W. MEEK,
Recorded: Nov 27 1857 - LEWELLEN MURPHY, Co Surv Parker Co TX

[74] Parker Co. TX - 30 - Before undersigned authority came DAVID HERRING as applicant and J. H. HEWETT and T. [?] C. BROWN two disinterested and respectable witnesses - all duly sworn and saith that applicant was bonafide settled upon vacant land on Aug 26 1856, date of enactment of act authorizing settlement of vacant land within limits of Mississippi & Pa-

cific R. R. - continues to reside within limits - claims right of purchase under sd. act.
Signed: DAVID HERRING, J. H. HEWETT, F.[?] C. BROWN
Sworn to & subscribed Feb 23 1857 before JOHN H. PRINCE, Co. Clerk by WM. M. GREEN, Dept.

Parker Co. TX - Field notes of survey of 160 acs. for DAVID HERRING by virtue of his preemption affidavit No. 30 - Situate on waters of Grindstone Creek, tributary of Brazos Riv. about 9 mi. S 68° W from Weatherford -

[75]   Beg. SW of SW cor. MONROE UPTON 160 ac. preemption survey
Surveyed: Nov 26 1857 - LEWELLEN MURPHY, Co Surv Parker Co TX
Chain Carriers: JOSEPH H. HEWETT, DAVID HERRING
Recorded: Nov 27 1857

[76]   Parker Co. TX - 58 - Before undersigned authority came THOMAS B. MARTIN as applicant and T. C. MORE and W. G. MORE two disinterested and respectable witnesses - all duly sworn and saith that applicant was bonafide settled upon vacant land on Aug 26 1856, date of enactment of act authorizing settlement of vacant land within limits of Mississippi & Pacific R. R. - continues to reside within limits - claims right of purchase under said act.
Signed: THOMAS "X" B. MARTIN [mark], W. G. "X" MORE [mark], G. C. "X" MORE [mark]
Sworn to and subscribed Feb 24 1857 before JOHN H. PRINCE, Clerk Co. Court Parker Co. by WM. M. GREEN, Dept.

Parker Co. TX - Field notes of survey of 160 acs. for THOMAS B. MARTIN by virtue of his preemption affidavit No. 58 - Situate on waters of Grindstone Creek, tributary of Brazos Riv.

[77]   about 6 mi. N 56° W from Weatherford - Beg. SE of SE cor. PETER WELDON 160 ac. preemption survey -
Surveyed: Sep 10 1857 - LEWELLEN MURPHY, Co Surv Parker Co TX
Chain Carriers: THOMAS. C. MORE, WILLIAM G. MORE
Recorded: Nov 28 1857 - LEWELLEN MURPHY, Co Surv Parker Co TX

[78]   "Oct 24 1874" [on top of this sheet in small letters]
Parker Co. TX - 47 - Before undersigned authority came W. G. MORE as applicant and A. M. GARY and STEPHEN KIDWELL two disinterested and respectable witnesses - all duly sworn and saith that applicant was bonafide settled upon vacant land on Aug 26 1856, date of enactment of act authorizing settlement of vacant land within limits of Mississippi & Pacific R. R. - continues to reside within limits - claims right of purchase under said act.
Signed: W. G. "X" MORE [mark], A. M. GARY, STEPHEN KIDWELL
Sworn to & subscribed Feb 24 1857 before JOHN H. PRINCE, Clerk Co. Court Parker Co. TX, by WM. M. GREEN, Dept

Parker Co. TX - Field notes of survey of 160 acs. for W. G. MORE by virtue of his preemption affidavit No. 47 - Situate on waters of Grindstone Creek, tributary of Brazos Riv. -

[79]   about 6 1/2 mi. N 67° W from Weatherford - Beg. SW from SE cor. T. C. MORE 160 ac. preemption survey - SW cor. STEPHEN KIDWELL preemption -
Surveyed: Sep 11 1857 - LEWELLEN MURPHY, Co Surv Parker Co TX
Chain Carriers: THOMAS B. MARTIN, THOMAS C. MORE
Recorded: Nov 28 1857

[80]   Parker Co. TX - Before JOHN H. PRINCE, Clerk Co. Court Parker Co. TX, came J. B. PINKSTON and after being duly sworn says that the preemption affidavit issued to J. B. PINKSTON by the Clerk of the Co. Court of Parker Co. TX is lost or mislaid, the same being No. 128 dated Mar 28 1857 - WM. C. BAKER and JOHN JONES being witnesses on same
Signed: J. B. PINKSTON
Sworn to & subscribed Oct 3 1857 before JOHN H. PRINCE, Clerk Co. Court Parker Co. TX

Parker Co. TX, - I, JOHN H. PRINCE, Clerk Co. Court of Parker Co. TX, hereby certify that on the 28th March 1857 I issued to J. B. PINKSTON a preemption affidavit No. 128 WM. C. BAKER and JOHN JONES being witnesses. Original issued under an act authorizing the location settlement of Mississippi & Pacific R.R. Reserve passed 26th August 1856
Signed: JOHN H. PRINCE, Clerk Co. Court Parker Co. TX
Dated: Oct 3 1857

Parker Co. TX - Have surveyed 160 acs. for J. B. PINKSTON by virtue of his affidavit No. 128 - Situate in Parker Co. on Patrick's Creek, waters of Brazos Riv. about 6 mi. S 45° W -

[81]   from Weatherford - Beg. NW of NW cor. JOHN JEMERSON 160 ac. survey -
Surveyed: Aug 4 1857 - LEWELLEN MURPHY, Co Surv Parker Co TX
Chain Carriers: LEVI CURRANT, G. W. PARSONS
Recorded: Nov 28 1857 - LEWELLEN MURPHY, Co Surv Parker Co TX

[82]   Parker Co. TX - 195 - Before undersigned authority came J. H. CROSS as applicant and B. HAYNES and ISAAC O. HEADLEY two disinterested and respectable witnesses - all duly sworn and saith that applicant was bonafide settled upon vacant land on Aug 26 1856, date of enactment of act authorizing settlement of vacant land within limits of Mississippi & Pacific R. R. - continues to reside within limits - claims right of purchase under said act.
Signed: J. H. CROSS, BLUFORD HAYNES, [HEADLEY doesn't sign]
Sworn to & subscribed Sep 5 1857 before JOHN H. PRINCE, Clerk Co. Court Parker Co. TX

Parker Co. TX - Have surveyed 160 acs. for J. H. CROSS by virtue of affidavit No. 195 - Situate in Parker Co. on head of Long's Creek, waters of Brazos Riv. about 10 mi. S 25° E from Weatherford - Beg. SE of N cor. 43,358,308 sq. vrs. surveyed for Leon Co. -

[83] Surveyed: Sep 5 1857 - ISAAC O. HEADLEY, D. S. P. C.
Chain Carriers: DANIEL METORD [?], JOHN PARKER
Recorded: Nov 28 1857

Parker Co. TX - 45 - Before JOHN MATLOCK, Chief Justice Parker Co. TX, appeared JESSE F. MONTGOMERY as applicant and JESSE W. FRANKLIN and JOHN HEFLEY two disinterested and respectable witnesses - all duly sworn and saith that applicant was bonafide settled upon vacant land on Aug 26 1856 - continues to reside thereon
Signed: JESSE F. MONTGOMERY, J. W. FRANKLIN, JOHN M. HEFLEY
Sworn to & subscribed Feb 14 1857 before JOHN MATLOCK, Chief Justice Parker Co. TX

[84] Parker Co. TX - Field notes of survey of 160 acs. for JESSE F. MONTGOMERY by virtue of his preemption affidavit No. 45 Situate in Parker Co. on waters of Walnut Creek, tributary West Fork Trinity Riv. - Beg. on E boundary line JOHN MONTGOMERY 160 ac. preemption survey -

[85] Surveyed: Mar 22 1857 - LEWELLEN MURPHY, Co Surv Parker Co TX
Chain Carriers: THOMAS J. LEWIS, JOHN MONTGOMERY
Recorded: Nov 28 1857 - LEWELLEN MURPHY, Co Surv Parker Co TX

Parker Co. TX - 43 - Before JOHN MATLOCK, Chief Justice Parker Co. TX, personally appeared JOHN MONTGOMERY as applicant and J. W. FRANKLIN and J. M. HEFLEY two disinterested and respectable witnesses - all duly sworn and saith that applicant was bonafide settled upon vacant land on Aug 26 1856, date of enactment of act authorizing settlement of vacant land within limits of Mississippi & Pacific R. R. - continues to reside within limits claims right of purchase under said act.

[86] Signed: JOHN MONTGOMERY, J. W. FRANKLIN, J. M. HEFLEY
Sworn to & subscribed Feb 14 1857 before JOHN MATLOCK, Chief Justice Parker Co. TX

Parker Co. TX - Have surveyed 160 acs. for JOHN MONTGOMERY by virtue of his preemption affidavit No. 43 - Situate in Parker Co. on waters of Walnut Creek, tributary West Fork Trinity Riv. Beg. NE of SE cor. 480 ac. survey -

[87] in name of WILLIAM HIGGINS -
Surveyed: Feb 14 1857 - LEWELLEN MURPHY, Co Surv Parker Co TX
Chain Carriers: JESSE F. MONTGOMERY, THOMAS J. LEWIS

Recorded: Nov 28 1857 - LEWELLEN MURPHY, Co Surv Parker Co TX

[88]   Parker Co. TX - 26 - Before JOHN MATLOCK, Chief Justice Parker Co. TX, personally appeared JOHN BUSTER as applicant and THOMAS CALWELL and WILLIAM ALLEN two disinterested and respectable witnesses - all duly sworn and saith that applicant was bonafide settled upon vacant land on Aug 26 1856, date of enactment of act authorizing settlement of vacant land within limits of Mississippi & Pacific R. R. - continues to reside within limits - claims right of purchase under said act.
Signed: JOHN BUSTER, THOMAS CALWELL, WILLIAM H. ALLEN
Sworn to & subscribed Feb 7 1857 before JOHN MATLOCK, Chief Justice Parker Co. TX

Parker Co. TX - Field notes of survey of 165 4/100 acs. for JOHN BUSTER by virtue

[89]   of his preemption affidavit No. 26 - Situate on waters of Walnut Creek, tributary West Fork Trinity Riv. - Beg. E of SW cor. THOMAS CALWELL 160 ac. survey -
Surveyed: Oct 5 1857 - LEWELLEN MURPHY, Co Surv Parker Co TX
Chain Carriers: JOHN BRISCOE, Jacob BRISCO

[90]   Recorded: Nov 2 1857 - LEWELLEN MURPHY, Co Surv Parker Co TX

Parker Co. TX - 182 - Before JOHN H. PRINCE, Clerk Co. Court Parker Co. TX, personally came MIYAMIN [?] M. BOGGS as applicant and JOHN SQUIRES and WM. SILLIVINT two disinterested and respectable witnesses - all duly sworn and saith that applicant was bonafide settled upon vacant land on Aug 26 1856, date of enactment of act authorizing settlement of vacant land within limits of Mississippi & Pacific R. R. - continues to reside within limits - claims right of purchase under said act.
Signed: MIYAMIN M. BOGGS, JOHN SQUIRES, WM. SILLIVINT
Sworn to & subscribed Jul 28 1857 before JOHN H. PRINCE, Clerk Co. Court Parker Co. TX

[91]   Parker Co. TX - Field notes of survey of 160 acs. for MIYAMIN M. BOGGS by virtue of his preemption affidavit No. 182 - Situate on waters of Clear Fork Trinity Riv. about 8 1/2 mi. N 12° W from Weatherford - Beg. SW from SW cor. WM. SILLIVINT 160 ac. preemption survey -
Surveyed: [no month] 28 1857 - LEWELLEN MURPHY, Co Surv Parker Co TX

[92]   Chain Carriers: JOSEPH HARRISON, ASHER E. ROBERTSON
Recorded: Nov 30 1857 - LEWELLEN MURPHY, Co Surv Parker Co TX

Parker Co. TX - 204 - Before undersigned authority came JOHN STULTZ as applicant and BALEY HILL and WM. P. DULANTY two dis-

interested and respectable witnesses - all duly sworn and saith that applicant was bonafide settled upon vacant land on Aug 26 1856, date of enactment of act authorizing settlement of vacant land within limits of Mississippi & Pacific R. R. - continues to reside within limits - claims right of purchase under said act.
Signed: JOHN STULTZ, WILLIAM P. DULANY, BALY HILL
Sworn to & subscribed Oct 13 1857 before JOHN H. PRINCE, Clerk Co. Court Parker Co. TX

[93] Parker Co. TX - Field notes of survey of 160 acs. for JOHN STULTZ by virtue of his preemption affidavit No. 204 - Situate on waters of Willow Branch Creek, tributary Clear Fork Trinity Riv. about 7 mi. N 30° W from Weatherford - Beg. NE from NW cor. WILLIAM P. DULANY 160 ac. preemption survey - Surveyed: Oct 12 1857 - LEWELLEN MURPHY, Co Surv Parker Co TX Chain Carriers: ADAM STULTS, WILLIAM P. DULANY

[94] Recorded: Nov 30 1857

Parker Co. TX - 130 - Before undersigned authority personally came WILLIAM P. DULANY as applicant and BAYLE HILL and DAVID STIMSON two disinterested and respectable witnesses - all duly sworn and saith that applicant was bonafide settled upon vacant land on Aug 26 1856, date of enactment of act authorizing settlement of vacant land within limits of Mississippi & Pacific R. R. - continues to reside within limits - claims right of purchase under said act.
Signed: WM. P. DULANY, BAILEY HILL, DAVID STIMSON
Sworn to & subscribed Mar 30 1857 before JOHN H. PRINCE, Clerk Co. Court Parker Co. TX

[95] Parker Co. TX - Field notes of survey of 160 acs. for WILLIAM P. DULANY by virtue of his preemption affidavit No. 130 Situate on waters of Willow Creek branch, tributary of Clear Fork Trinity Riv. about 6 1/2 mi. N 37° W from Weatherford - Beg. NE of NE cor. PETER WELDON 160 ac. preemption survey -
Surveyed: Oct 12 1857 - LEWELLEN MURPHY, Co Surv Parker Co TX

[96] Chain Carriers: JOHN STULTZ, ADAM STULTZ
Recorded: Nov 30 1857 - LEWELLEN MURPHY, Co Surv Parker Co TX

Parker Co. TX - 57 - Before CHARLES GELDON, Notary Public in and for aforesaid co., personally came WILLIAM H. C. CABBINESS as applicant and ELIZABETH CABBINESS and JAMES JOHNSON two disinterested and respectable witnesses - all duly sworn and saith that applicant was bonafide settled upon vacant land on Aug 26 1856, date of enactment of act authorizing settlement of vacant land within limits of Mississippi & Pacific R. R. - continues to reside within limits - claims right of purchase under said act.

[no signatures]
In testimony whereof I hereunto sign my name and affix my seal of office this May 7 1857 - CHARLES GELDON, Notary Public

Parker Co. TX - Field notes of survey of 160 acs. for WILLIAM H. C. CABBINESS by virtue of his preemption affidavit No. 57 -

[97] Situate in Parker Co. on waters Clear Fork Trinity Riv. - Beg. NW from SW cor. JOHN A. CANAFAX 160 ac. survey -
Surveyed: Mar 26 1857 - LEWELLEN MURPHY, Co Surv Parker Co TX
Chain Carriers: A. M. ROBERTSON, J. A. J. HARRISON
Recorded: Dec 14 1857- LEWELLEN MURPHY, Co Surv Parker Co TX

[98] Parker Co. TX - 52 - Before CHARLES GELDON, Notary Public in and for aforesaid co., personally came JNO. M. PATTERSON as applicant and JAMES SPROULS and ZACHARIAH BURRIS two disinterested and respectable witnesses - all duly sworn and saith that applicant was bonafide settled upon vacant land on Aug 26 1856 - continues to reside thereon -
Signed: JOHN M. PATTERSON, JAMES SPROULS, ZACHARIAH "X" BURRIS [mark]
Sworn to & subscribed Apr 6 1857 before CHARLES GELDON, Notary Public

Parker Co. TX - Field notes of survey of 160 acs. for JOHN M. PATTERSON by virtue of his preemption affidavit No. 52 - Situate in Parker Co. on waters Walnut Creek, tributary West Fork Trinity Riv. -

[99] Beg. on NE cor. JESSE W. FRANKLIN 160 ac. preemption survey - NW cor. of JAMES SPROULS preemption survey - W boundary line WM. COPELANDs preemption -
Surveyed: Apr 8 1857 - LEWELLEN MURPHY, Co Surv Parker Co TX
Chain Carriers: JAMES SPROULS, [no other name]

[100] Recorded: Dec 14 1857 - LEWELLEN MURPHY, Co Surv Parker Co TX

Parker Co. TX - 89 - Before JOHN MATLOCK, Chief Justice Parker Co. TX, personally came LOUISA LEONARD as applicant and WM. J. ELLIS and QUINTEN N. ANDERSON two disinterested and respectable witnesses - all duly sworn and saith that applicant was bonafide settled upon vacant land on Aug 26 1856, - continues to reside thereon -
Signed: LOUISA LEONARD, WILLIAM J. ELLIS, QUINTEN N. ANDERSON
Sworn to & subscribed Mar 21 1857 before JOHN MATLOCK, Chief Justice Parker Co. TX

Parker Co. TX - Field notes of survey of 160 acs. for LOUISA LEONARD by virtue of her preemption affidavit No. 89 -

[101] Situate in Parker Co. waters of Walnut Creek, tributary

West Fork Trinity Riv. - Beg. S of NE cor. ALLEN C. HILL 160 ac. preemption survey - N boundary line of QUINTON N. ANDERSONs preemption -
Surveyed: Apr 1 1857 - LEWELLEN MURPHY, Co Surv Parker Co TX
Chain Carriers: ROBERT A. HENDERSON, SAMUEL SEVIER LEONARD
Recorded: Dec 14 1857 - LEWELLEN MURPHY, Co Surv Parker Co TX

[102] Parker Co. TX - 25 - Before JOHN MATLOCK, Chief Justice Parker Co. TX., personally came MARY LEONARD as applicant and THOMAS COLWELL and WILLIAM ALLEN two disinterested and respectable witnesses - all duly sworn and saith that applicant was bonafide settled upon vacant land on Aug 26 1856, date of enactment of act authorizing settlement of vacant land within limits of Mississippi & Pacific R. R. - continues to reside within limits - claims right of purchase under said act.
Signed: MARY "X" LEONARD [mark], THOMAS "X" COLWELL [mark], WILLIAM H. ALLEN
Sworn to & subscribed Feb 7 1857 before JOHN MATLOCK, Chief Justice Parker Co. TX.

Parker Co. TX - Field notes of survey of 160 acs. for MARY LEONARD by virtue of her preemption affidavit No. 25 - Situate in Parker Co. -

[103] on Walnut Creek, tributary West Fork Trinity Riv. - Beg. on SE cor. of LOUISA LEONARD 160 ac. preemption survey -
Surveyed: Apr 1 1857 - LEWELLEN MURPHY, Co Surv Parker Co TX
Chain Carriers: SAMUEL S. LEONARD, ROBERT A. HENDERSON
Recorded: Dec 14 1857 - LEWELLEN MURPHY, Co Surv Parker Co TX

[104] Parker Co. TX - 2 - Before undersigned authority came JAMES D. CARR as applicant and JAMES F. COLE and EZRA MULKIN two disinterested and respectable witnesses - all duly sworn and saith that applicant was bonafide settled upon vacant land on Aug 26 1856, date of enactment of act authorizing settlement of vacant land within limits of Mississippi & Pacific R. R. - continues to reside within limits - claims right of purchase under said act.
Signed: JAMES D. CARR, J. F. COLE, EZRA MULKIN
Sworn to & subscribed Oct 26 1857 before JOHN P. COLE, Notary Public Parker Co. TX

Parker Co. TX - Field notes of survey of 136 5/10 acs. for JAMES D. CARR by virtue of his preemption affidavit No. 2 - Situate in Parker Co. on waters Clear Fork Trinity Riv. about 11 mi. S 74° E from Weatherford - Beg. N of ENE [sic] cor. J. G. WRAY 320 ac. survey -

[105] Surveyed: Oct 27 1857 - LEWELLEN MURPHY, Co Surv Parker Co TX
Chain Carriers: JAMES N. BRIGHT, FRANCIS S. BLODGET
Recorded: Dec 14 1857 - LEWELLEN MURPHY, Co Surv Parker Co TX

Parker Co. TX - 167 - Before undersigned authority personally came SETON MAGERS as applicant and ISAAC GLASS and DAVID ROSE two disinterested and respectable witnesses - all duly sworn and saith that applicant was bonafide settled upon vacant land on Aug 26 1856, date of enactment of act authorizing settlement of vacant land within limits of Mississippi & Pacific R. R. - continues to reside within limits - claims right of purchase under said act.

[106] Signed: SETON MAGERS, ISAAC GLASS, DAVID "X" ROSE [mark] Sworn to & subscribed Jun 7 1857 before JOHN H. PRINCE, Clerk Co. Court Parker Co. TX

Parker Co. TX - Field notes of survey of 160 acs. for SETON MAGERS [MAYORS ?] by virtue of his preemption affidavit No. 167 Situate in NE portion of the county on Clear Fork Trinity Riv. - Beg. on W boundary line JOHN HAUPE [?] 320 ac. survey - SE cor. DAVID C. ROSE 160 ac. preemption survey

[107] cor. on W. boundary of JOHN HANPIS [?] survey -
Surveyed: Dec 2 1857 - LEWELLEN MURPHY, Co. Surv Parker Co TX
Chain Carriers: WILLIAM E. BURKE, WILLIAM BAKER
Recorded: Dec 14 1857 - LEWELLEN MURPHY, Co Surv Parker Co TX

Parker Co. TX - 161 - Before undersigned authority personally came JOHN GORDON as applicant and ISAAC BRISCO and N. G. LEE two disinterested and respectable witnesses - all duly sworn and saith that applicant was bonafide settled upon vacant land on Aug 26 1856, date of enactment of act authorizing settlement of vacant land within limits of Mississippi & Pacific R. R. - continues to reside within limits - claims right of purchase under said act.
Signed: JOHN "X" GORDON [mark], ISAAC "X" BRISCO [mark], N. G. LEE
Sworn to & subscribed May 26 1857 before JOHN H. PRINCE, Clerk Co. Court Parker Co. TX

[108] Parker Co. TX - Field notes of survey of 160 acs. for JOHN GORDON by virtue of his preemption affidavit No. 161 - Situate in Parker Co. on headwaters Clear Fork Trinity Riv. about 12 1/2 mi. N 28° W from Weatherford - Beg. SW from SW cor. ISAAC BRISCO 160 ac. preemption survey -
Surveyed: Dec 7 1857 - LEWELLEN MURPHY, Co Surv Parker Co TX
Chain Carriers: ALFRED GORDON, UPTON C. BLACKWELL

[109] Recorded: Dec 15 1857 - LEWELLEN MURPHY, Co Surv Parker Co TX

Parker Co. TX - Before undersigned authority personally came JACOB A. WHITTEN as applicant and JOHN CLARY and R. C. BETTY two disinterested and respectable witnesses - all duly sworn and saith that applicant was bonafide settled upon vacant land

on Aug 26 1856, date of enactment of act authorizing settlement of vacant land within limits of Mississippi & Pacific R. R. - continues to reside within limits - claims right of purchase under said act.
Signed: J. A. WHITTEN, R. C. BETTY, JOHN "X" CLARY [mark]
Sworn to & subscribed Mar 19 1857 before JOHN H. PRINCE, Clerk Co. Court Parker Co. TX

[110] Parker Co. TX - Field notes of survey of 160 acs. for J. A. WHITTEN by virtue of his preemption affidavit No. 114 - Situate in Parker Co. on waters Rock Creek, tributary Brazos Riv. - Beg. SE of SE cor. JOHN H. BUTLER 160 ac. survey -
Surveyed: Nov 4 1857 - LEWELLEN MURPHY, Co Surv Parker Co TX
Chain Carriers: JOHN CLARY, ISAAC BETTY
Recorded: Dec 15 1857 - LEWELLEN MURPHY, Co Surv Parker Co TX

[111] Parker Co. TX - 180 - Before undersigned authority personally came W. T. BLASSINGAME as applicant and S. L. GILLILAND and I. O. HEADLEY two disinterested and respectable witnesses - all duly sworn and saith that applicant was bonafide settled upon vacant land on Aug 26 1856, date of enactment of act authorizing settlement of vacant land within limits of Mississippi & Pacific R. R. - continues to reside within limits claims right of purchase under said act.
Signed: W. T. BLASSINGAME, S. L. GILLILAND, ISAAC O. HEADLEY
Sworn to & subscribed Jul 9 1857 before JOHN H. PRINCE, Clerk Co. Court Parker Co. TX by WM. M. GREEN, Dept.

Parker Co. TX - Field notes of survey of 160 acs. for W. T. BLASSINGAME by virtue of his preemption affidavit No. 180 - Situate in Parker Co. on waters Clear Fork Trinity Riv. - Beg. W & N of SW cor. DAVID C. ROSE 160 ac. preemption survey -

[112] Surveyed: Dec 2 1857 - LEWELLEN MURPHY, Co Surv Parker Co TX
Chain Carriers: LEWIS P. MC DONALD, WILLIAM C. MOORE
Recorded: Dec 15 1857 - LEWELLEN MURPHY, Co Surv Parker Co TX

[113] Parker Co. TX - 165 - Before undersigned authority personally came W. J. MAYO as applicant and M. D. TACKITT and JAMES A. MILLER two disinterested and respectable witnesses - all duly sworn and saith that applicant was bonafide settled upon vacant land on Aug 26 1856, date of enactment of act authorizing settlement of vacant land within limits of Mississippi & Pacific R. R. - continues to reside within limits claims right of purchase under said act.
Signed: W. J. MAYO, M. D. TACKITT, JAMES A. MILLER
Sworn to & subscribed June 1 1857 before JOHN H. PRINCE, Clerk Co. Court Parker Co. TX

Parker Co. TX - Field notes of survey of 160 acs. for W. J. MAYO by virtue of his preemption affidavit No. 165 - Situate in Parker Co. on waters Clear Fork Trinity Riv. about 12 mi. N 20° W from Weatherford - Beg. S of NW cor. ISAAC BRISCO 160 ac. preemption survey -

[114] Surveyed: Dec 8 1857 - LEWELLEN MURPHY, Co Surv Parker Co TX
Chain Carriers: M. D. TACKITT, UPTON C. BLACKWELL
Recorded: Dec 15 1857 - LEWELLEN MURPHY, Co Surv Parker Co TX

Parker Co. TX - 66 - Before JOHN MATLOCK, Chief Justice Parker Co., personally came as LIDDY GORE applicant and WOODSON D. HENRY and JAMES H. SMITH two disinterested and respectable witnesses - all duly sworn and saith that applicant was bonafide settled upon vacant land on Aug 26 1856, date of enactment of act authorizing settlement of vacant land within limits of Mississippi & Pacific R. R. - continues to reside within limits claims right of purchase under said act.

[115] Signed: LIDDY GORE, WOODSON D. HENRY, JAMES H. SMITH
Sworn to & subscribed Feb 26 1857 before JOHN MATLOCK, Chief Justice Parker Co.

Parker Co. TX - Field notes of survey of 160 acs. for LIDDY GORE by virtue of her preemption affidavit No. 66 - Situate in Parker Co. waters of Walnut Creek, tributary West Fork Trinity Riv. about 17 1/2 N 25° E from Weatherford - Beg. E of NE cor. ABRAHAM BIRDWELL 160 ac. preemption survey -

[116] N boundary line Parker Co.
Surveyed: Dec 5 1857 - LEWELLEN MURPHY, Co Surv Parker Co TX
Chain Carriers: RICHARD B. SMITH, JOHN B. THOMAS
Recorded: Dec 15 1857 - LEWELLEN MURPHY, Co Surv Parker Co TX

Parker Co. TX - 106 - Before JOHN MATLOCK, Chief Justice Parker Co. TX, personally came ROBERT M. WALKER as applicant and SAMUEL H. WALKER and E. H. CROMPTON two disinterested and respectable witnesses - all duly sworn and saith that applicant was bonafide settled upon vacant land on Aug 26 1856, date of enactment of act authorizing settlement of vacant land within limits of Mississippi & Pacific R. R. - continues to reside within limits claims right of purchase under said act.

[117] Signed: ROBERT M. "X" WALKER [mark], SAMUEL H. "X" WALKER [mark], E. H. CROMPTON
Sworn to & subscribed Oct 31 1857 before JOHN MATLOCK, Chief Justice Parker Co. TX

Parker Co. TX - Field notes of survey of 160 acs. for ROBERT M. WALKER by virtue of his preemption affidavit No. 106 - Situate on waters of Walnut Creek, tributary West Fork Trinity Riv. about 13 1/2 mi. N 30° E from Weatherford - Beg. S of SW cor. JOHN DUNCAN 160 ac. preemption survey -

[118] N boundary of SAMUEL H. WALKERs preemption -
Surveyed: Dec 3 1857 - LEWELLEN MURPHY, Co Surv Parker Co TX
Chain Carriers: WILLIAM NATIONS, ENOCH H. CROMPTON
Recorded: Dec 15 1857 - LEWELLEN MURPHY, Co Surv Parker Co TX

[119] Parker Co. TX - 57 - Before JOHN MATLOCK, Chief Justice Parker Co. TX, personally came STEPHEN NEWSON as applicant and WILLIAM PENNINGTON and HENRY BEEDLE two disinterested and respectable witnesses - all duly sworn and saith that applicant was bonafide settled upon vacant land on Aug 26 1856, date of enactment of act authorizing settlement of vacant land within limits of Mississippi & Pacific R. R. - continues to reside within limits - claims right of purchase under said act.
Signed: STEPHEN NEWSON, WILLIAM PENNINGTON, HENRY BEADLE
Sworn to & subscribed Feb 20 1857 before JOHN MATLOCK, Chief Justice Parker Co. TX

[120] Parker Co. TX - Field notes of survey of 160 acs. for STEPHEN NEWSON by virtue of his preemption affidavit No. 57 - Situate on waters Ash Creek, tributary West Fork Trinity Riv. about 13 mi. N 52° E from Weatherford - Beg. SE from SE cor. LOVING CLIFTON 144 4/10 ac. preemption survey -
Surveyed: Sep 28 1857 - LEWELLEN MURPHY, Co Surv Parker Co TX
Chain Carriers: CHRISTOPHER BEDWELL, THOMAS N. RASH

[121] Recorded: Dec 15 1857 - LEWELLEN MURPHY, Co Surv Parker Co TX

Parker Co. TX - 199 - Before JOHN H. PRINCE, Clerk Co. Court Parker Co. TX, personally came G. W. MEEK as applicant and M. O. BARTEN and W. T. BARTEN two disinterested and respectable witnesses - all duly sworn and saith that applicant was bonafide settled upon vacant land on Aug 26 1856, date of enactment of act authorizing settlement of vacant land within limits of Mississippi & Pacific R. R. - continues to reside within limits claims right of purchase under said act.
Signed: G. W. "X" MEEK [mark], W. T. BARTEN, M. O. BARTEN
Sworn to & subscribed Sep 8 1857 before JOHN H. PRINCE, Clerk Co. Court Parker Co. TX

[122] Parker Co. TX - Field notes of survey of 160 acs. for G. W. MEEK by virtue of his preemption affidavit No. 199 - Situate SW part of Parker Co. on Brazos Riv.- Beg. E of SW cor. MARY MEEK 160 ac. preemption survey -
Surveyed: Nov 9 1857 - LEWELLEN MURPHY, Co Surv Parker Co TX
Chain Carriers: JACOB MEEK, JOHN WESLEY MEEK

[123] Recorded: Dec 22 1857 - LEWELLEN MURPHY, Co Surv Parker Co TX

Parker Co. TX - 113 - Before undersigned authority personally came JOHN CLARY as applicant and W. C. MC ADAMS and JOHN H.

BUTLER two disinterested and respectable witnesses - all duly sworn and saith that applicant was bonafide settled upon vacant land on Aug 26 1856, date of enactment of act authorizing settlement of vacant land within limits of Mississippi & Pacific R. R. - continues to reside within limits - claims right of purchase under said act.
Signed: JOHN "X" CLARY [mark], W. C. "X" MC ADAMS [mark], JOHN H. BUTLER
Sworn to & subscribed Mar 19 1857

Parker Co. TX - Field notes of survey of 160 acs. for JOHN CLARY by virtue of his preemption affidavit No. 113 -

[124] Situate on waters Rock Creek, tributary Brazos Riv.- Beg. W of SW cor. JACOB A. WHITTEN 160 ac. preemption survey
Surveyed: Nov 4 1857 - LEWELLEN MURPHY, Co Surv Parker Co TX
Chain Carriers: ISAAC BETTY, JACOB A. WHITTEN
Recorded: Dec 22 1857 - LEWELLEN MURPHY, Co Surv Parker Co TX

[125] Parker Co. TX - 219 - Before undersigned authority personally came JOHN M. TAYLOR as applicant and ISOM CRANFIL and GEORGE COPELAND two disinterested and respectable witnesses - all duly sworn and saith that applicant was bonafide settled upon vacant land on Aug 26 1856, date of enactment of act authorizing settlement of vacant land within limits of Mississippi & Pacific R. R. - continues to reside within limits claims right of purchase under said act.
Signed: JOHN M. TAYLOR, ISOM CRANFIL, GEORGE COPELAND
Sworn to & subscribed Nov 16 1857 before JOHN H. PRINCE, Clerk Co. Court Parker Co. TX

Parker Co. TX - Field notes of survey of 160 acs. for JOHN M. TAYLOR by virtue of his preemption affidavit No. 219 - Situate in NW part of Parker Co. on waters of Rock Creek, tributary Brazos Riv. about 11 mi. N 45° W from Weatherford -

[126] Beg. NW from SW cor. DANIEL V. KIRBIE 160 ac. preemption survey -
Surveyed: Oct 31 1857 - LEWELLEN MURPHY, Co Surv Parker Co TX
Chain Carriers: DAVID WHITE, GEORGE COPELAND
Recorded: Dec 22 1857 - LEWELLEN MURPHY, Co Surv Parker Co TX

[127] Parker Co. TX - 157 - Before undersigned authority personally came CALVIN L. BANDY as claimant and JOHN B. KERBY and ISAAC O. HEADLEY two disinterested and respectable witnesses all duly sworn and saith that applicant was bonafide settled upon vacant land on Aug 26 1856, date of enactment of act authorizing settlement of vacant land within limits of Mississippi & Pacific R. R. - continues to reside within limits claims right of purchase under said act.
Signed: CALVIN L. BANDY, JOHN B. KEARBY, ISAAC O. HEADLEY

Sworn to & subscribed May 20 1857 before JOHN H. PRINCE, Clerk Co. Court Parker Co. TX

"The JAMES H. WARFIELD 671 ac. survey covers the T. BALIMAN survey which is supposed to be null and void" [in left margin beside this entry]

Parker Co. TX - Field notes of survey of 160 acs. for CALVIN L. BANDY by virtue of his preemption affidavit No. 157 - Situate on waters Patrick's Creek, tributary Brazos Riv. - Beg. SE from N cor. J. BALIMAN 640 ac. survey -

[128] Surveyed: Nov 21 1857 - LEWELLEN MURPHY, Co Surv Parker Co TX
Chain Carriers: JAMES JACKSON, JOHN W. BRASHEARS
Recorded: Dec 23 1857 - LEWELLEN MURPHY, Co Surv Parker Co TX

[129] Parker Co. TX - 218 - Before undersigned authority personally came WILLIAM BAKER as applicant and LEWIS P. MC DONALD and CALVIN LYNCHE two disinterested and respectable witnesses - all duly sworn and saith that applicant was bonafide settled upon vacant land on Aug 26 1856, date of enactment of act authorizing settlement of vacant land within limits of Mississippi & Pacific R. R. - continues to reside within limits claims right of purchase under said act.
Signed: WILLIAM BAKER, LEWIS P. MC DONALD, CALVIN LYNCH

Sworn to & subscribed Nov 28 1857 before JOHN H. PRINCE, Clerk Co. Court Parker Co. TX, by B. F. WALKER, Dept.

Parker Co. TX - Field notes of survey of 160 acs. for WILLIAM BAKER by virtue of his preemption affidavit No. 218 - Situate on Clear Fork Trinity Riv. - Beg. W of NE cor. JOHN SNYDER 320 ac. survey & on N. boundary said survey -

[130] NE cor. WILLIAM WILSON 160 ac. preemption survey - S. boundary line of LEWIS P. MC DONALD 282 ac. survey -
Surveyed: Dec 1 1857 - LEWELLEN MURPHY, Co Surv Parker Co TX
Chain Carriers: CALVIN LYNCH, LEWIS P. MC DONALD
Recorded: Dec 23 1857 - LEWELLEN MURPHY, Co Surv Parker Co TX

[131] Parker Co. TX - 159 - Before undersigned authority personally came FRANCIS LEFLETT as applicant and WILLIAM WELCH and WASHINGTON ROY two disinterested and respectable witnesses - all duly sworn and saith that applicant was bonafide settled upon vacant land on Aug 26 1856, date of enactment of act authorizing settlement of vacant land within limits of Mississippi & Pacific R. R. - continues to reside within limits claims right of purchase under said act.
Signed: FRANCIS LEFLET, WILLIAM "X" WELCH [mark], WASHINGTON "X" ROY [mark]

Sworn to & subscribed May 21 1857 before JOHN H. PRINCE, Clerk
Co. Court Parker Co. TX

Parker Co. TX - Field notes of survey of 160 acs. for FRANCIS
LEFLET by virtue of his preemption affidavit No. 159 - Situate
in SW part of Parker Co. on waters Patrick's Creek, tributary
Brazos Riv. - Beg. NW from NE cor. CALVIN L. BANDY 160 ac.
preemption survey -

[132] Surveyed: Nov 21 1857 - LEWELLEN MURPHY, Co Surv Parker
Co TX
Chain Carriers: JOHN W. BRASHEARS, WILLIAM JACKSON
Recorded: Dec 23 1857 - LEWELLEN MURPHY, Co Surv Parker Co TX

[133] Parker Co. TX - 158 - Before undersigned authority personally came JOHN B. KEARBY as applicant and ISAAC O. HEADLEY
and CALVIN L. BANDY two disinterested and respectable witnesses all duly sworn and saith that applicant was bonafide settled upon vacant land on Aug 26 1856, date of enactment of act
authorizing settlement of vacant land within limits of Mississippi & Pacific R. R. - continues to reside within limits
claims right of purchase under said act.
Signed: JOHN B. KEARBY, ISAAC O. HEADLEY, CALVIN L. BANDY
Sworn to & subscribed May 20 1857 before JOHN H. PRINCE, Clerk
Co. Court Parker Co. TX

Parker Co. TX - Field notes of survey of 83 35/100 for JOHN B.
KIRBY by virtue of his preemption affidavit No. 158 - Situate
SW part Parker Co. on waters of Patrick's Creek, tributary
Brazos Riv. about 8 mi. S 38° W from Weatherford - Beg. SE
from E or NE cor -

[134] FRANCIS LEFLET 160 ac. survey -
Surveyed: Nov 23 1857 - LEWELLEN MURPHY Co Surv Parker Co TX
Chain Carriers: STEPHEN BRANNAN, WILLIAM JACKSON
Recorded: Dec 23 1857 - LEWELLEN MURPHY, Co Surv Parker Co TX

[135] Parker Co. TX - 160 - Before undersigned authority personally came ISAAC BRISCO as applicant and NICHOLAS G. LEE and
JOHN GORDON two disinterested and respectable witnesses - all
duly sworn and saith that applicant was bonafide settled upon
vacant land on Aug 26 1856, date of enactment of act authorizing settlement of vacant land within limits of Mississippi &
Pacific R. R. - continues to reside within limits claims right
of purchase under said act.
Signed: ISAAC "X" BRISCO [mark], JOHN "X" GORDON [mark],
NICHOLAS G. LEE
Sworn to & subscribed May 26 1857 before JOHN H. PRINCE, Clerk
Co. Court Parker Co. TX

Parker Co. TX - Field notes of survey of 160 acs. for ISAAC
BRISCO by virtue of his preemption affidavit No. 160 - Situate

NW part of Parker Co. on waters of Clear Fork Trinity Riv. about 12 1/2 mi. N 26° W from Weatherford - Beg. SW of NW cor. J. M. JENKINS 320 ac. survey -

[136] Surveyed: Oct 8 1857 - LEWELLEN MURPHY, Co Surv Parker Co TX
Chain Carriers: JAMES C. EDWARDS, ISOM BRISCO
Recorded: Dec 24 1857 - LEWELLEN MURPHY, Co Surv Parker Co TX

Parker Co. TX - No. [blank] - Before undersigned authority personally came FRANCIS S. BLODGET as applicant and JAMES F. COLE and J. A. LEDBETTER two disinterested and respectable witnesses - all duly sworn and saith that applicant was bonafide settled upon vacant land on Aug 26 1856, date of enactment of act authorizing settlement of vacant land within limits of Mississippi & Pacific R. R. - continues to reside within limits claims right of purchase under said act.

[137] Signed: FRANCIS S. BLODGET, J. F. COLE, J. A. LEDBETTER
Sworn to & subscribed Aug 17 1857 before J. P. COLE, Notary Public in and for Parker Co. TX

Parker Co. TX - Field notes of survey of 160 acs. for FRANCIS S. BLODGET by virtue of his preemption affidavit No. 1 - Situate in SE part of co. on waters of Clear Fork of Trinity Riv. about 9 1/2 mi. S 68° E from Weatherford - Beg. N of SW cor. SAMUEL LEAKE 320 ac. survey -

[138] Surveyed: Oct 22 1857 - LEWELLEN MURPHY, Co Surv Parker Co TX
Chain Carriers: JOHN H. PHELPS, JAMES D. BLODGET
Recorded: Dec 24 1857 - LEWELLEN MURPHY, Co Surv Parker Co TX

Parker Co. TX - 13 - Before undersigned authority personally came JOSEPH REEVES as applicant and R. S. PORTER Junr. and WM. PATTERSON two disinterested and respectable witnesses - all duly sworn and saith that applicant was bonafide settled upon vacant land on Aug 26 1856, date of enactment of act authorizing settlement of vacant land within limits of Mississippi & Pacific R. R. - continues to reside within limits - claims right of purchase under said act.
Signed: JOSEPH REEVES, R. S. PORTER, Junr., WILLIAM PATTERSON

[139] Sworn to & subscribed Feb 25 1857 before J. J. BEEMAN, Notary Public in and for Parker Co. TX

Parker Co. TX - Field notes of survey of 160 acs. for JOSEPH REEVES by virtue of his preemption affidavit No. 13 - Situate on Grindstone Creek, tributary of Brazos Riv. about 9 mi. N 87° W from Weatherford - Beg. E of NE cor. ISAAC BURROWS 160 ac. preemption survey

[140] Surveyed: Nov 12 1857 - LEWELLEN MURPHY, Co Surv Parker Co TX
Chain Carriers: ROBERT F. PORTER, WILLIAM C. HALL
Recorded: Dec 24 1857 - LEWELLEN MURPHY, Co Surv Parker Co TX

Parker Co. TX - 27 - Before undersigned authority personally came WILLIAM D. KING as applicant and N. J. HOLDER and E. B. DAVIDSON two disinterested and respectable witnesses - all duly sworn and saith that applicant was bonafide settled upon vacant land on Aug 26 1856, date of enactment of act authorizing settlement of vacant land within limits of Mississippi & Pacific R. R. - continues to reside within limits - claims right of purchase under said act.
Signed: WM. D. KING, N. J. HOLDER, E. B. DAVIDSON

[141] Sworn to & subscribed Feb 21 1857 before JOHN H. PRINCE, Clerk Co. Court Parker Co. TX

Parker Co. TX - Have surveyed for W. D. KING 160 acs. by virtue of affidavit No. 27 - Situate in Parker Co. on waters Clear Fork Trinity Riv. - Beg. SW from SW cor. JAMES WILLIAMS 320 ac. survey -
Surveyed: Aug 26 1857 - LEWELLEN MURPHY, Co Surv Parker Co TX
Chain Carriers: SAM. W. KING, W. D. KING
Recorded: Dec 28 1857 - LEWELLEN MURPHY, Co Surv Parker Co TX

[142] Parker Co. TX - 97 - Before JOHN MATLOCK, Chief Justice Parker Co. TX, personally came MARTHA JANE GODBEHERE as applicant and CALVIN LINCE and SETON MAGERS two disinterested and respectable witnesses - all duly sworn and saith that applicant was bonafide settled upon vacant land on Aug 26 1856, date of enactment of act authorizing settlement of vacant land within limits of Mississippi & Pacific R. R. - continues to reside within limits - claims right of purchase under said act.
Signed: MARTHA J. "X" GODBEHERE [mark], CALVIN LINCH, SETON MAGORS
Sworn to & subscribed Aug 6 1857 before JOHN MATLOCK, Chief Justice Parker Co. TX

Parker Co. TX - Field notes of survey of 160 acs. for MARTHA JANE GODBEHERE by her preemption virtue affidavit No. 97 - Situate in Parker Co. on waters of Clear Fork Trinity Riv. about 7 mi. N 33° E from Weatherford - Beg. on [torn] N. boundary

[143] JOHN HANTE [?] 320 ac. survey -
Surveyed: Aug 12 1857- LEWELLEN MURPHY, Co Surv Parker Co TX
Chain Carriers: WILLIAM L. BLASSINGAME, LEWIS P. MC DONALD
Recorded: Dec 28 1857 - LEWELLEN MURPHY, Co Surv Parker Co TX

[144] Parker Co. TX - 37 - Before CHARLES GELDON, Notary Pub-

lic in and for the co. aforesaid, personally came THOMAS GUTTIREC as applicant and P. J. BURROWS and B. F. BOSWELL two disinterested and respectable witnesses - all duly sworn and saith that applicant was bonafide settled upon vacant land on Aug 26 1856, date of enactment of act authorizing settlement of vacant land within limits of Mississippi & Pacific R. R. - continues to reside within limits - claims right of purchase under said act.
Signed: THOMAS GUTTERY, PHILIP J. BURROW, B. F. BOSWELL
Sworn to & subscribed Mar 13 1857 before CHARLES GELDON, Notary Public

Parker Co. TX - Field notes of survey of 36 5/10 ac. for THOMAS GUTTERY by virtue of his preemption affidavit No. 37 - Situate in NE part of co. on waters of Ash Creek, tributary of West Fork Trinity Riv. - Beg. S of NE cor. 320 ac. preemption survey

[145] in name JAMES WITCHER - W boundary line of LOVING CLIFTON preemption survey -
Surveyed: Sep 28 1857 - LEWELLEN MURPHY, Co Surv Parker Co TX
Chain Carriers: SHADE CANTRELL, JOHN GUTTERY
Recorded: Dec 28 1857 - LEWELLEN MURPHY, Co Surv Parker Co TX

[146] Parker Co. TX - 86 - Before undersigned authority personally came JOHN H. BUTLER as applicant and J. S. STEPHENS and W. C. MC ADAMS two disinterested and respectable witnesses - all duly sworn and saith that applicant was bonafide settled upon vacant land on Aug 26 1856, date of enactment of act authorizing settlement of vacant land within limits of Mississippi & Pacific R. R. - continues to reside within limits claims right of purchase under said act.
Signed: JOHN H. BUTLER, J. S. "X" STEPHENS [mark], W. C. "X" MC ADAMS [mark]
Sworn to & subscribed Feb 28 1857 before JOHN H. PRINCE, Clerk Co. Court Parker Co. TX

Parker Co. TX - Field notes of survey of 160 acs. for JOHN H. BUTLER by virtue of his preemption affidavit No. 86 - Situate on Rock Creek, tributary of Brazos Riv. about 14 mi. N 68° W from Weatherford - Beg. W from SW cor. DANIEL V. KIRBIE 160 ac. preemption survey -

[147] Surveyed: Nov 4 1857 - LEWELLEN MURPHY, Co Surv Parker Co TX
Chain Carriers: JACOB A. WHITTEN, ISAAC BETTY
Recorded: Dec 28 1857 - LEWELLEN MURPHY, Co Surv Parker Co TX

[148] Parker Co. TX - 92 - Before JOHN MATLOCK, Chief Justice Parker Co. TX, personally came HOWARD HAYES as applicant and JAMES WIMBLY and ROBERT WRIGHT two disinterested and respectable witnesses - all duly sworn and saith that applicant was

bonafide settled upon vacant land on Aug 26 1856, date of enactment of act authorizing settlement of vacant land within limits of Mississippi & Pacific R. R. - continues to reside within limits claims right of purchase under said act.
Signed: HOWARD HAYES, JAMES WIMBERLY, ROBERT WRIGHT
Sworn to & subscribed Feb 27 1857 before JOHN MATLOCK, Chief Justice Parker Co. TX

Parker Co. TX - Field notes of survey of 160 acs. for HOWARD HAYES by virtue of his preemption affidavit No. 92 - Situate in NE part Parker Co. on waters of Walnut Creek, tributary West Fork Trinity Riv. about 16 1/2 mi. N 43° E from Weatherford - Beg. on NW cor -

[149] ROBERT SHORT 160 ac. preemption survey - "it is likewise the SW cor. of ROBERT J. BILLINGSLEA 160 preemption survey" -
Surveyed: Apr 15 1857 - LEWELLEN MURPHY, Co Surv Parker Co TX
Chain Carriers: JAMES WIMBLY, SAMUEL HAND
Recorded: Dec 28 1857 - LEWELLEN MURPHY, Co Surv Parker Co TX

[150] Parker Co. TX - 54 - Before undersigned authority personally came BENJAMIN REYNOLDS as applicant and AUGER PRICE and ROBERT BROWN two disinterested and respectable witnesses - all duly sworn and saith that applicant was bonafide settled upon vacant land on Aug 26 1856, date of enactment of act authorizing settlement of vacant land within limits of Mississippi & Pacific R. R. - continues to reside within limits claims right of purchase under said act.
Signed: BENJAMIN "X" REYNOLDS [mark], ANGER "X" PRICE [mark], ROBERT BROWN
Sworn to & subscribed Feb 24 1857 before JOHN H. PRINCE, Clerk Co. Court Parker Co. TX by WM. M. GREEN, Dept.

Parker Co. TX - Field notes of survey of 160 acs. for BENJAMIN R. REYNOLDS by virtue of his affidavit No. 54 - Situate in Parker Co. S Fork waters Clear Fork Trinity Riv. - Beg. W of NW cor. PETER KIRK 320 ac. survey -

[151] cor. JAMES KIDWELL 160 ac. survey -
Surveyed: Aug 21 1857 ISAAC O. HEADLEY, D. S. P. C.
Chain Carriers: JOHN JAMES, B. R. REYNOLDS
Recorded: Dec 29 1857 - LEWELLEN MURPHY, Co Surv Parker Co TX

Parker Co. TX - 11 - Before undersigned authority personally came WILLIAM PATTERSON as claimant and ROBERT S. PORTER Jun and JOSEPH REEVES two disinterested and respectable witnesses - all duly sworn and saith that applicant was bonafide settled upon vacant land on Aug 26 1856, date of enactment of act authorizing settlement of vacant land within limits of Mississippi & Pacific R. R. - continues to reside within limits - claims right of purchase under said act.

Signed: WILLIAM PATTESON, R. S. PORTER, JOSEPH REEVES

[152] Sworn to & subscribed Feb 25 1857 before J. J. BEEMAN, Notary Public in and for Parker Co.

Parker Co. TX - Field notes of survey of 160 acs. for WILLIAM PATTERSON by virtue of his preemption affidavit No. 11 - Situate on waters Grindstone Creek, tributary of Brazos Riv. about 9 3/4 mi. N 80° W from Weatherford - Beg. NW from SW cor. ROBERT S. PORTER 160 preemption survey -
Surveyed: Apr 14 1857 - LEWELLEN MURPHY, Co Surv Parker Co TX
Chain Carriers: WILLIAM PATTERSON, ROBERT S. PORTER

[153] Recorded: Dec 30 1857 - LEWELLEN MURPHY, Co Surv Parker Co TX

Parker Co. TX - 213 - Before JOHN H. PRINCE, Clerk Co. Court Parker Co., personally came DAVID C. ROSE as applicant and WM. COLEMAN and J. H. SEWELL two disinterested and respectable witnesses - all duly sworn and saith that applicant was bonafide settled upon vacant land on Aug 26 1856, date of enactment of act authorizing settlement of vacant land within limits of Mississippi & Pacific R. R. - continues to reside within limits claims right of purchase under said act.
Signed: DAVID "X" C. ROSE [mark], WILLIAM "X" COLEMAN [mark], J. H. SEWELL
Sworn to & subscribed Nov 28 1857 before JOHN H. PRINCE, Clerk Co. Court Parker Co. TX

Parker Co. TX - Field notes of survey of 160 acs. for DAVID C. ROSE by virtue of his preemption affidavit No. 213 -

[154] Situate on Clear Fork Trinity Riv. about 6 1/4 N 25° E from Weatherford - Beg. on NW cor. of the heirs of JOHN W. HAWPE 320 ac. survey - S boundary line of J. THOMAS survey -
Surveyed: Nov 30 1857 - LEWELLEN MURPHY, Co Surv Parker Co TX
Chain Carriers: WILLIAM C. MOORE, SETON MAYORS

[155] Recorded: Dec 30 1857 - LEWELLEN MURPHY, Co Surv Parker Co TX

Parker Co. TX - 125 - Before undersigned authority personally came SINGLETON GILBERT as applicant and WILSON LITTLEFIELD and L. J. GILBERT two disinterested and respectable witnesses - all duly sworn and saith that applicant was bonafide settled upon vacant land on Aug 26 1856, date of enactment of act authorizing settlement of vacant land within limits of Mississippi & Pacific R. R. - continues to reside within limits - claims right of purchase under said act.
Signed: SINGLETON GILBERT, L. J. "X" GILBERT [mark], WILSON "X" LITTLEFIELD [mark]

Sworn to & subscribed Mar 28 1857 before JOHN H. PRINCE, Clerk Co. Court Parker Co. TX

Parker Co. TX - Field notes of survey of 109 acs. for SINGLETON GILBERT

[156] by virtue of his preemption affidavit No 125 - Situate on SW side of Brazos Riv. about 15 mi. S 71° W from Weatherford - Beg. on E cor. WILSON LITTLEFIELD 160 ac. preemption survey - N boundary SAMUEL LITTLEFIELD 160 ac. preemption survey - E cor. LEMUEL J. GILBERT 160 ac. survey
Surveyed: Nov 9 1857 - LEWELLEN MURPHY, Co Surv Parker Co TX
Chain Carriers: LEMUEL J. GILBERT, WILSON LITTLEFIELD

[157] Recorded: Dec 30 1857 - LEWELLEN MURPHY, Co Surv Parker Co TX

Parker Co. TX - Before JOHN MATLOCK, Chief Justice Parker Co. TX, personally came HUGH BROWN as applicant and JAMES SILLIVINT and JOSEPH WALKER two disinterested and respectable witnesses to me well known all of whom being to me duly sworn the said applicant HUGH BROWN deposeth and saith that he was bonafide settled upon vacant land previous to the 26th Aug 1856 and that he commenced said settlement in the summer of 1855 as a young man over the age of seventeen years and that he claims the right of purchase of said settlement under an act authorizing the sale of vacant land within limits of Mississippi & Pacific R. R. - continues to reside within limits - claims right of purchase under said act.
Signed: HUGH BROWN, JOSEPH WALKER, WILLIAM S. SILLIVINT [?]

[158] Sworn to & subscribed Mar 27 1857 before JOHN MATLOCK, Chief Justice Parker Co. TX

Parker Co. TX - Field notes of survey of 160 acs. for HUGH BROWN by virtue of his preemption affidavit No. 92 - Situate in N part of county on waters of Clear Fork Trinity Riv. about 10 1/2 mi. N from Weatherford - Beg. NE of NW cor. WILLIAM SILLIVINT 160 ac. preemption survey -
Surveyed: Oct 7 1857 - LEWELLEN MURPHY, Co Surv Parker Co TX
Chain Carriers: WILLIAM SILLIVINT, FRANCIS M. SILLIVINT

[159] Recorded: Dec 30 1857 - LEWELLEN MURPHY, Co Surv Parker Co TX

Parker Co. TX - 24 - Before undersigned authority personally came OLIVER CHILDERS as applicant and DANIEL LEE and ELI LEE two disinterested and respectable witnesses - all duly sworn and saith that applicant was bonafide settled upon vacant land on Aug 26 1856, date of enactment of act authorizing settlement of vacant land within limits of Mississippi & Pacific R. R. - continues to reside within limits - claims right of pur-

chase under said act.
Signed: OLIVER CHILDERS, DANIEL LEE, ELI LEE
Sworn to & subscribed Feb 21 1857 before JOHN H. PRINCE, Clerk Co. Court Parker Co. TX

"Resurveyed and recorded in Bk A p 198" [left margin in ink]

[160] Denton Dist. TX - Survey No. 3 of 160 acs. for OLIVER CHILDERS by virtue of his preemption certificate issued to him by the Co. Clerk of Parker Co. No. 24 - Situate at line and being in Parker Co. in Upper Cross Timbers on waters of Clear Fork Trinity Riv. about 4 mi. N from Weatherford - Beg. E of SE cor. JOHN ADAMS survey -
Surveyed: Feb 21 1857 WILLIAM MARKLEY [?] T.C.C.
[Chain Carriers ?]: JOHN VARDY, OLIVER CHILDERS

[161] Recorded: Jan 5 1858 - LEWELLEN MURPHY, Co Surv Parker Co TX

Parker Co. TX - 100 - Before undersigned authority personally came HIRAM FRANKLIN as applicant and G. W. FOX and JANE COLLIN two disinterested and respectable witnesses - all duly sworn and saith that applicant was bonafide settled upon vacant land on Aug 26 1856, date of enactment of act authorizing settlement of vacant land within limits of Mississippi & Pacific R. R. - continues to reside within limits - claims right of purchase under said act.
Signed: HIRAM FRANKLIN, G. W. FOX, JANE "X" COLLIN [mark]
Sworn to & subscribed Feb 28 1857 before JOHN H. PRINCE, Clerk Co. Court Parker Co. TX

"This survey is relocated and recorded in Bk A p 224 this Nov 12 1861 - R. H. HAWKINS, Co. Surveyor" [in ink left margin]

[162] Parker Co. TX - Have surveyed 160 acs for HIRAM FRANKLIN by virtue of his affidavit No. 100 - Situate in Parker Co. on S Fork waters of Clear Fork Trinity Riv. about 6 mi. S 50° E from Weatherford - Beg. N from SW cor. JANE COLLIN 160 ac. survey, W boundary of same -
Surveyed: Aug 28 1857 - ISAAC O. HEADLEY, D. S. P. C.
Chain Carriers: RICHARD N. JOHNSON, JOHN W. OWEN

[163] Recorded: Jan 5 1858 - LEWELLEN MURPHY, Co Surv Parker Co TX

Parker Co. TX - Personally appeared before Me, LEWELLEN MURPHY, Co. Surveyor, WILLIAM NIX, who being duly sworn deposeth and saith that he believed the land upon which he had settled and has made an improvement is vacant and unappropriated and that he is entitled to the same by virtue of an act of Congress of Texas proved Jan 22 1845 granting to settlers on vacant public domain preemption privileges and he further deposes and says that he settled on said land on or about the Dec 14 1853 and that he applied within the time prescribed by

[164] Law to a legally authorized surveyor to have his pre-emption surveyed and that after repeated applications he could not succeed in having his preemption completely surveyed and recorded up to this time.
Signed: WILLIAM NIX
Sworn to & subscribed Jan 11 1858 before LEWELLEN MURPHY, Co. Surv. Parker Co.

Parker Co. TX - Field notes of survey of 318 acs. for WILLIAM NIX by virtue of foregoing affidavit - Situate in Parker Co. on waters of Silver Creek, tributary West Fork Trinity Riv. - Beg. on NW cor. of W. B. BRENT 320 ac. survey No. 19

[165] NE boundary line of ADAM L. LOWDERS 320 ac. survey No. 23 S boundary line R. N. DOBIE 320 ac. survey No. 25 - W boundary line of JOHN H. MOORE 320 ac. survey No. 20 -
Surveyed: Jan 12 1858 - LEWELLEN MURPHY, Co Surv Parker Co TX
Chain Carriers: JOSEPH A. WOODDALL, NICOLAS J. WOODROME

[166] Recorded: Feb 1 1858 - LEWELLEN MURPHY, Co Surv Parker Co TX

Parker Co. TX - 71 - Before JOHN MATLOCK, Chief Justice Parker Co. TX, personally came JAMES WIMBLEY as applicant and HOWARD HAYS and ROBERT WRIGHT two disinterested and respectable witnesses - all duly sworn and saith that applicant was bonafide settled upon vacant land on Aug 26 1856 - continues to reside thereon
Signed: JAMES WIMBLEY, HOWARD HAYS, ROBERT WRIGHT
Sworn to & subscribed Feb 27 1857 before JOHN MATLOCK, Chief Justice Parker Co. TX

[167] Parker Co. TX - Field notes of survey of 160 acs. for JAMES WIMBLY by virtue of his preemption affidavit No. 71 - Situate in NE part Parker Co. on waters Walnut Creek, tributary West Fork Trinity Riv. - Beg. S of NW cor. LEMUEL FRANKS 141 87/110 preemption survey - Cor. in ROBERT WRIGHTs W boundary line

[168] - W cor. LEMUEL FRANKS preemption -
Surveyed: [no month] 4 1858 - LEWELLEN MURPHY, Co Surv Parker Co TX
Chain Carriers: HOWARD HAYS, ROBERT J. BILLINGSLEA
Recorded: Feb 5 185 - LEWELLEN MURPHY, Co Surv Parker Co TX

[NOTE: THE NEXT PAGE IS THE BACK SIDE OF PREVIOUS PAGE NO. "168" BUT IS NUMBERED "179"]

[179] Parker Co. TX - 239 - Before undersigned authority per-

sonally came WM. C. PRINCE as applicant and T. M. PRINCE Sen and ISAAC O. HEADLEY two disinterested and respectable witnesses all duly sworn and saith that applicant was bonafide settled upon vacant land on Aug 26 1856, date of enactment of act authorizing settlement of vacant land within limits of Mississippi & Pacific R. R. - continues to reside within limits claims right of purchase under said act.
Signed: WM. C. PRINCE, T. M. PRINCE Sen., ISAAC O. HEADLEY
Sworn to & subscribed Feb 8 1858 before JOHN H. PRINCE, Clerk Co. Court Parker Co. TX

Parker Co. TX - Field notes of survey of 160 acs. for WM. C. PRINCE by virtue of his preemption affidavit No. 239 -

[180] Situate in NE part Parker Co. on divide between waters of Silver Creek and Ash Creek, tributaries of West Fork Trinity Riv. - Beg. NE of SE cor. WILLIAM D. HAILEY 160 ac. survey - W boundary line MEMUCAN HUNT 320 ac. survey -
Surveyed: [no month] 7 [no year] - LEWELLEN MURPHY, Co Surv Parker Co TX
Chain Carriers: JOHN TYLER, MARTIN V. SHULTS

[181] Recorded: Feb 19 1858 - LEWELLEN MURPHY, Co Surv Parker Co TX

Parker Co. TX - 28 - Before CHARLES GILDON, Notary Public in and for aforesaid co. personally came MARTIN SHULTZ as applicant and JAMES HOGGAN [?] and WILLIAM HOGGAN [?] two disinterested and respectable witnesses - all duly sworn and saith that applicant was bonafide settled upon vacant land on Aug 26 1856, date of enactment of act authorizing settlement of vacant land within limits of Mississippi & Pacific R. R. - continues to reside within limits - claims right of purchase under said act.
Signed: MARTIN "X" SHULTZ [mark], JAMES "X" HOGGAN [mark], WILLIAM "X" HOGGAN [mark]
Sworn to & subscribed Mar 5 1857 before CHARLES GILDON, Notary Public

[182] Parker Co. TX - Field notes of survey of 160 acs. for MARTIN SHULTS by virtue of his preemption affidavit No. 28 - Situate on waters of a tributary of the West Fork of Trinity Riv. about 15 1/2 mi. N 60° E from Weatherford - Beg. NW of NE cor. WILLIAM PRINCE 160 ac. preemption survey - E boundary line of B. F. BOSWELL 160 ac. preemption survey -
Surveyed: Jan 14 1858 - LEWELLEN MURPHY, Co Surv Parker Co TX
Chain Carriers: JOHN R. FLETCHER [?], WADE HAMPTON SHULTZ

[183] Recorded: Jan 14 1858 - LEWELLEN MURPHY, Co Surv Parker Co TX

[NOTE: THE WRITING IN THE REMAINDER OF THIS BOOK HAS BECOME VERY DIFFICULT TO READ WITH THE NAMES EXTREMELY HARD TO DECIPHER]

Parker Co. TX - 45 - Before CHARLES GILDON, Notary Public in and for aforesaid co. personally came A. E. ROBERTSON as applicant and ISAAC PRICE and J. T. HARRISON two disinterested and respectable witnesses - all duly sworn and saith that applicant was bonafide settled upon vacant land on Aug 26 1856 - continues to reside thereon
Signed: A. E. ROBERTSON, ISAAC "X" PRICE [mark], J. T. HARRISON
Sworn to & subscribed Mar 7 1857 before CHARLES GILDON, Notary Public

[184] Parker Co. TX - Field notes of survey of 160 acs. for ASHUR E. ROBERTSON by virtue of his preemption affidavit No. 45 Situate in NW part of Co. on waters of Willow Branch, tributary Clear Fork Trinity Riv. about 7 1/4 mi. N 18° W from Weatherford - Beg. SW of SW cor. ___?___ BOGGS 160 ac. preemption survey -
Surveyed: Oct 10 1857 - LEWELLEN MURPHY, Co Surv Parker Co TX
Chain Carriers: ___?___ ___?___, JAMES C. EDWARDS

[185] Recorded: Feb 23 1858 - LEWELLEN MURPHY, Co Surv Parker Co TX

Parker Co. TX - 11 - Before JOHN MATLOCK, Chief Justice Parker Co. TX, personally came JAMES W. ERWIN as applicant and WILLIAM SILLIVANT and CORRELL [?] LITTLETON [?] two disinterested and respectable witnesses - all duly sworn and saith that applicant was bonafide settled upon vacant land on Aug 26 1856, date of enactment of act authorizing settlement of vacant land within limits of Mississippi & Pacific R. R. - continues to reside within limits - claims right of purchase under said act.
Signed: JAMES W. ERWIN, WILLIAM SILLIVANT, CORRELL [?] LITTLETON [?]
Sworn to & subscribed Jan 11 1858 before JOHN MATLOCK, Chief Justice Parker Co. TX

[186] Parker Co. TX - Field notes of survey of 160 acs. for JAMES W. ERWIN by virtue of his preemption affidavit No. 11 - Situate in [blank] part of Parker Co. on waters of Clear Fork Trinity Riv. about 13 mi. from town of Weatherford - Beg. S of NW cor. STEPHEN _?_ ERWIN 160 ac. preemption survey
Surveyed: Jan 27 1858 - LEWELLEN MURPHY, Co Surv Parker Co TX
Chain Carriers: WILLIAM A. ERWIN, STEPHEN L. ERWIN

[187] Recorded: Feb 23 1858 - LEWELLEN MURPHY, Co Surv Parker Co TX

Parker Co. TX - 153 - Before undersigned authority personally came WILLIAM BARNES as applicant and WILLIAM EUBANK and J. M. EVANS two disinterested and respectable witnesses - all duly sworn and saith that applicant was bonafide settled upon vacant land on Aug 26 1856, date of enactment of act authorizing settlement of vacant land within limits of Mississippi & Pacific R. R. - continues to reside within limits - claims right of purchase under said act.
Signed: WILLIAM BARNES, WILLIAM EUBANKS, J. M. EVANS
Sworn to & subscribed May 8 1857 before JOHN H. PRINCE, Clerk Co. Court Parker Co. TX, by WM. M. GREEN, Dept.

[188] Parker Co. TX - Field notes of survey of 160 acs. for WILLIAM BARNES by virtue of his preemption affidavit No. 153 - Situate on waters of Antoine Creek, tributary of Brazos Riv. about 10 mi. ?W from Weatherford - Beg. on E cor. FRANCISO SANCHES 160 ac. preemption survey -
Surveyed: Feb 18 1858 - LEWELLEN MURPHY, Co Surv Parker Co TX
Chain Carriers: __?__ CRETSINGER, M. J. S. WAMPLER

[189] Recorded: Feb 23 1858 - LEWELLEN MURPHY, Co Surv Parker Co TX

Parker Co. TX - 27 - Before CHARLES GILDON, Notary Public in and for aforesaid co. personally came WILLIAM HOGGARD as applicant and JNO. G. [?] REYNOLDS and JAMES HOGGARD two disinterested and respectable witnesses - all duly sworn and saith that applicant was bonafide settled upon vacant land on Aug 26 1856, date of enactment of act authorizing settlement of vacant land within limits of Mississippi & Pacific R. R. - continues to reside within limits - claims right of purchase under said act.
Signed: WILLIAM "X" HOGGARD [mark], JOHN G. [?] REYNOLDS, JAMES "X" HOGGARD [mark]
Sworn to & subscribed Mar 5 1857 before CHARLES GILDON, Notary Public

Parker Co. TX - Field notes of survey of 80 acs. for WILLIAM HOGGARD

[190] by virtue of his preemption affidavit No. 27 - Situate on waters of Ash Creek, tributary of West Fork Trinity Riv. about 16 mi. N 58° E from Weatherford - Beg. E of SW cor. JONATHAN Y. REYNOLDS 160 ac. preemption survey -
Surveyed: Sep 29 1857 - LEWELLEN MURPHY, Co Surv Parker Co TX
Chain Carriers: M. T. PASCHAL, MARTIN B. SHULTS
Recorded: Feb 23 1858 - LEWELLEN MURPHY, Co Surv Parker Co TX

[191] Parker Co. TX - 63 - Before CHARLES GILDON, Notary Public in and for aforesaid co. personally came A. L. HILL as applicant and H. G. CAUTRSLK [?] and J. A. WOODALL two disinterested and respectable witnesses - all duly sworn and saith

that applicant was bonafide settled upon vacant land on Aug 26 1856, date of enactment of act authorizing settlement of vacant land within limits of Mississippi & Pacific R. R. - continues to reside within limits - claims right of purchase under said act.
[NO SIGNATURES]
Sworn to & subscribed Nov 21 1857 before CHARLES GILDON, Notary Public

Parker Co. TX - Field notes of survey of 154 84/100 acs. for A. L. HILL by virtue of his preemption affidavit - Situate in NE part of Parker Co. on waters of Silver Creek, tributary of West Fork Trinity Riv. - Beg. E of SE cor. L. M. RODENALL [?] 640 ac. survey No. 21 -

[192] J. WILCOX survey -
Surveyed: Jan 12 1858 - LEWELLEN MURPHY, Co Surv Parker Co TX
Chain Carriers: WILLIAM NIX, JOSEPH A. WOODALL
Recorded: Feb 23 1858 - LEWELLEN MURPHY, Co Surv Parker Co TX

Parker Co. TX - 112 - Before JOHN MATLOCK, Chief Justice Parker Co. TX, personally came STEPHEN S. ERWIN as applicant and WILLIAM SILLIVINT [?] and CARROLL SILLIVINT [?] two disinterested and respectable witnesses - all duly sworn and saith that applicant was bonafide settled upon vacant land on Aug 26 1856, date of enactment of act authorizing settlement of vacant land within limits of Mississippi & Pacific R. R. - continues to reside within limits - claims right of purchase under said act.

[193] Signed: S L ERWIN, WILLIAM SILLIVINT, CARRALE SILLIVINT
Sworn to & subscribed Jan 11 1858 before JOHN MATLOCK

Parker Co. TX - Field notes of survey of 160 acs. for STEPHEN L. ERWIN by virtue of his preemption affidavit No. 112 - Situate in NW part of Parker Co. on waters Clear Fork Trinity Riv. about 12 1/2 mi. NW from Weatherford - Beg. on NW cor. SAMUEL WALKER 160 ac. preemption survey -

[194] Surveyed: Jan 27 1858 - LEWELLEN MURPHY, Co Surv Parker Co TX
Chain Carriers: NICOLAS G. [?] LEE, WILLIAM A. ERWIN
Recorded: Feb 23 1858 - LEWELLEN MURPHY, Co Surv Parker Co TX

Parker Co. TX - 122 - Before undersigned authority personally came ANDERSON GREEN as applicant and JOHN SQUIRES and JOHN W. MURPHY two disinterested and respectable witnesses - all duly sworn and saith that applicant was bonafide settled upon vacant land on Aug 26 1856, date of enactment of act authorizing settlement of vacant land within limits of Mississippi & Pacific R. R. - continues to reside within limits - claims right of purchase under said act.

Signed: ANDERSON GREEN, JOHN SQUIRES, JOHN W. MURPHY

[195] Sworn to & subscribed Mar 28 1857 before JOHN H PRINCE, Clerk Co. Court Parker Co. TX

Parker Co. TX - Field notes of survey of 160 acs. for ANDERSON GREEN by virtue of his preemption affidavit No. 122 - Situate on Clear Fork Trinity Riv. about 7 mi. N 13° E from Weatherford - Beg. SE of SE cor. JNO. A. CANNAFAX 160 ac. preemption survey - ALFRED GREENs SW cor.
Surveyed: Jan 21 1858 - LEWELLEN MURPHY, Co Surv Parker Co TX
Chain Carriers: WILLIAM A. BOYD, ALFRED ? GREEN

[196] Recorded: Jan 23 1858 - LEWELLEN MURPHY, Co Surv Parker Co TX

Parker Co. TX - 143 - Before undersigned authority personally came SAMUEL CATSINGER as applicant and JAMES BEDFRED and ISAAC SEILA [?] two disinterested and respectable witnesses - all duly sworn and saith that applicant was bonafide settled upon vacant land on Aug 26 1856, date of enactment of act authorizing settlement of vacant land within limits of Mississippi & Pacific R. R. - continues to reside within limits - claims right of purchase under said act.
Signed: SAML. CATSINGER, JAMES BEDFRED, ISAAC "X" IOLA [mark]
Sworn to & subscribed Apr 23 1857 before JOHN H. PRINCE, Clerk Co. Court Parker Co. TX

Parker Co. TX - Field notes of survey of 160 acs. for DANIEL [?] CATSINER by virtue of his preemption -

[197] affidavit No. 143 - Situate on waters of San Antoine Creek, tributary Brazos Riv. about 10 mi. S 5° W from Weatherford - Beg. W from S cor. JEROME A. GARDNER 160 ac. preemption survey - NW boundary of Silas ? preemption survey -
Surveyed: Feb 16 1858 - LEWELLEN MURPHY, Co Surv Parker Co TX
Chain Carriers: THOMAS BEDFORD, WILLIAM EUBANKS
Recorded: Feb 23 1857 - LEWELLEN MURPHY, Co Surv Parker Co TX

[198] Parker Co. TX - 174 - Before undersigned authority personally came THOMAS JACKSON as applicant and JAMES R. CAMPBELL and JAMES C. EDWARDS two disinterested and respectable witnesses - all duly sworn and saith that applicant was bonafide settled upon vacant land on Aug 26 1856, date of enactment of act authorizing settlement of vacant land within limits of Mississippi & Pacific R. R. - continues to reside within limits claims right of purchase under said act.
Signed: THOS. JACKSON, JAMES R. CAMPBELL, JAMES C. EDWARDS
Sworn to & subscribed Jul 4 1857 before JOHN H. PRINCE, Clerk Co. Court Parker Co. TX

Parker Co. TX - Field notes of survey of 160 ac. for THOMAS

JACKSON by virtue of his preemption affidavit No. 174 - Situate in dividing edge between the Clear Fork and the South Fork of Trinity Riv. about 3 1/2 mi. NE from Weatherford - Beg. [bottom of page torn]

[199]   cor. JOHN SNYDER survey - JOHNSON WOOSLEY 320 ac. survey
Surveyed: Jan 25 1858 - LEWELLEN MURPHY, Co Surv Parker Co TX
Chain Carriers: ELIJAH GRISHAM, JAMES HOPKINS
Recorded: Jul 23 1858 - LEWELLEN MURPHY, Co Surv Parker Co TX

Parker Co. TX - 234 - This day appeared before me JONATHAN W. MURPHY as applicant and JOHN SQUIRE and ISAAC GLASS two disinterested and respectable witnesses - all duly sworn and saith that applicant was bonafide settled upon vacant land on Aug 26 1856, date of enactment of act authorizing settlement of vacant land within limits of Mississippi & Pacific R. R. - continues to reside within limits - claims right of purchase under said act.

[200]   Signed: JOHN W. MURPHY, ISAAC GLASS, JOHN SQUIRES
Sworn to & subscribed Sep 5 1857 before JOHN H. PRINCE, Clerk Co. Court Parker Co. TX

Parker Co. TX - Field notes of survey of 160 acs. for JOHN W. MURPHY by virtue of his affidavit No. 234 - Situate on waters of Clear Fork Trinity Riv. about 9 1/2 mi. N 12° E from Weatherford Beg. S of NE cor. [torn] BURRIS 160 ac. survey - [badly torn]

[201]   Surveyed: Feb 6 1858 - LEWELLEN MURPHY, Co Surv Parker Co TX
Chain Carriers: JOHN SQUIRES, WILL A. BOYD
Recorded: Feb 23 1858 - LEWELLEN MURPHY, Co Surv Parker Co TX

Parker Co. TX - 36 - Before undersigned authority personally came B. F. BOSWELL as applicant and P. H. BURROW and THOMAS GATTERY [?] two disinterested and respectable witnesses - all duly sworn and saith that applicant was bonafide settled upon vacant land on Aug 26 1856, date of enactment of act authorizing settlement of vacant land within limits of Mississippi & Pacific R. R. - continues to reside within limits - claims right of purchase under said act. [rest of page torn]

[PAGES MISSING]

[204]   Parker Co. TX - Field notes of survey of 160 acs. for CHARLES A. CABBINESS by virtue of his preemption affidavit No. 78 taken before JOHN MATLOCK, Chief Justice of Parker Co. on 9th March 1857 - Situate in Parker Co. on waters of Clear Fork Trinity Riv. - Beg. SW from SW cor. W. H. C. CABBINESS 160 ac. preemption survey -

Surveyed: Apr 26 1857
Chain Carriers: [names torn off]

[205] Recorded: Feb 22 1858 - LEWELLEN MURPHY, Co Surv Parker Co TX

Parker Co. TX - Before JOHN H. PRINCE, Clerk Co. Court Parker Co. TX, personally came JOHN BOYD as applicant and I O HEADLEY and SAML. R. BARBER two disinterested and respectable witnesses all duly sworn and saith that applicant was bonafide settled upon vacant land on Aug 26 1856, date of enactment of act authorizing settlement of vacant land within limits of Mississippi & Pacific R. R. - continues to reside within limits claims right of purchase under said act.
Signed: JOHN "X" BOYD [mark], ISAAC O HEADLEY, SAMUEL R BARBER
Sworn to & subscribed Feb 12 1857

Parker Co. TX - Have surveyed 160 acs. in the name of [torn]

[206] by virtue of his affidavit No. 202 - Situate in Parker Co. on waters of Brazos Riv. about 6 mi. S from Weatherford - Beg. NW from N cor. COLUMBUS R. PATTEN 738 ac. survey -
Surveyed: Sep 12 1857 - ISAAC O. HEADLEY, D. S. P. C.
Chain Carriers: WILLIAM W. CRISWELL, ROBT. H. BOYD
[no recorded date]

Parker Co. TX - 152 - Before undersigned authority personally came ISAM CRANFIELL as applicant and W. B. ANDERSON [?] and SAMUEL J. KIRBEE [?] two disinterested and respectable witnesses all duly sworn and saith that applicant was bonafide settled upon vacant land on Aug 26 1856, date of enactment of act authorizing settlement of vacant land within limits of Mississippi & Pacific R. R. - continues to reside within limits claims right of purchase under said act.

[207] Signed: Isom CRANFIELD, W. B. TANDIAN [?], SAMUEL J. KIRBEE
Sworn to & subscribed ? 4 1857 before JOHN H. PRINCE, Clerk Co. Court Parker Co. TX

Parker Co. TX - Field notes of survey of 160 acs. for ISOM CRANFIELD by virtue of his preemption affidavit No. 152 - Situate in Parker Co. on waters of Rock Creek, tributary Brazos Riv. about 10 mi. N 54° W from Weatherford - Beg. N of NW cor. DAVID WHITE 160 ac. preemption survey -

[208] Surveyed: Jan 30 1858 - LEWELLEN MURPHY, Co Surv Parker Co TX
Chain Carriers: DAVID WHITE, GEORGE COPELAND
Recorded: Feb 27 1858 - LEWELLEN MURPHY, Co Surv Parker Co TX

Parker Co. TX - 39 - Before CHARLES GILDON, Notary Public in

and for aforesaid co. personally came A. HENDRICK as applicant and LEVI CHILMAN [?] and CABELE [?] PIERCE two disinterested and respectable witnesses - all duly sworn and saith that applicant was bonafide settled upon vacant land on Aug 26 1856, date of enactment of act authorizing settlement of vacant land within limits of Mississippi & Pacific R. R. - continues to reside within limits - claims right of purchase under said act.
Signed: ALBERT HENDRICKS, LEVI ____ILMAN, CEBEA [?] PEARCE

[209] Sworn to & subscribed Mar 18 1857 before CHARLES GILDON, Notary Public

Parker Co. TX - Field notes of survey of 160 acs. for A. HENDRICKS which is the amount he is entitled to by virtue of his preemption certificate No. 39 - Situate in Parker Co. on West Prong Red Bear Creek, tributary Clear Fork Trinity Riv. - Beg. N of SW cor. BLUFORD HAINES 320 ac. survey -
Feb 17 1857 - J. E. JENKINS, Surveyor, certifies foregoing survey made by him
Chain Carriers: B. HARRIS, J. A. GLENNE [?]
Recorded: Mar 1 1858 - LEWELLEN MURPHY, Co Surv Parker Co TX

[210] Parker Co. TX - 12 - Before undersigned authority personally came FRANCISCO SANCHES as applicant and two disinterested and respectable witnesses [NO NAMES] - all duly sworn and saith that applicant was bonafide settled upon vacant land on Aug 26 1856, date of enactment of act authorizing settlement of vacant land within limits of Mississippi & Pacific R. R. - continues to reside within limits - claims right of purchase under said act.
Signed: FRANCISCO SANCHES, M. F. P. WAMPLER, JAMES KEEL
Sworn to & subscribed May 9 1857 before R. A. EDDLEMAN, Notary Public in and for aforesaid co.

"This survey is preempted by WILLIAM IRBY and recorded in Bk A p 211 Sept 17 1861 - R. A. HAWKINS, Co. Surveyor" [in left margin of this sheet]

Parker Co. TX - Field notes of survey of 160 acs. for FRANCISCO SANCHES by virtue of his preemption affidavit No. 12 - Situate in Parker Co. on waters of San Antoine Creek, tributary of Brazos Riv. about 10 mi. S 12° W from Weatherford - Beg. NW from W cor. SAMUEL CRETSINGER 160 ac. preemption survey -

[211] Surveyed: Feb 18 1858 - LEWELLEN MURPHY, Co Surv Parker Co TX
Chain Carriers: WILLIAM H. MARTIN, WILLIAM EUBANKS
Recorded: Mar 1 1858 - LEWELLEN MURPHY, Co Surv Parker Co TX

Parker Co. TX - 112 - Before JOHN H. PRINCE, Clerk Co. Court

Parker Co. TX personally came JAMES A. WILMETH as applicant and L. J. GILBERT and WILSON LITTLEFIELD two disinterested and respectable witnesses - all duly sworn and saith that applicant was bonafide settled upon vacant land on Aug 26 1856, date of enactment of act authorizing settlement of vacant land within limits of Mississippi & Pacific R. R. - continues to reside within limits - claims right of purchase under said act

[212] Signed: JAMES A. WILMETH, L. J. "X" GILBERT [mark], WILSON "X" LITTLEFIELD [mark]
Sworn to & subscribed Nov 10 1857 before JOHN H. PRINCE, Clerk Co. Court Parker Co. TX

Parker Co. TX - Field notes of survey [no acreage given] for JAMES A. WILMETH by virtue of his preemption affidavit No. 112 - Situate in Parker Co. on E side Brazos Riv. - Beg. on NW cor. ASA POE 160 ac. survey -
Surveyed: Sep 16 1857 - L. E. SMITH, Dept Surv Parker Co TX
Chain Carriers: A. J. ___?___, J. T. WELMITH

[213] Recorded: Mar 1 1858 - LEWELLEN MURPHY, Co Surv Parker Co TX

Parker Co. TX - 89 - Before undersigned authority personally came J. M. GIBSON as applicant and NOAH STAGGS and GEORGE W. STAGGS two disinterested and respectable witnesses - all duly sworn and saith that applicant was bonafide settled upon vacant land on Aug 26 1856, date of enactment of act authorizing settlement of vacant land within limits of Mississippi & Pacific R. R. - continues to reside within limits - claims right of purchase under said act.
Signed: J. M. GIBSON, NOAH STAGGS, GEORGE W. STAGGS
Sworn to & subscribed Feb 28 1857 before JOHN H. PRINCE, Clerk Co. Court Parker Co. TX

Parker Co. TX - Field notes of survey of 160 acs. for J. M. GIBSON by virtue of his preemption affidavit No. 89 - Situate on waters of San Antoine Creek, tributary of Brazos Riv. - "The Buffalo Bayo Brazos & Colorado Railroad Co. 160 ac. survey now covers the JOSEPH LOGSDON 160 ac. survey - supposed to be vacant" [in left margin this sheet]

[214 ?] about 17 1/2 mi. S from Weatherford - Beg. N of SE cor. JOSEPH FERGSON [?] 160 ac. preemption survey -
Surveyed: Feb 19 1858 - LEWELLEN MURPHY, Co Surv Parker Co TX
Chain Carriers: ABSALAM W. CLARY, JAMES BEVERLY
Recorded: Mar 1 1858 - LEWELLEN MURPHY, Co Surv Parker Co TX

Parker Co. TX - 35 - Before J. J. BEEMAN, Notary Public in and for aforesaid co. personally came J. F. WAMPLER as claimant and VOLENTINE S. [?] WAMPLER and WILLIAM HOPKINS two disinterested and respectable witnesses - all duly sworn and saith that applicant was bonafide settled upon vacant land on Aug 26 1856, date of enactment of act authorizing settlement of vacant land within limits of Mississippi & Pacific R. R. - continues to reside within limits - claims right of purchase under said act.

[215] [NO SIGNATURES]
Sworn to & subscribed Jan 4 1858 before J. J. BEEMAN, Notary Public

Parker Co. TX - Field notes of survey of 160 acs. for M. J. S. WAMPLER by virtue of his preemption affidavit No. 35 - Situate on waters of San Antoine Creek, tributary Brazos Riv about 8 mi. from Weatherford - Beg. SW from S cor. JOHN JAMES AUSBURN 160 ac. preemption survey
Surveyed: Feb 18 1858 - LEWELLEN MURPHY, Co Surv Parker Co TX
Chain Carriers: WILLIAM T. LAYNE, M. J. S. WAMPLER

[new sheet -page no. torn] Recorded: Mar 1 1858 - LEWELLEN MURPHY, Co Surv Parker Co TX

Parker Co. TX - Before undersigned authority personally came JOHN MATTHEWS as applicant and D. H. SISK and D. T. BROGDON two disinterested and respectable witnesses - all duly sworn and saith that applicant was bonafide settled upon vacant land on Aug 26 1856, date of enactment of act authorizing settlement of vacant land within limits of Mississippi & Pacific R. R. - continues to reside within limits - claims right of purchase under said act.
Signed: JOHN MATTHEWS, S. H. SISK, D. T. BROGDEN
Sworn to & subscribed Jan 28 1858 before JOHN H. PRINCE, Clerk Co. Court Parker Co. TX

[217] Parker Co. TX - Field notes of survey of 160 for JOHN MATTHEWS by virtue of his preemption affidavit - Situate in S part of Parker Co. on waters of Long Creek, tributary of Brazos Riv. - Beg. E cor. J. W. GILPIN 160 ac. preemption survey -
Chain Carriers: J. J. ___?___, D. J. ___?___
Recorded: Mar [no day] 1858 - LEWELLEN MURPHY, Co Surv Parker Co TX

[new sheet - no number] Parker Co. TX - 232 - Before JOHN H. PRINCE, Clerk Co. Court personally came GEORGE W. GILPIN as claimant and MARTIN WALKER and D. H. SISK two disinterested and respectable witnesses - all duly sworn and saith that applicant was bonafide settled upon vacant land on Aug 26 1856, date of enactment of act authorizing settlement of vacant land within limits of Mississippi & Pacific R. R. - continues to reside within limits - claims right of purchase under said act
Signed: GEO. W. GILPHIN, MARTIN WALKER, D. H. SISK

Sworn to & subscribed Jan 27 1858 before JOHN H. PRINCE, Clerk Co. Court Parker Co. TX

Parker Co. TX - Field notes of survey of 160 acs. for GEORGE W. GILPHIN by virtue of his preemption affidavit No. 232 - Situate on waters of Long Creek, tributary of Brazos Riv. about 14 mi. from Weatherford - Beg. SE -

[219] from S cor. Leon Co. School land 43,359,370 sq. vrs. survey -
Surveyed: Feb 12 1858 - LEWELLEN MURPHY, Co Surv Parker Co TX
Chain Carriers: THOMAS PARKINSON, MARTIN WALKER
Recorded: Mar 1 1858 - LEWELLEN MURPHY, Co Surv Parker Co TX

Parker Co. TX - 174 - Before JOHN H. PRINCE, Clerk Co. Court Parker Co. TX

[220] personally came SILAS SMITH as applicant and SAML. R. BARBER and ROBT. C. HART two disinterested and respectable witnesses - all duly sworn and saith that applicant was bonafide settled upon vacant land on Aug 26 1856, date of enactment of act authorizing settlement of vacant land within limits of Mississippi & Pacific R. R. - continues to reside within limits claims right of purchase under said act.
Signed: SILAS SMITH, SAML. R. BARBER, ROBT. C. HART
Sworn to & subscribed Jul 11 1858 before JOHN H. PRINCE, Clerk Co. Court Parker Co. TX

Parker Co. TX - Field notes of survey of 160 acs. for SILAS SMITH by virtue of his preemption affidavit 174 - Situate in SW part Parker Co. on waters of San Antoine Creek, tributary of Brazos Riv. about 11 mi. S 10° W from Weatherford - Beg. on S cor. JEROME GORDON 160 ac. preemption survey -

[221] Surveyed: Feb 16 1858 - LEWELLEN MURPHY, Co Surv Parker Co TX
Chain Carriers: THOMAS BEDFORD [?], HENRY H. DYER
Recorded: Mar 1 1858 - LEWELLEN MURPHY, Co Surv Parker Co TX

Parker Co. TX - 34- Before J. J. BEEMAN, Notary Public in and for aforesaid co. personally came WILLIAM C. HALL as applicant and JOSEPH REEVES and C. C. BLAIN two disinterested and respectable witnesses - all duly sworn and saith that applicant was bonafide settled upon vacant land on Aug 26 1856, date of enactment of act authorizing settlement of vacant land within limits of Mississippi & Pacific R. R. - continues to reside within limits - claims right of purchase under said act.

[222] Signed: WILLIAM C. HALL, JOSEPH REEVES, C. C. BLAN [?]
Sworn to & subscribed Feb 8 1858 before J. J. BEEMAN, Notary Public

Parker Co. TX - Field notes of survey of 160 acs. for WILLIAM C. HALL by virtue of his preemption affidavit No. 36 - Situate on waters of Grindstone Creek, tributary of Brazos Riv. about 9 1/2 N 87° W from Weatherford - Beg. ___ from NW cor. ISRAEL BURROWS 160 ac. preemption survey - [page torn]

[223] Surveyed: Feb 9 1858 - LEWELLEN MURPHY, Co Surv Parker Co TX
Chain Carriers: WILLIAM C. HALL, JOSEPH REEVES
Recorded: Mar 1 1858 - LEWELLEN MURPHY, Co Surv Parker Co TX

Parker Co. TX - 240 - Before undersigned authority personally came JOSIAH F. BLACKWELL as applicant and D. H. SISK and JOSEPH ROBINSON two disinterested and respectable witnesses -

[NOTE: REST OF PAGE TORN- THIS WAS THE LAST SHEET OF THIS VOLUME]

PARKER COUNTY PRE-EMPTION RECORD "C"
1856 - 1858

[1]   "PREEMPTION BOOK C"

State of Texas
County of Parker
    I have surveyed 53 acs. of land for A. H. ONSTOTT by virtue of his affidavit No. 253 taken before JOHN H. PRINCE, Clerk of of [sic] Parker County and dated March the 4th A.D. 1858. Situated in Parker County ["on the" - blotted out] about 9 miles S 5° E from the town of Weatherford on Spring Creek a tributary of the Brazos River. Beg. ?W from NE cor. & N boundary of T. J. SHAW 143 ac. survey - E or [sic] SE cor. J. S. STROUDS preemption -
Surveyed: Mar 4 1858
Chain Carriers: JOHN S. [?] RAY, T. J. SHAW
"I the undersigned do hereby certify" [torn]

[REMAINDER OF PAGE TORN]

[2]   Surveyed: by ISAAC O. HEADLEY, D. S. P. C. T.
Recorded: Mar 5 185[torn] - LEWELLEN MURPHY, Co Surv Parker Co TX

The State of Texas | No. 256
County of Parker | Before the undersigned authority this
                          day came DAVID MOORE as applicant and
S. R. BARBER and JOSEPH ROBINSON two disinterested respectable witnesses known to me. All of whom being duly sworn say upon their oath that applicant was bonafide settled upon land they believe to be vacant at the date of an act to authorize the location sale and settlement of the Mississippi & Pacific Rail Road Reserve passed the 26th of August 1856 and yet resides upon same
                            DAVID MOORE
                            SAMUEL R. BARBER
                            JOSEPH ROBINSON
Sworn to & subscribed to before me to [torn] certify which I have hereunto set my hand and office seal this [date and signature torn off]

[3]   Parker Co. TX - Have surveyed 160 acs. for DAVID MOORE by virtue affidavit No. 256 taken before JOHN H. PRINCE, Clerk of Parker Co. and dated March 4 1858 - Situate in Parker Co. on waters of Red Bear Creek, waters of the Brazos Riv. about 6 mi. S from Weatherford - Beg. SW from NW cor. JOHN BOYD 160 ac. survey -
Surveyed: Mar 4 1858 - ISAAC O. HEADLEY, D. S. P. C. T.
Chain Carriers: JOHN MOOR, J. J. [?] BRISCO

[4]   Recorded: Mar 5 1858 - LEWELLEN MURPHY, Co Surv Parker Co TX

Parker Co. TX. - No. 166 - Before the undersigned authority this day came M. D. TACKETT as applicant and W. J. MAYO and JAMES A. MILLER two disinterested respectable witnesses known to me. Applicant was bonafide settled upon land believe to be vacant at date of act to authorize location sale & settlement of the Mississippi & Pacific R. R. Reserve passed Aug 26 1856 and still resides thereon
Signed: M. D. TACKITT, W. J. MAYO, JAMES A. MILLER
Sworn to & subscribed Jun 1 1857 before JOHN H. PRINCE, Clerk Co. Court Parker Co. TX

[Page No. torn] Parker Co. TX - Have surveyed 160 acs. for M. D. TACKITT by virtue his preemption affidavit No. 166 - Situate on waters of Clear Fork Trinity Riv. about 12 mi. N 16° W from Weatherford - Beg. SE of SE cor. ISAAC BRISCO 160 ac. preemption survey -
Surveyed: Aug 2 1857 R. J. BILLINGSLEA, D. S. P. C.
Chain Carriers: N. G. [?] LEE, J. H. TACKITT

[6]   Recorded: Mar 7 1858 - LEWELLEN MURPHY, Co Surv Parker Co TX

Parker Co. TX. - No. 145 - Before the undersigned authority this day came JOSEPH HART as applicant and STEPHEN HART and ROBERT C. HART two disinterested respectable witnesses known to me. Applicant was bonafide settled upon land believed to be vacant at date of act to authorize the location sale & settlement of the Mississippi & Pacific R. R. Reserve passed Aug 26 1856 and still resides thereon
Signed: JOSEPH HART, STEPHEN HART, R. C. HART
Sworn to & subscribed [no month] 27 1857 before JOHN H PRINCE, Clerk Co. Court Parker Co. TX

[7]   Parker Co. TX - Have surveyed 160 acs. for JOSEPH HART by virtue his affidavit No. 145 - Situate in Parker Co. about 6 mi. S from Weatherford on waters of Red Bear Creek, tributary of Brazos Riv. - Beg. at N or NE cor. JOHN BOYD 160 ac. survey - SW cor. TILLMAN BOYD 160 ac. survey & S boundary line of same -
Surveyed: Mar 2 1858 - ISAAC O. HEADLEY, D. S. P. C. T.
Chain Carriers: WILLIAM R. EMERRY, AMESLEY PARSONS

[8]   Recorded: Mar 8 1858 - LEWELLEN MURPHY, Co Surv Parker Co TX

Parker Co. TX. - No. 46 - Before me, JOHN MATLOCK, Chief Justice Parker Co. TX, appeared GEORGE LEE as applicant and LINZY LEWIS and WALDEN WALTERS two disinterested respectable witnesses known to me. Applicant was bonafide settled upon land believed to be vacant on Aug 26 1856 and still resides thereon.

[9] Signed: GEORGE LEE, LINZY LEWIS, WALDEN WALTERS
Sworn to & subscribed Feb 16 1857 before JOHN MATLOCK, Chief Justice Parker Co. TX

"The NW cor. of GEORGE LEEs 160 ac. preemption survey begins on SW cor. of 960 ac. survey of land made in the name of the Heirs of JACOB AARON" [along right margin this page]

Parker Co. TX - Field notes of survey of 160 acs. for GEORGE LEE by virtue his preemption affidavit No. 46 - Situate in District of Denton Parker Co. in the Upper Cross Timbers on waters of Clear Fork Trinity Riv about 2 1/2 mi. N 15° E from Weatherford Beg. SE from SE cor JOHN ADAMS 320 ac preemption survey -

[10] Surveyed: Feb 21 1857 - WILLIAM L. LIVELY, Dept. Surv. Denton L. D.
Chain Carriers: J. B. GILLILAND, JOHN JONES
Recorded: Mar 8 1858 - LEWELLEN MURPHY, Co Surv Parker Co TX

Parker Co. TX. - No. 47 - Before JOHN MATLOCK, Chief Justice Parker Co. TX, personally appeared DANIEL LEE as applicant and LINZY LEWIS and WALDEN WALTERS two disinterested respectable witnesses known to me. Applicant was bonafide settled upon land believed to be vacant on Aug 26 1856 and still resides thereon.

[11] Signed: DANIEL LEE, LINZY LEWIS, WALDEN WALTERS
Sworn to & subscribed Feb 16 1857 before JOHN MATLOCK, Chief Justice Parker Co. TX

Dist. of Denton TX - Survey No. 2 - Have surveyed 160 acs. for DANIEL -

[12] LEE by virtue his preemption certificate No. 47 - Situate in Parker Co. in Cross Timbers on waters of Clear Fork Trinity Riv. about 2 mi. N 15° E from Weatherford - Beg. on SE cor. of GEO. LEE survey -
Surveyed: Feb 21 1857 - WILLIAM LIVELY, Dept Surv Denton L D
Chain Carriers: J. B. GILLILAND, JOHN JONES

[13] Recorded: Mar 8 1858 - LEWELLEN MURPHY, Co Surv Parker Co TX

Parker Co. TX. - Before JOHN MATLOCK, Chief Justice Parker Co. TX came WILLIAM J. WOMACK as applicant and THOMAS J. WOMACK and EZEKIALL L. A. ENSEY two disinterested respectable witnesses known to me. Applicant was bonafide settled upon land believed to be vacant at date of act to authorize location sale & settlement of the Mississippi & Pacific R. R. Reserve passed Aug 26 1856 and still resides thereon.

[14] Signed: WILLIAM J. WOMACK, THOMAS J. WOMACK, EZEKIEL L. A. ENSEY
Sworn to & subscribed Feb 17 1858 before JOHN MATLOCK, Chief Justice Parker Co. TX

Parker Co. TX - Field Notes survey of 160 acs. for WILLIAM J. WOMACK by virtue affidavit No. [blank] - Situate on waters of Walnut Creek, tributary West Fork Trinity Riv. - Beg. on SW cor. T. J. WOMACK preemption survey -

[15] Surveyed: Mar 5 1858 - R. J. BILLINGSLEA, D. S. P. C. T.
Chain Carriers: JNO. A. NEILL, E. ENSEY
Recorded: Mar 5 1858 - LEWELLEN MURPHY, Co Surv Parker Co TX

Parker Co. TX. - No. 69 - Before JOHN MATLOCK, Chief Justice Parker Co. TX came LEFTRIDGE J. FRANCIS as applicant and JAMES J. BARKER and JOSEPH BARKER two disinterested respectable witnesses known to me. Applicant was bonafide settled upon land believed to be vacant on Aug 26 1856 and still resides thereon

[16] Signed: LEFTRIDGE J. FRANCIS, JAMES J. BARKER, JOSEPH BARKER
Sworn to & subscribed Feb 26 1857 before JOHN MATLOCK, Chief Justice Parker Co. TX

[NOTE: THE MISSISSIPPI & PACIFIC RESERVE IS NOT REFERRED TO IN ALL THE AFFIDAVITS OF BOOK "C"]

Parker Co. TX - Field notes survey of 160 acs. for L J FRANCIS by virtue affidavit No. 69 - Situate on waters of Clear Fork, tributary of West Fork Trinity Riv. - Beg. on NW cor. JOSEPH BARKERS 320 ac. preemption survey -

[17] Surveyed: Mar 6 1858 - R. J. BILLINGSLEA, D. S. P. C. T.
Chain Carriers: ISAAC GLASS, J. W. GODFREY
Recorded: Mar 8 1858 - LEWELLEN MURPHY, Co Surv Parker Co TX

Parker Co. TX. - No. 99 - Before the undersigned authority this day came HIRAM PINNEL as applicant and T. B. MARTIN and PETER WELDON two disinterested respectable witnesses known to me. Applicant was bonafide settled upon land believed to be vacant at date of act to authorize location sale & settlement of the Mississippi & Pacific R. R. Reserve passed Aug 26 1856 and still resides thereon.

[18] Signed: HIRAM PINNEL, T. B. "X" MARTIN [mark], P WELDON
Sworn to & subscribed [no month] 28 1857 before JOHN H PRINCE, Clerk Co Court Parker Co TX

Parker Co. TX - Have surveyed 160 acs. for HIRAM PINNEL by virtue affidavit No. 99 - Situate in Parker Co. about 8 mi. N 45° W from Weatherford on head of Grindstone Creek, waters of Brazos Riv. - Beg. NE from NE cor. PETER WELDON 160 ac. survey

[19] Surveyed: Mar 1 1858 - ISAAC O. HEADLEY, D. S. P. C. T.
Chain Carriers: PETER WELDON, R. M. MEADOR
Recorded: Mar 8 1858 - LEWELLEN MURPHY, Co Surv Parker Co TX

Parker Co. TX. - No. 96 - Before the undersigned authority this day came LYDIA FOLLY as applicant and JAMES HORTON and G. W. FOX two disinterested respectable witnesses known to me. Applicant was bonafide settled upon land believed to be vacant at date of act to authorize location sale & settlement of the Mississippi & Pacific R. R. Reserve passed Aug 26 1856 and still resides thereon.

[20] Signed: LYDIA "X" FOLLY [mark], G W FOX, JAMES W HORTON
Sworn to & subscribed Feb 28 1857 before JOHN H. PRINCE, Clerk Co Court Parker Co TX

Parker Co. TX - Have Surveyed 100 acs. for LYDIA FOLLY by virtue affidavit No. 96 - Situate in Parker Co. on waters of Clear Fork of Trinity Riv. - Beg. at NE cor. JAMES WILLIAMS 320 ac. survey

[21] Surveyed: Aug 26 1857 - ISAAC O. HEADLEY, D. S. P. C. T.
Chain Carriers: G. W. FOX, WESLEY FRANKLIN
Recorded: Mar 9 1858 - LEWELLEN MURPHY, Co Surv Parker Co TX

Parker Co. TX. - No. 98 - Before the undersigned authority this day came JANE COLLIE as applicant and G. W. FOX and HIRAM FRANKLIN two disinterested respectable witnesses known to me. Applicant was bonafide settled upon land believed to be vacant at date of act to authorize location sale & settlement of the Mississippi & Pacific R. R. Reserve passed Aug 26 1856 and still resides thereon.

[22] Signed: JANE "X" COLLIE [mark], HIRAM FRANKLIN, G W FOX
Sworn to & subscribed Feb 28 1857 before JOHN H. PRINCE, Clerk Co. Court Parker Co. TX

Parker Co. TX - Have surveyed 160 acs. for JANE COLLIE by virtue her affidavit No. 98 - Situate in Parker Co on S Fork waters of Trinity Riv. about 7 mi. S 60° E from Weatherford - Beg. W & S from SW cor. LIDIA FOLLY 100 ac. survey -

[23] Surveyed: Aug 28 1857 - ISAAC O. HEADLEY, D. S. P. C. T.
Chain Carriers: RICHARD N. JOHNSON, J. W. OWEN
Recorded: Mar 9 1858 - LEWELLEN MURPHY, Co Surv Parker Co TX

[NOTE: FOLLOWING SURVEY DOES NOT HAVE AFFIDAVIT PRECEDING IT]

Parker Co. TX - Have surveyed for WILLIAM N. COZORT 160 acs. by virtue affidavit No. 6 taken before JOHN H. PRINCE, Clerk Co. Court Parker Co. TX and dated Feb 10 1857 - Situate in Parker Co. on waters of Trinity Riv. about -

[24] 3 1/2 mi. S 50o˜ E from Weatherford - Beg. S from SW cor. ABRAHAM PIPKIN 160 ac. survey -
Surveyed: May 25 1857 - ISAAC O. HEADLEY, D. S. P. C. T.
Chain Carriers: ASER PIPKIN, PHILLIP B. PIPKIN

"I, the undersigned do hereby certify that the survey designated by the foregoing plat & field notes was made by me according to law and that the limits, boundaries and corners together with the marks, natural and artificial are truly described therein - Given under my hand this 25th day of May 1857 - ISAAC O. HEADLEY, D. P. S. P. C.

[25] Recorded: Mar 27 1858 - LEWELLEN MURPHY, Co Surv Parker Co TX

Parker Co. TX. - No. 172 - Before the undersigned authority this day came EZRA MULKINS as applicant and ISAAC O. HEADLEY and JAMES TINSLEY two disinterested respectable witnesses known to me. Applicant was bonafide settled upon land believed to be vacant at date of act to authorize location sale & settlement of the Mississippi & Pacific R. R. Reserve passed Aug 26 1856 and still resides thereon.
Signed: EZRA MULKINS, JAMES TINSLEY, ISAAC O. HEADLEY
Sworn to & subscribed Jun 29 1857 before JOHN H. PRINCE, Clerk Co. Court Parker Co. TX

Parker Co. TX - Have surveyed 132 acs. for EZRA MULKINS by virtue affidavit No. 172 - Situate in Parker Co. -

[26] about 12 mi. S. 60° E from Weatherford - Beg. at NW cor R. C. HIBBERT 320 ac. survey - E boundary line of JOHN M. SPEARMAN 320 ac. survey -
Surveyed: Jan 21 1858 - ISAAC O. HEADLEY, D. S. P. C. T.
Chain Carriers: JOHN W. MULKINS, MILES A. PEACH [?]
Recorded: Mar 18 1858 - LEWELLEN MURPHY, Co Surv Parker Co TX

[27] Parker Co. TX - No 134 - Before the undersigned authority this day came JOHN C. CHAPMAN as applicant and GEORGE K. ELKINS and P. S. HALL two disinterested respectable witnesses known to me. Applicant was bonafide settled upon land believed to be vacant at date of act to authorize location sale & settlement of the Mississippi & Pacific R. R. Reserve passed Aug 26 1856 and still resides thereon.
Signed: JOHN C. CHAPMAN, GEORGE K. ELKINS, P. S. HALL
Sworn to & subscribed Apr 4 1857 before JOHN H. PRINCE, Clerk Co. Court Parker Co. TX

Parker Co. TX - Have surveyed 160 acs. for JOHN C. CHAPMAN by virtue affidavit No. 134 -

[28] Situate in Parker Co. about 2 1/2 mi. N 45° W from Weatherford on waters of Clear Fork Trinity Riv. - Beg. NW from NW cor. Parker Co. 320 ac. survey -
Surveyed: Feb 20 1858 - ISAAC O. HEADLEY, D. S. P. C. T.
Chain Carriers: WM. TRIMBLE, JACKSON FIDDLER
Recorded: May 3 1858 - LEWELLEN MURPHY, Co Surv Parker Co TX

[29] Parker Co. TX - No 117 - Before the undersigned authority this day came JEROME A. GARDNER as applicant and I. O. HEADLEY and SAML. R. BARBER two disinterested respectable witnesses known to me. Applicant was bonafide settled upon land believed to be vacant at date of act to authorize location sale & settlement of the Mississippi & Pacific R. R. Reserve passed Aug 26 1856 and still resides thereon.
Signed: J. A. GARDNER, SAMUEL R. BARBER, ISAAC O. HEADLEY
Sworn to & subscribed Mar 27 1857 before JOHN H. PRINCE, Clerk Co Court Parker Co TX

Parker Co. TX - Field notes of survey of 160 acs. for JEROME A. GARDNER by virtue his preemption affidavit -

[30] No 117 - Situate on waters of San Antoine Creek, tributary Brazos Riv. about 10 1/4 mi. S 4° W from Weatherford - Beg. NW of N or NE cor. JAMES CLAYTON 320 ac. survey - N. cor. SILAS SMITH survey -
Surveyed: Feb 16 1858 - LEWELLEN MURPHY, Co Surv Parker Co TX
Chain Carriers: HENRY H. DYER, THOMAS BEDFORD

[31] Recorded: May 4 1858 - LEWELLEN MURPHY, Co Surv Parker Co TX

Parker Co. TX. - No. 29 - Before me, J. J. BEEMAN, Notary Public in and for aforesaid Co., appeared HENRY S. SISK as claimant and G. W. STAGGS and DANIEL H. SISK two disinterested respectable witnesses known to me. Applicant was bonafide settled upon land believed to be vacant at date of act to authorize location sale & settlement of the Mississippi & Pacific R. R. Reserve passed Aug 26 1856 and still resides thereon.
[NO SIGNATURES]
Sworn to & subscribed Sep 14 1857 before J. J. BEEMAN, Notary Public

[32] Parker Co. TX - Have surveyed 160 acs. for H. S. SISK by virtue affidavit No. 29 - Situate in Parker Co. about 6 mi. S 25° E from Weatherford - Beg. NE from N or NE cor. JESSE THOMAS 320 ac. survey -
Surveyed: Feb 20 1858 - ISAAC O. HEADLEY, D. S. P. C. T.
Chain Carriers: WALTER BATY, R. E. BYRD

[33]   Recorded: May 5 1858 - LEWELLEN MURPHY, Co Surv Parker
Co TX

Parker Co. TX. - No. 156 - Before the undersigned authority
this day came G. W. HOLLINGSWORTH as applicant and ASER PIPKIN
and W. N. COZORT two disinterested respectable witnesses known
to me Applicant was bonafide settled upon land believed to be
vacant at date of act to authorize location   sale & settlement
of the Mississippi & Pacific R. R. Reserve   passed Aug 26 1856
and still resides thereon.
Signed: G W HOLLINGSWORTH, W N "X" COZORT [mark], ASER PIPKIN
Sworn to & subscribed May 18 1857 before JOHN H. PRINCE, Clerk
Co Court Parker Co TX

[34]   Parker Co. TX - Have surveyed 160 acs. for G. W.
HOLLINGSWORTH by virtue his affidavit No. 156 - Situate in
Parker Co. about 2 1/2 mi. S 30° E from Weatherford - Beg. SW
from SW cor. HENRY INNMAN 160 ac. survey -
Surveyed: Mar 2 1858 - ISAAC O. HEADLEY, D. S. P. C. T.
Chain Carriers: E. H. CRUMPTON, ASER PIPKIN
Recorded: May 5 1858 - LEWELLEN MURPHY, Co Surv Parker Co TX

[35]   Parker Co. TX - No 196 - Before the undersigned authority this day came BLUFORD HAYNES as applicant and T. F. JONES
and GEORGE STAGGS two disinterested respectable witnesses
known to me.   Applicant   was bonafide   settled upon land believed to be vacant at date of act to authorize location sale
& settlement of the Mississippi & Pacific R. R. Reserve passed
Aug 26 1856 and still resides thereon.
Signed: BLUFORD HAYNES, S. [?] F. JONES, G. W. STAGGS
Sworn to & subscribed Sep 5 1857 before JOHN H. PRINCE, Clerk
Co Court Parker Co TX

Parker Co. TX - Have surveyed 160 acs. for BLUFORD HAYNES by
virtue affidavit No. 196 - Situate in Parker Co. about 2 1/2
mi. S from Weatherford -

[36]   Beg. at E cor. WM. C. GILLISPEE 480 ac. survey -
Surveyed: Mar 2 1858 - ISAAC O. HEADLEY, D. S. P. C. T.
Chain Carriers: L. MC CARTY, WM. MC CARTY
Recorded: May 5 1858 - LEWELLEN MURPHY, Co. Surv. Parker Co TX

[37]   Parker Co. TX - No 242 - Before the undersigned authority this day came JAS. R. BROWN as applicant and JOHN H PHELPS
and C. C. MC CARVER two disinterested respectable witnesses
known to me. Applicant was bonafide settled upon land believed to be vacant at date of act to authorize location sale
& settlement of the Mississippi & Pacific R. R. Reserve passed
Aug 26 1856 and still resides thereon.
Signed: JAMES R. BROWN, J. H. PHELPS, C. C. MC CARVER
Sworn to & subscribed Feb 20 1858 before JOHN H. PRINCE, Clerk
Co Court Parker Co TX

[38] Parker Co. TX - Have surveyed 160 acs. for JAMES R. BROWN by virtue affidavit No. 212 [?] - Situate in Parker Co. about 10 mi. S 80° E from Weatherford on Clear Fork Trinity Riv. - Beg. W from NW cor. JAMES CARR 136 ac. survey
Surveyed: Mar 20 1858 - ISAAC O. HEADLEY, D. S. P. C. T.
Chain Carriers: JAMES BRIGHT, WILSON WOOD

[39] Recorded: May 5 1858 - LEWELLEN MURPHY, Co Surv Parker Co TX

Parker Co. TX. - No. 7 - Before the undersigned authority this day came ABSALUM SPARKS as applicant and ISAAC O. HEADLEY and N. B. HOLDER two disinterested respectable witnesses known to me Applicant was bonafide settled upon land believed to be vacant at date of act to authorize location sale & settlement of the Mississippi & Pacific R. R. Reserve passed Aug 26 1856 and still resides thereon.
Signed: ABSALUM SPARKS, ISAAC O. HEADLEY, N. B. HOLDER
Sworn to & subscribed Feb 16 1857 before JOHN H. PRINCE, Clerk Co Court Parker Co TX

[40] Parker Co. TX - Have surveyed 160 acs. for ABSALUM SPARKS by virtue affidavit No. 7 - Situate in Parker Co. about 3 mi. S 59° E from Weatherford on waters of Clear Fork Trinity Riv. Beg. E from SW cor. & in S. boundary of A. MORE 160 ac. survey
Surveyed: Feb 26 1858 - ISAAC O. HEADLEY, D. S. P. C. T.
Chain Carriers: N. B. HOLDER, JOHN SHANKS

[41] Recorded: May 6 1858 - LEWELLEN MURPHY, Co Surv Parker Co TX

[NOTE: THE AFFIDAVIT FOR THE FOLLOWING SURVEY APPEARS AFTER THE FIELD NOTES]

Parker Co. TX - Field Notes survey of 160 acs. for STEPHEN BEDFORD by virtue his preemption affidavit No. 142 taken before JOHN H. PRINCE, Clerk Co. Court Parker Co. TX on Feb 11 1858 - Situate on Spring Creek, tributary Brazos Riv. about 12 mi. S 4° W from Weatherford - Beg. on S cor. JAMES BEDFORD 148 ac. survey - W cor. BENJAMIN F. IRBYES survey - SE boundary line of JAMES CLAYTON 320 ac. survey -

[42] Surveyed: Feb 19 1858 - LEWELLEN MURPHY, Co Surv Parker Co TX
Chain Carriers: THOMAS BEDFORD, DANIEL CRETSINGER
Recorded: May 6 1858 - LEWELLEN MURPHY, Co Surv Parker Co TX

Parker Co. TX. - No. 142 - Before me, JOHN H. PRINCE, Clerk Co. Court Parker Co. TX, came STEPHEN BEDFORD as applicant and ISAAC SEELA and DANIEL CRETSINGER two disinterested respectable witnesses known to me. Applicant was bonafide settled upon land believed to be vacant at date of act to authorize location sale & settlement of the Mississippi & Pacific R. R. Reserve passed Aug 26 1856 and still resides thereon.

[43] Signed: STEPHEN BEDFORD [WITNESSES DID NOT SIGN]
Sworn to & subscribed Feb 19 1858 before JOHN H. PRINCE, Clerk Co Court Parker Co TX

Parker Co. TX. - No. 144 - Before JOHN H. PRINCE, Clerk Co. Court Parker Co. TX, came STEPHEN BEDFORD and after being duly sworn says that JAMES BEDFORD did on the 22nd day of April 1857 prove by his own oath and oaths of ISAAC LEELA [sic] and DANL. CRETSINGER, two disinterested and respectable witnesses, prove that he was bonafide settled upon land they believe to be vacant at date of act to authorize location sale and settlement of the Mississippi & Pacific R. R. Reserve passed Aug 26th 1856 and that upon said proof he received his preemption affidavit which is lost or

[44] misplaced so that the same cannot be found this 19th Feb 1858
Signed: STEPHEN BEDFORD, agent for JAMES BEDFORD
Sworn to & subscribed before me to certify which I have hereunto set my hand and official seal this 19th Feb 1858 - JOHN H. PRINCE, Clerk Co Court Parker TX

Parker Co. TX - Field notes of survey of 148 acs. for JAMES BEDFORD by virtue his preemption affidavit No. 144 - Situate on Spring Creek, tributary Brazos Riv. about 12 mi. SW from Weatherford - Beg. NE from W cor. BENJAMIN F. IRBY 200 ac. survey & N boundary of same -

[45] I. SEALA preemption line - SE boundary line of JAMES CLAYTON 320 ac. survey -
Surveyed: Feb 19 1858 - LEWELLEN MURPHY, Co Surv Parker Co TX
Chain Carriers: THOMAS BEDFORD, DANIEL CRETSINGER
Recorded: May 6 1858 - LEWELLEN MURPHY, Co Surv Parker Co TX

[46] Parker Co. TX - No 149 - Before JOHN H. PRINCE, Clerk Co. Court Parker Co. TX, came THOMAS DRAPER as applicant and ISAAC O. HEADLEY and DANIEL H. SISK two disinterested respectable witnesses known to me. Applicant was bonafide settled upon land believed to be vacant at date of act to authorize location sale & settlement of the Mississippi & Pacific R. R. Reserve passed Aug 26 1856 and still resides thereon.
Signed: THOS. R. DRAPER, D. H. SISK, ISAAC O. HEADLEY
Sworn to & subscribed Apr 29 1857 before JOHN H. PRINCE, Clerk Co Court Parker Co TX

Parker Co. TX - Field notes survey of 160 acs. for THOMAS R. DRAPER by virtue his preemption affidavit No. 149 -

[47]   Situate in SE part Parker Co. on waters of San Antoine Creek, tributary Brazos Riv. - Beg. NE from N or NE cor. JAMES BEVERLY 74 3/10 ac. survey -
Surveyed: May 8 1858 - LEWELLEN MURPHY, Co Surv Parker Co TX
Chain Carriers: THOMAS L. RHODES, DANIEL H. SISK

[48]   Recorded: May 8 1858 - LEWELLEN MURPHY, Co Surv Parker Co TX

Parker Co. TX. - No. 41 - Before CHARLES GILDON, Notary Public in and for aforesaid co., appeared ALFA [or ALSA] LONG as applicant and JAMES LONG and JOHN BLACK two disinterested respectable witnesses known to me. Applicant was bonafide settled upon land believed to be vacant at date of act to authorize location sale & settlement of the Mississippi & Pacific R. R. Reserve passed Aug 26 1856 and still resides thereon. Signed: ALFA "X" LONG, JAMES "X" LONG, [no signature for 3rd witness]
Sworn to & subscribed Mar 21 1857 before CHARLES GILDON, Notary Public

[49] Parker Co. TX - Field notes of survey of 113 3/10 acs. for ALFA LONG by virtue her preemption affidavit No. 41 - Situate in Parker Co. on waters of Silver Creek, tributary West Fork Trinity Riv. about 10 mi. N ? from Weatherford - Beg. W & S of SW cor. MEMUCAN HUNT 160 ac. survey - SW cor. & S boundary line of JOHN BLACKs 113 3/10 ac. preemption survey

[50]   Surveyed: Apr 14 1857 - LEWELLEN MURPHY, Co Surv Parker Co TX
Chain Carriers: B. S. DUNNAGAN, JAMES P. JOHNSON
Recorded: May 10 1858 - LEWELLEN MURPHY, Co Surv Parker Co TX

Parker Co. TX. - No. 67 - Before JOHN MATLOCK, Chief Justice Parker Co. TX, appeared SARAH BLYTHE as applicant and WOODSON HENRY and JAMES H. SMITH two disinterested respectable witnesses known to me. Applicant was bonafide settled upon land believed to be vacant at date of act to authorize location sale & settlement of the Mississippi & Pacific R. R. Reserve passed Aug 26 1856 and still resides thereon.

[51]   Signed: SARAH BLYTHE, WOODSON D. HENRY, JAMES H. SMITH
Sworn to & subscribed Feb 26 1857 before JOHN MATLOCK, Chief Justice Parker Co TX

Denton Land Dist. TX - Have surveyed 160 acs. for SARAH BLYTHE by virtue her preemption certificate No. 67 - Situate in Parker Co in Denton Land Dist. on waters of Walnut Creek - Beg. SW from 25 mi. tree in N boundary line of Parker Co. -

[52]   Surveyed: Apr 20 1857 - L. E. CAMP, D. S. D. L. D.
Chain Carriers: T. H. LUCKEY, W. D. CRISWELL

Recorded: May 10 1858 - LEWELLEN MURPHY, Co Surv Parker Co TX

[53] Parker Co. TX. - No. 65 - Before JOHN MATLOCK, Chief Justice Parker Co. TX, appeared CALVIN M. CRISWELL as applicant and WOODSON D. HENRY and JAMES H. SMITH two disinterested respectable witnesses known to me. Applicant was bonafide settled upon land believed to be vacant at date of act to authorize location sale & settlement of the Mississippi & Pacific R. R. Reserve passed Aug 26 1856 and still resides thereon. Signed: CALVIN M. CRISWELL, WOODSON D. HENRY, JAMES H. SMITH Sworn to & subscribed Feb 26 1857 before JOHN MATLOCK, Chief Justice Parker Co TX

[54] Denton Land Dist. TX - Have surveyed 160 acs. for C. M. CRISWELL by virtue his preemption certificate No. 65 - Situate in Denton Land Dist. in Parker Co. on waters of Walnut Creek - Beg. at SE cor. SARAH BLYTHE preemption survey -
Surveyed: Apr 21 1857 - L. E. CAMP, D. S. D. L. D.
Chain Carriers: T. H. LUCKEY, W. D. CRISWELL

[55] Recorded: May 10 1858 - LEWELLEN MURPHY, Co Surv Parker Co TX

Parker Co. TX. - No. 8 - Before the undersigned authority this day came NATHAN B. HOLDER as applicant and I. O. HEADLEY and ABSALOM SPARKS two disinterested respectable witnesses known to me. Applicant was bonafide settled upon land believed to be vacant at date of act to authorize location sale & settlement of the Mississippi & Pacific R. R. Reserve passed Aug 26 1856 and still resides thereon.

[56] Signed: N. B. HOLDER, ABSALOM SPARKS, ISAAC O. HEADLEY Sworn to & subscribed Feb 16 1857 before JOHN H. PRINCE, Clerk Co Court Parker Co TX

Parker Co. TX - Have surveyed 160 acs. for N. B. HOLDER by virtue affidavit No. 8 - Situate in Parker Co. about 4 mi. S 40° E from Weatherford on waters of Clear Fork Trinity Riv. - Beg. SW from SW cor. J. P. COFFMAN 80 ac. survey -

[57] Surveyed: Feb 2 1858 - ISAAC O. HEADLEY, D. S. P. C. T.
Chain Carriers: E. B. DAVIDSON, A. SPARKS
Recorded: May 12 1858 - LEWELLEN MURPHY, Co Surv Parker Co TX

Parker Co. TX. - No. 44 - Before CHARLES GILDON, Notary Public in and for aforesaid Co. personally came JOHN A. PRICE as applicant and ISAAC PRICE and A. E. ROBERTSON two disinterested respectable witnesses known to me. Applicant was bonafide settled upon land believed to be vacant at date of act to authorize location sale & settlement of the Mississippi & Pacific R. R. Reserve passed Aug 26 1856 and still resides thereon.

[58]   Signed: JNO. A. "X" PRICE [mark], ISAAC "X" PRICE [mark], A. E. ROBERTSON
Sworn to & subscribed Mar 27 1857 before CHARLES GILDON, Notary Public

Parker Co. TX - Field notes survey of -

[59]   160 acs. for JOHN A. PRICE by virtue his preemption affidavit No. 44 - Situate on headwaters of Willow Branch, tributary Clear Fork Trinity Riv. about 7 1/2 mi. N 37° W from Weatherford - Beg. on N boundary line WILLIAM P. DULANEY 160 ac. preemption survey -
Surveyed: May 15 1858 - LEWELLEN MURPHY, Co Surv Parker Co TX
Chain Carriers: REASON M. MEADOR, BALEY HILL

[60]   Recorded: May 17 1858 - LEWELLEN MURPHY, Co Surv Parker Co TX

Parker Co. TX. - No. 56 - Before the undersigned authority this day came ROBERT BROWN as applicant and ANGER PRICE and WM. HOWARD two disinterested respectable witnesses known to me. Applicant was bonafide settled upon land believed to be vacant at date of act to authorize location sale & settlement of the Mississippi & Pacific R. R. Reserve passed Aug 26 1856 and still resides thereon.

[61]   Signed: ROBERT BROWN, ANGER "X" PRICE [mark], WILLIAM HOWARD
Sworn to & subscribed Feb 24 1857 before JOHN H. PRINCE, Clerk Co Court Parker Co TX

Parker Co. TX - Have surveyed 160 acs. for ROBERT BROWN including his improvements by virtue his affidavit No. 56 - Situate in Parker Co. on headwaters of Red Bear Creek, tributary Brazos Riv. - Beg. NE from NE cor. JEREMIAH POSEY 160 ac. survey

[62]   Surveyed: Apr 14 1858 - ISAAC O. HEADLEY, D. S. P. C. T.
Chain Carriers: WILLIAM HOWARD, ELI BROWN
Recorded: May 31 1858 - LEWELLEN MURPHY, Co Surv Parker Co TX

[63]   Parker Co. TX - No 225 - Before JOHN H. PRINCE, Clerk Co. Court Parker Co. came ISAAC GLASS as applicant and JOHN BURROWS and WM. L. WILSON two disinterested respectable witnesses known to me. Applicant was bonafide settled upon land believed to be vacant at date of act to authorize location sale & settlement of the Mississippi & Pacific R. R. Reserve passed Aug 26 1856 and still resides thereon.
Signed: ISAAC GLASS, JOHN BURROWS, WM. L. WILSON
Sworn to & subscribed Jan 19 1858 before JOHN H. PRINCE, Clerk Co Court Parker Co TX

[64] Parker Co. TX - Have surveyed 160 acs. for ISAAC GLASS including his improvements by virtue affidavit No. 225 - Situate in Parker Co. about 8 mi. NE from Weatherford on waters of Clear Fork Trinity Riv. - Beg. at SE cor. of L. P. MC DONNAL 282 ac. survey - SW cor. CALVIN LYNCH 160 ac. survey - Surveyed: Mar 11 1858 - ISAAC O. HEADLEY, D. S. P. C. T.
Chain Carriers: DAVID BROWN, D. C. ROSE

[65] Recorded: May 31 1858 - LEWELLEN MURPHY, Co Surv Parker Co TX

Parker Co. TX. - No. 10 - Before the undersigned authority this day came JOHN H. PHELPS as applicant and SOLOMON DERRETT and J. P. COLE two disinterested respectable witnesses known to me. Applicant was bonafide settled upon land believed to be vacant at date of act to authorize location sale & settlement of the Mississippi & Pacific R. R. Reserve passed Aug 26 1856 and still resides thereon.
Signed: JOHN H. PHELPS, SOLOMON DERRETT, JOHN P. COLE

[66] Sworn to & subscribed Feb 16 1857 before JOHN H PRINCE, Clerk Co Court Parker Co TX, by WM. M. GREEN, Dept.

Parker Co. TX - Field notes of survey of 160 acs. for JOHN H. PHELPS by virtue his preemption affidavit No. 10 - Situate on waters of Clear Fork Trinity Riv. about 10 mi. S 85° E from Weatherford - Beg. E of NW cor. ELIZA OTIER [OXIER ?] 320 ac. survey -

[67] Surveyed: Oct 26 1857 - LEWELLEN MURPHY, Co Surv Parker Co TX
Chain Carriers: HARRISON BROWN, JEREMIAH THOMPSON
Recorded: May 31 1858 - LEWELLEN MURPHY, Co Surv Parker Co TX

Parker Co. TX. - No. 114 - Before the undersigned authority this day came JAMES YOUNG BLOOD [sic] as applicant and DAVID WHITE and GEORGE COPELAND two disinterested respectable witnesses known to me. Applicant was bonafide settled upon land believed to be vacant at date of act to authorize location sale & settlement of the Mississippi & Pacific R. R. Reserve passed Aug 26 1856 and still resides thereon.

[68] Signed: JAMES "X" YOUNGBLOOD [mark], DAVID WHITE, GEORGE COPELAND
Sworn to & subscribed Dec 7 1857 before JOHN H. PRINCE, Clerk Co Court Parker Co TX

Parker Co. TX - Field notes of survey of 160 acs. for JAMES YOUNGBLOOD by virtue his preemption affidavit No. 114 - Situate on waters of -

[69] Rock Creek, tributary Brazos Riv. about 10 3/4 mi. NW

from Weatherford - Beg. NW from SE cor. JOHN M. TAYLOR 160 ac. survey
Surveyed: Jan 30 1858 - LEWELLEN MURPHY, Co Surv Parker Co TX
Chain Carriers: JOSEPH MANLEY, DAVID WHITE
Recorded: May 31 1858 - LEWELLEN MURPHY, Co Surv Parker Co TX

[END OF BOOK "C"]

PRE-EMPTION RECORD "D" PARKER COUNTY
1857

[1] PREEMPTION BOOK D

The State of Texas | No. 38
County of Parker | Before the undersigned authority this day came JONATHAN H. WALKER as applicant and WILLIAM SILLIVENT and WILLIAM TAYLOR, two disinterested and respectable witnesses and to me well known. All of whom being by me duly sworn the said applicant JONATHAN H. WALKER deposeth and saith that he was bonafide settled upon vacant land on the 26th day of August A. D. 1856 and that he continues to reside upon the same from the time of such settlement up to the date hereof. The said WILLIAM SILLIVENT and WILLIAM TAYLOR deposeth and say that the applicant JONATHAN H. WALKER was bonafide settled upon vacant land on the 26th day of August A. D. 1856 and that he continues to reside upon the same from the time of such settlement up to this date Feb 14 1857.

JONATHAN H. WALKER
WILLIAM SILLIVENT
WILLIAM TAYLOR

Sworn to & subscribed before me to certify which I have hereunto signed my name and the seal of the county court hereon impressed at Weatherford on this the 14th day of February A D 1857.

JOHN MATLOCK,
Chief Justice
Parker County Texas

[2] Parker Co. TX - Field notes of survey of 160 acs. for JONATHAN H. WALKER by virtue of his preemption affidavit No. 38 Situate in Parker Co. on waters of Clear Fork Trinity Riv. - Beg. N of NW cor. WILLIAM TAYLOR 160 ac. preemption survey - Surveyed: Feb 16 1857 - LEWELLEN MURPHY, Dept Surv Denton L D
Chain Carriers: WILLIAM TAYLOR, BENJAMIN J. STACKS

[3] Recorded: Jun 4 1857 - LEWELLEN MURPHY, Co Surv Parker Co TX

Parker Co. TX - No. 91 - Before me, JOHN MATLOCK, Chief Justice Parker Co. TX, this day personally came WILLIAM J. SILLIVENT as applicant and JOSEPH WALKER and HUGH BROWN, two disinterested and respectable witnesses. All of whom deposeth and saith that applicant was bonafide settled upon vacant land on the 26th day of August A. D. 1856 and continues to reside upon the same
Signed: WILLIAM J. SILLIVENT, JOSEPH WALKER, HUGH BROWN
Sworn to and subscribed Mar 27 1857 before JOHN MATLOCK, Chief Justice Parker Co TX

[4]   Parker Co. TX - Field notes of survey of 160 acs. for
WILLIAM J. SILLIVENT by virtue his preemption affidavit No. 91
- Situate in Parker Co. on waters Walnut Creek, tributary West
Fork Trinity Riv. - Beg. N of SW cor. WILLIAM HIGGINS 160 ac.
survey and W boundary of same -

[5]   Surveyed: Mar 28 1857 - LEWELLEN MURPHY, Dept Surv
Denton Land Dist
Chain Carriers: JAMES CULLWELL, FRANCIS MARION HARRIS
Recorded: Jun 4 1857 - LEWELLEN MURPHY Co Surv Parker Co TX

Parker Co. TX - No. 86 - Before JOHN MATLOCK, Chief Justice
Parker Co. TX, this day personally came JAMES CULWELL as applicant and JOSHUA CALDWELL and JOHN P. ALLEN, two disinterested and respectable witnesses. Said applicant JAMES CALDWELL
deposeth and saith that the land upon which he cultivated and
improved is vacant public land and that he commenced said settlement and improvement in the Spring of 1855 and continues to
cultivate the same from the commencement of said settlement up
to the present date as a single man over the age of seventeen
years.

[6]   Signed: JAMES COLWELL, JOSHUA COLWELL, JOHN PERRY ALLEN
Sworn to & subscribed Mar 19 1857 before JOHN MATLOCK, Chief
Justice Parker Co TX

Denton Land Dist. TX - Field notes of survey of 160 acs. for
JAMES COLWELL by virtue of his preemption affidavit No. 86 -
Situate in Parker Co. on waters of Walnut Creek, tributary
West Fork Trinity Riv. - Beg. at NW cor. HEZEKIAH CALWELL 160
ac. preemption survey -

[7]   Surveyed: Mar 19 1857 - LEWELLEN MURPHY, Dept Surv
Denton Land Dist
Chain Carriers: JOHN PERRY ALLEN, MERRICK BARTLETT
Recorded: Jun 5 1857 - LEWELLEN MURPHY, Co Surv Parker Co TX

Tarrant Co. TX - I, JOHN W. GODFREY do Solemnly swear that I
was on the land that I claim on the 13th of Dec. 1853 and believe it to be vacant land and still claim 320 acs. by virtue
of the preemption Law this March 21st 1854. Affix my hand and
scroll for seal
Signed: JOHN W. GODFREY
Sworn to & subscribed Mar 24 1854 before J. E. JENKINS, Dept
Surv Robertson Land Dist

[8]   Robertson Land Dist. TX - Mar 24 1854 - Survey for JOHN
W. GODFREY of the Dist. of Tarrant Co. 320 acs. of land lying
on Clear Fork Trinity Riv. by virtue of his preemption claim -
Beg. N of NE cor. JOSEPH BARKERs 320 ac. survey -
Surveyed by J. E. JENKINS, Dept. Surv. R. L. Dist.
Chain Carriers: DAVID STIMPSON, JOSEPH BARKER

Recorded: Jun 5 1857 - LEWELLEN MURPHY, Co Surv Parker Co TX

Robertson Land Dist. TX - I, JAMES J. BARKER do Solemnly swear that on or about the 13th of Dec 1853 I was settled upon the land I claim as a preemptionist and believe the same to be vacant and unappropriated this March 24th 1854
Signed: JAMES J. BARKER

[9]   Sworn to & subscribed to Mar 25 1854 before J E JENKINS, Dept Surv Robertson Land Dist

Robertson Land Dist. TX - Mar 25 1854 - Survey for JAMES J. BARKER of the Territory of Tarrant Co. 320 acs. of land lying on waters Clear Fork Trinity Riv. by virtue of his preemption claim Beg. at SW cor. JOHN W. GODFREY's 320 ac. survey -
Surveyed by J. E. JENKINS, Dept. Surv. R. L. Dist.
Chain Carriers: DAVID STIMPSON, J. W. GODFREY
Recorded: Jun 5 1857 - LEWELLEN MURPHY, Co Surv Parker Co TX

Parker Co. TX - No. 25 - Before CHARLES GILDON, Notary Public in and for aforesaid co. personally appeared THOS. CULWELL as applicant and SAML. S. LEONARD

[10]   and WM. H. ALLEN, two disinterested and respectable witnesses. All of whom deposeth and saith that applicant was bonafide settled upon vacant land before the 26th day of August A. D. 1856 and continues to reside upon the same
Signed: THOS "X" CULWELL [mark], SAMUEL S LEONARD, W H ALLEN
Sworn to & subscribed Feb 23 1857 before CHARLES GILDON, Notary Public

Parker Co. TX - Field notes of survey of 160 acs. for THOMAS CULWELL by virtue of his preemption affidavit No. 25 - Situate in Parker Co. on waters of Walnut Creek, tributary West Fork Trinity Riv. -

[11]   Beg. S of NE cor. HEZEKIAH CULWELL 160 ac. preemption survey - E boundary line JAMES CULWELL 160 ac. preemption survey S boundary line WILLIAM H. ALLENs preemption survey -
W boundary line of THOMAS CULWELL Jr. 160 ac. survey -
Surveyed: Mar 23 1857 - LEWELLEN MURPHY, Dept Surv Denton Land Dist
Chain Carriers: MERRICK BARTLETT, WILLIAM H ALLEN, THOMAS CULWELL

[12]   Recorded: Jun 5 1857 - LEWELLEN MURPHY, Co Surv Parker Co TX

Parker Co. TX - No. 85 - Before JOHN MATLOCK, Chief Justice Parker Co. TX, this day personally came JOSHUA CALDWELL as applicant and JAMES CALDWELL and JOHN P. ALLEN, two disinterested and respectable witnesses. said applicant says land upon

which he is now bonafide settled is vacant public land & commenced said settlement in the fall of 1855 and he has cultivated and improved the same from the commencement unto the present date as a single man over the age of seventeen years.
Signed: JOSHUA COLDWELL, JAMES COLDWELL, JOHN PERRY ALLEN

[13]   Sworn to & subscribed Mar 19 1857 before JOHN MATLOCK, Chief Justice Parker Co TX

Parker Co. TX - Field notes of survey of 104 2/10 acs. for JOSHUA CULWELL by virtue his preemption affidavit No. 85 - Situate in Parker Co. on waters of Walnut Creek, tributary West Fork Trinity Riv. - Beg. E of SW cor. THOMAS ALLEN 160 ac. preemption survey - N boundary line JOHN PERRY ALLENs 160 preemption survey -

[14]   Surveyed: Mar 20 1857 - LEWELLEN MURPHY, Dept Surv Denton Land Dist
Chain Carriers: SOLOMON HEINES, THOMAS ALLEN
Recorded: Jun 5 1857 - LEWELLEN MURPHY, Co Surv Parker Co TX

Parker Co. TX - No. 12 - Before the undersigned authority this day came GEORGE W. LIGHT as applicant and JAMES HUDSON and WILLIAM WILSON, two disinterested and respectable witnesses. All of whom deposeth and saith that applicant was bonafide settled upon vacant land on the date of an act to authorize the location & settlement of the Mississippi & Pacific R. R. Reserve passed August 26th A. D. 1856 and has continued to reside upon the same

[15]   Signed: GEORGE "X" W. LIGHT [mark], WM. WILSON, JAMES HUDSON
Sworn to & subscribed Feb 16 1857 before JOHN H. PRINCE, Clerk Co Court Parker Co TX

Parker Co. TX - Field notes of survey of 160 acs. for GEORGE W. LIGHT by virtue his preemption affidavit No. 12 - Situate in Parker Co. on waters of Grindstone Creek, tributary Brazos Riv.- Beg. NW from NW cor. JANE MOSS 160 ac. preemption survey

[16]   Surveyed: Mar 5 1857 - LEWELLEN MURPHY, Dept Surv Denton Land Dist
Chain Carriers: A. J. DYCHE, HOWELL R. MOSS
Recorded: Jun 6 1857 - LEWELLEN MURPHY, Co Surv Parker Co TX

Parker Co. TX - 10 - Before the undersigned authority this day came ROBERT S. PORTER Senr as claimant and JOSEPH REAVES and WILLIAM PATISON, two disinterested and respectable witnesses. All of whom deposeth and saith that applicant was bonafide settled upon vacant land on the date of an act to authorize the location & settlement of the Mississippi & Pacific R. R. Reserve passed August 26th A. D. 1856 and has continued to reside upon the same

[17] Signed: R. S. PORTER, JOSEPH REEVES, WILLIAM PATTERSON
Sworn to & subscribed Feb 25 1857 before J. J. BEEMAN, Notary
Public

Denton Land Dist. TX - Field notes of survey of 160 acs. for
ROBERT S. PORTER by virtue his preemption affidavit No. 10 -
Situate in Parker Co. on waters of Grindstone Creek, tributary
Brazos Riv. - Beg. NE from NW cor. JOHN F. PORTER 160 ac. preemption survey -

[18]   Surveyed: Feb 25 1857 - LEWELLEN MURPHY, Dept Surv
Denton Land Dist
Chain Carriers: A. J. DYCHE, JOHN C. HIGHTOWER
Recorded: Jun 6 1857 - LEWELLEN MURPHY, Co Surv Parker Co TX

Parker Co. TX - No. 57 - Before JOHN MATLOCK, Chief Justice
Parker Co. TX, this day personally came AMBERS ANGELY as applicant and ZACHARIAH BURRIS and THOMAS BURRIS, two disinterested and respectable witnesses. All   of whom deposeth and
saith that applicant was bonafide settled upon vacant land on
the 26th day of August A. D. 1856 and continues to reside upon
the same

[19] Signed: AMBERS ANGELY, ZACHARIAH BURRIS, THOMAS BURRIS
Sworn to & subscribed Feb 25 1857 before JOHN MATLOCK, Chief
Justice Parker Co TX

Parker Co. TX - Field notes of survey of 160 acs. for AMBERS
ANGELY by virtue his preemption affidavit No. 57 - Situate in
Parker Co. on waters of Walnut Creek, tributary West Fork
Trinity Riv. - Beg. on NW cor. WILLIAM COPELAND 160 ac. preemption survey -

[20]   Surveyed: Mar 19 1857   - LEWELLEN MURPHY, Dept Surv
Denton Land Dist
Chain Carriers: JAMES SPROULS, ISAAC DENTON PLUMMLEE
Recorded: Jun 6 1857 - LEWELLEN MURPHY, Co Surv Parker Co TX

Parker Co. TX - No. 150 - Before the undersigned authority
this day came DANIEL V. KIRBIE as applicant and WILLIAM B.
FONDREN and ISAM CRANFIELD, two disinterested and respectable
witnesses. All of whom deposeth and saith that applicant was
bonafide settled upon vacant land on the date of an act to authorize the location & settlement of the Mississippi & Pacific
R. R. Reserve passed August 26th A. D. 1856 and has continued
to reside upon the same

[21] Signed: DANIEL V. KIRBIE, W. B. FONDREN, ISOM CRANFILL
Sworn to & subscribed May 4 1857 before JOHN H. PRINCE, Clerk
Co Parker Co

Parker Co. TX - Field notes of survey of 160 acs. for DANIEL V. KIRBIE by virtue his preemption affidavit No. 150 - Situate in Parker Co. on waters of Rock Creek, tributary Brazos Riv. - Beg. NW from NW cor. PETER WELDEN 160 ac. preemption survey -

[22] Surveyed: May 1 1857 - LEWELLEN MURPHY, Dept Surv Denton Land Dist.
Chain Carriers: JOHN M. TAYLOR, ISOM CRANFIELD
Recorded: Jun 6 1857 - LEWELLEN MURPHY, Co Surv Parker Co TX

Parker Co. TX - No. 97 - Before the undersigned authority this day came PETER WELDEN as applicant and THOS. B. MARTIN and HIRAM PINNELL, two disinterested and respectable witnesses. All of whom deposeth and saith that applicant was bonafide settled upon vacant land on the date of an act to authorize the location & settlement of the Mississippi & Pacific R. R. Reserve passed August 26th A. D. 1856 and has continued to reside upon the same

[23] Signed: P. WELDEN, THOMAS B. "X" MARTIN [mark], HIRAM PINNELL
Sworn to & subscribed Feb 28 1857 before JOHN H. PRINCE, Clerk Co Court Parker Co

Parker Co. TX - Field notes of survey of 160 acs. for PETER WELDEN by virtue his preemption affidavit No. 97 - Situate in Parker Co. on waters of Grindstone Creek, tributary Brazos Riv. Beg. NE from NE cor. JAMES H. PORTER 160 ac. preemption survey -

[24] Surveyed: Apr 29 1857 - LEWELLEN MURPHY, Dept Surv Denton Land Dist
Chain Carriers: HIRAM PINNELL, JONATHAN S. LEE
Recorded: Jun 6 1857 - LEWELLEN MURPHY, Co Surv Parker Co TX

[25] Parker Co. TX - No. 72 - Before the undersigned authority this day came J. J. BEEMAN as applicant and JAMES KIDWELL and GEORGE LEE, two disinterested and respectable witnesses. All of whom deposeth and saith that applicant was bonafide settled upon vacant land on the date of an act to authorize the location & settlement of the Mississippi & Pacific R. R. Reserve passed August 26th A. D. 1856 and has continued to reside upon the same
Signed: J. J. BEEMAN, JAMES "X" KIDWELL [mark], GEORGE LEE
Sworn to & subscribed Feb 26 1857 before JOHN H. PRINCE, Clerk Co Court Parker Co, by WM. M. GREEN, Dept.

Parker Co. TX - Field notes of survey of 160 acs. for J. J. BEEMAN by virtue his preemption affidavit No. 72 - Situate in Parker Co. -

[26] on waters of S Fork of Clear Fork Trinity Riv. - Beg.

SE from NE cor. JAMES H. SEWELL 320 ac. preemption survey -
Surveyed: May 2 1857 - LEWELLEN MURPHY, Dept Surv Denton Land Dist
Chain Carriers: JAMES JOHNSON, HENRY C. PRICE
Recorded: Jun 8 1857 - LEWELLEN MURPHY, Co Surv Parker Co TX

[27] Parker Co. TX - No. 18 - Before the undersigned authority this day came ANGUIS M. POE as applicant and A. J. DYCHE and JAMES HUDSON, two disinterested and respectable witnesses. All of whom deposeth and saith that applicant was bonafide settled upon vacant land on the date of an act to authorize the location & settlement of the Mississippi & Pacific R. R. Reserve passed August 26th A. D. 1856 and has continued to reside upon the same
Signed: A. M. POE, A. J. DYCHE, JAMES HUDSON
Sworn to & subscribed Feb 17 1857 before JOHN H. PRINCE, Clerk Co Court Parker Co, by WM. M. GREEN, Dept.

Parker Co. TX - Field notes of survey of 160 acs. for ANGUIS M. POE by virtue his preemption affidavit No. 18 - Situate in Parker Co. -

[28] on waters of Brazos Riv. - Beg. SW of SW cor. ASA GILMORE 160 ac. preemption survey -
Surveyed: Mar 12 1857 - LEWELLEN MURPHY, Dept Surv Denton Land Dist
Chain Carriers: JOHN W. POE, JOHN TURREN
Recorded: Jun 8 1857 - LEWELLEN MURPHY, Co Surv Parker Co TX

[29] Parker Co. TX - No. 9 - Before CHARLES GILDON, Notary Public in and for aforesaid co. personally appeared THOMAS RILEY as applicant and ROBERT WRIGHT and LEMUEL FRANKS, two disinterested and respectable witnesses. All of whom deposeth and saith that applicant was bonafide settled upon vacant land on August 26th A. D. 1856 and has continued to reside upon the same
Signed: THOMAS RILEY, ROBERT WRIGHT, LEMUEL FRANKS
Sworn to & subscribed Feb 17 1857 before CHARLES GILDON, Notary Public

Parker Co. TX - Field notes of survey of 160 acs. for THOMAS RILEY by virtue his preemption affidavit No. 9 -

[30] Situate in Parker Co. on waters of Walnut Creek, tributary West Fork Trinity Riv. - Beg. S of NE cor. LEMUEL FRANKS 141 8/10 ac. preemption survey -
Surveyed: Apr 3 1857 - LEWELLEN MURPHY, Dept Surv Denton Land Dist
Chain Carriers: JAMES WIMBLEY, ANDREW JACKSON
Recorded: Jun 8 1857 - LEWELLEN MURPHY, Co Surv Parker Co TX

[31] Parker Co. TX - No. 6 - Before the undersigned authority

this day came JAMES H. PORTER as claimant and JOSEPH REEVES and R. S. PORTER Senr., two disinterested and respectable witnesses. All of whom deposeth and saith that applicant was bonafide settled upon vacant land on the date of an act to authorize the location & settlement of the Mississippi & Pacific R. R. Reserve passed August 26th A. D. 1856 and has continued to reside upon the same
Signed: JAMES H. PORTER, JOSEPH REEVES, R. S. PORTER, Senr.
Sworn to & subscribed Feb 25 1857 before J. J. BEEMAN, Notary Public

Denton Land Dist. TX - Field notes of survey of 160 acs. for JAMES H. PORTER by virtue his preemption affidavit No. 6 -

[32] Situate in Parker Co. on Grindstone Creek, tributary Brazos Riv. - Beg. SE from NW cor. ROBERT S. PORTER 160 ac. preemption survey & N. boundary line of same -
Surveyed: Feb 25 1857 - LEWELLEN MURPHY, Dept Surv Denton Land Dist
Chain Carriers: A. J. DYCHE, JOHN C. HIGHTOWER

[33] Recorded: Jun 8 1857 - LEWELLEN MURPHY, Co Surv Parker Co TX

Parker Co. TX - No. 42 - Before JOHN MATLOCK, Chief Justice Parker Co., personally appeared J. W. FRANKLIN as applicant and JOHN MONTGOMERY and J. M. HEFLEY, two disinterested and respectable witnesses. All of whom deposeth and saith that applicant was bonafide settled upon vacant land on the date of an act to authorize the location & settlement of the Mississippi & Pacific R. R. Reserve passed August 26th A. D. 1856 and has continued to reside upon the same
Signed: J. W. FRANKLIN, JOHN MONTGOMERY, J. M. HEFLEY
Sworn to & subscribed Feb 14 1857 before JOHN MATLOCK, Chief Justice Parker Co.

[34] Parker Co. TX - Field notes of survey of 160 acs. for JESSE W. FRANKLIN by virtue his preemption affidavit No. 42 - Situate in Parker Co. on waters of Walnut Creek, tributary West Fork Trinity Riv. - Beg. NE of NE cor. SALLY ASBURRY ENSEY 77 6/10 ac. preemption survey -
Surveyed: Feb 14 1857 - LEWELLEN MURPHY, Dept Surv Denton Land Dist

[35] Chain Carriers: ZACHARIAH BURRIS, THOMAS VERNON
Recorded: Jun 8 1857 - LEWELLEN MURPHY, Co Surv Parker Co TX

Parker Co. TX - No. 13 - Before the undersigned authority this day came WILLIAM WILSON as applicant and GEORGE W. LIGHT and JAMES HUDSON, two disinterested and respectable witnesses. All of whom deposeth and saith that applicant was bonafide settled upon vacant land on the date of an act to authorize the loca-

tion & settlement of the Mississippi & Pacific R. R. Reserve passed August 26th A. D. 1856 and has continued to reside upon the same
Signed: WM. WILSON, JAMES HUDSON, G. W. "X" LIGHT [mark]

[36] Sworn to & subscribed Feb 16 1857 before JOHN H PRINCE, Clerk Co Court Parker Co, by WM. M. GREEN, Dept.

Denton Land Dist. TX - Field notes of survey of 160 acs. for WILLIAM WILSON by virtue his preemption affidavit No. 13 - Situate in Parker Co. on waters of Grindstone Creek, tributary Brazos Riv.- Beg. SW from SE cor. GEORGE W. LIGHT 160 ac. preemption survey -

[37] Surveyed: Mar 6 1857 - LEWELLEN MURPHY, Dept Surv Denton Land Dist
Chain Carriers: ISRAEL BURROWS, WILLIAM WILSON
Recorded: Jun 8 1857 - LEWELLEN MURPHY, Co Surv Parker Co TX

Parker Co. TX - No. 7 - Before the undersigned authority this day came CHRISTOPHER C PORTER as claimant and ROBERT S PORTER, Senr. and A J DYCHE, two disinterested and respectable witnesses. All of whom deposeth and saith that applicant was bonafide settled upon vacant land on the date of an act to authorize the location & settlement of the Mississippi & Pacific R. R. Reserve passed August 26th A. D. 1856 and has continued to reside upon the same
Signed: C. C. PORTER, R. S. PORTER, A. J. DYCHE

[38] Sworn to & subscribed Feb 25 1857 before J. J. BEEMAN, Notary Public

Parker Co. TX - Field notes of survey of 160 acs. for CHRISTOPHER C. PORTER by virtue his preemption affidavit No. 7 - Situate in Parker Co. on waters Grindstone Creek, tributary Brazos Riv.- Beg. N of NW cor. WILLIAM C. BAKER 160 ac. preemption survey

[39] Surveyed: Feb 25 1857 - LEWELLEN MURPHY, Dept Surv Denton Land Dist
Chain Carriers: JOHN C. HIGHTOWER, JOHN F. PORTER
Recorded: Jun 8 1857 - LEWELLEN MURPHY, Co Surv Parker Co TX

Parker Co. TX - No. 62 - Before the undersigned authority this day came L. D. MEEK as applicant and JOHN W. MEEK and LEVI CURRENT, two disinterested and respectable witnesses. All of whom deposeth and saith that applicant was bonafide settled upon vacant land on the date of an act to authorize the location & settlement of the Mississippi & Pacific R. R. Reserve passed August 26th A. D. 1856 and has continued to reside upon the same

[40]   Signed: L D MEEK, JOHN W MEEK, LEVI "X" CURRANT [mark]
Sworn to & subscribed Feb 25 1857 before JOHN H. PRINCE, Clerk
Co Court Parker Co., by WM. M. GREEN, Dept.

Parker Co. TX - Field notes of survey of 160 acs. for L D MEEK
by virtue his preemption affidavit No. 62 - Situate in Parker
Co. on Brazos Riv.- Beg. SW from SW cor. ANGUIS M. POE 160 ac.
preemption survey -

[41]   Surveyed: Mar 11 1857 - LEWELLEN MURPHY, Dept Surv
Denton Land Dist
Chain Carriers: HENRY MEEK, JOHN W. MEEK
Recorded: Jun 8 1857 - LEWELLEN MURPHY, Co Surv Parker Co TX

[42]   Parker Co. TX - No. 60 - Before the undersigned authority this day came MARY MEEK as applicant and JOHN W. MEEK and
L. D. MEEK, two disinterested and respectable witnesses. All
of whom deposeth and saith that applicant was bonafide settled
upon vacant land on the date of an act to authorize the location & settlement of the Mississippi & Pacific R. R. Reserve
passed August 26th A. D. 1856 and has continued to reside upon
the same
Signed: MARY "X" MEEK [mark], JOHN W. MEEK, L. D. MEEK
Sworn to & subscribed Feb 25 1857 before JOHN H. PRINCE, Clerk
Co Court Parker Co, by WM. M. GREEN, Dept.

Parker Co. TX - Field notes of survey of 160 acs. for MARY
MEEK by virtue her preemption affidavit No. 60 - Situate in
Parker Co. on Brazos Riv.- Beg. SE -

[43]   from S cor. L. D. MEEK 160 ac. preemption survey -
Surveyed: Mar 10 1857 - LEWELLEN MURPHY, Dept Surv Denton Land
Dist
Chain Carriers: JOHN W. MEEK, HENRY MEEK
Recorded: Jun 9 1857 - LEWELLEN MURPHY, Co Surv Parker Co TX

Parker Co. TX - No. 61 - Before the undersigned authority this
day came JOHN W. MEEK -

[44]   as applicant and LEVI CURRENT and L.   D. MEEK, two disinterested and respectable witnesses. All of whom deposeth and
saith that applicant was bonafide settled upon vacant land on
the date of an act to authorize the location & settlement of
the Mississippi & Pacific R. R. Reserve passed August 26th A D
1856 and has continued to reside upon the same
Signed: JOHN W. MEEK, LEVI "X" CURRENT [mark], L. D. MEEK
Sworn to & subscribed Feb 25 1857 before JOHN H. PRINCE, Clerk
Co Court Parker Co, by WM. M. GREEN, Dept.

Parker Co. TX - Field notes of survey of 160 acs. for JOHN
WESLEY MEEK by virtue his preemption survey No. 61 - Situate
in Parker Co. on waters of Rock Creek, tributary of Brazos

Riv.- Beg. NW of NW cor. ANGUIS M. POE 160 ac. preemption survey -

[45] Surveyed: Mar 9 1857 - LEWELLEN MURPHY, Dept Surv Denton Land Dist
Chain Carriers: HENRY MEEK, JACOB MEEK
Recorded: Jun 9 1857 - LEWELLEN MURPHY, Co Surv Parker Co Tx

[46] Parker Co. TX - No. 94 - Before the undersigned authority this day came WILLIAM C. BAKER as applicant and WILLIAM HOWARD and WM. M. GREEN, two disinterested and respectable witnesses. All of whom deposeth and saith that applicant was bonafide settled upon vacant land on the date of an act to authorize the location & settlement of the Mississippi & Pacific R. R. Reserve passed August 26th A. D. 1856 and has continued to reside upon the same
Signed: WM. C. BAKER, WILLIAM HOWARD, WM. M. GREEN
Sworn to & subscribed Feb 28 1857 before JOHN H. PRINCE, Clerk Co Court Parker Co

Parker Co. TX - Field notes of survey of 160 acs. for WILLIAM C. BAKER by virtue his preemption affidavit No. 94 -

[47] Situate in Parker Co. on waters of Grindstone Creek, tributary Brazos Riv.- Beg. NW from NW cor. ROBERT P. BAKER 160 ac. preemption survey -
Surveyed: Mar 4 1857 - LEWELLEN MURPHY, Dept Surv Denton Land Dist
Chain Carriers: ASHLEY N. DENTON, MONROE UPTON
Recorded: Jun 9 1857 - LEWELLEN MURPHY, Co Surv Parker Co Tx

[48] Parker Co. TX - No. 69 - Before the undersigned authority this day came ALEXANDER N. BRASHEARS as applicant and JOHN GRISHAM and EPHRAYM MARTIN, two disinterested and respectable witnesses. All of whom deposeth and saith that applicant was bonafide settled upon vacant land on the date of an act to authorize the location & settlement of the Mississippi & Pacific R. R. Reserve passed August 26th A. D. 1856 and has continued to reside upon the same
Signed: ALEXANDER M. BRASHEARS, JOHN GRISHAM, EPHRAIM MARTIN
Sworn to & subscribed Feb 26 1857 before JOHN H. PRINCE, Clerk Co Court Parker Co, by WM. M. GREEN, Dept

Parker Co. TX - Field notes of survey of 160 acs. for ALEXANDER N. BRASHEARS by virtue his preemption affidavit No. 69 -

[49] Situate in Parker Co. on waters of Grindstone Creek, tributary of Brazos Riv.- Beg. on N cor. JOHN GRISHAM [?] 160 ac. preemption survey -
Surveyed: Mar 13 1857 - LEWELLEN MURPHY, Dept Surv Denton Land Dist
Chain Carriers: NATHAN GRISHAM, JOHN W. BRASHEARS

[50]   Recorded: Jun 9 1857 - LEWELLEN   MURPHY, Co Surv Parker Co Tx

Parker Co. TX - No. 37 - Before the undersigned authority this day came ROBERT P. BAKER   as applicant and JAMES M.   UPTON and MONROE UPTON, two disinterested and respectable witnesses. All of whom deposeth and saith that applicant was bonafide settled upon vacant land on the date of an act   to authorize the location & settlement of the   Mississippi & Pacific R.   R. Reserve passed August 26th A. D. 1856 and has continued to reside upon the same
Signed: R. P. BAKER, MONROE UPTON, JAMES M. UPTON
Sworn to & subscribed Feb 23 1857 before JOHN H. PRINCE, Clerk Co Court Parker Co, by WM. M. GREEN, Dept

Parker Co. TX - Field   notes of survey of 160   acs. for ROBERT P. BAKER -

[51]   by virtue his preemption affidavit No.   37 - Situate in Parker Co.   on waters   of Grindstone   Creek, tributary   Brazos Riv. Beg. NW from N cor. of the Leon Co. School 960 ac. survey
Surveyed: Mar 3 1857 - LEWELLEN MURPHY, Dept   Surv Denton Land Dist
Chain Carriers: WILLIAM C. BAKER, MILTON IKARD
Recorded: Jun 9 1857 - LEWELLEN MURPHY, Co Surv Parker Co Tx

[52]   Parker Co. TX - No. 28 - Before the undersigned authority this day came J.   H.   HEWETT as applicant and   DAVID HERING and F. C. BROWN, two disinterested   and respectable witnesses. All of whom   deposeth and   saith that   applicant was   bonafide settled upon vacant land   on the date   of an act   to authorize the location & settlement of   the Mississippi & Pacific   R. R. Reserve passed August   26th A.   D. 1856   and has continued   to reside upon the same
Signed: J. H. HEWETT, DAVID HERRING, F. C. BROWN
Sworn to & subscribed Feb 23 1857 before JOHN H. PRINCE, Clerk Co Court Parker Co, by WM. M. GREEN, Dept

Parker Co. TX - Field   notes of survey of 160   acs. for JOSEPH H. HEWETT by virtue of his preemption affidavit No. 28 -

[53]   Situate   in Parker Co.   on waters of   Grindstone Creek, tributary Brazos Riv.- Beg. S   of SW cor. ROBERT P.   BAKER 160 ac. preemption survey -
Surveyed: Mar 16 1857 - LEWELLEN MURPHY, Dept Surv Denton Land Dist
Chain Carriers: ISAAC B. MAJORS, DAVID HERRING

[54]   Recorded: Jun 9 1857 - LEWELLEN   MURPHY, Co Surv Parker Co Tx

Parker Co. TX - No. 11 - Before the undersigned authority this

day came JAMES HUDSON as applicant and WILLIAM WILSON and GEORGE W. LIGHT, two disinterested and respectable witnesses. All of whom deposeth and saith that applicant was bonafide settled upon vacant land on the date of an act to authorize the location & settlement of the Mississippi & Pacific R. R. Reserve passed August 26th A. D. 1856 and has continued to reside upon the same
Signed: JAMES HUDSON, WM. WILSON, G. W. "X" LIGHT [mark]
Sworn to & subscribed Feb 16 1857 before JOHN H. PRINCE, Clerk Co Court Parker Co, by WM. M. GREEN, Dept

Parker Co. TX - Field notes of survey -

[55] of 160 acs. for JAMES HUDSON by virtue his preemption affidavit No. 11 - Situate in Parker Co. on waters of Grindstone Creek, tributary Brazos Riv.- Beg in the bed of Grindstone Creek on NE cor. & the N boundary line YOUNG WARREN 160 ac. preemption survey -
Surveyed: Mar 7 1857 - LEWELLEN MURPHY, Dept Surv Denton Land Dist
Chain Carriers: WILLIAM P. WILSON, ASA GILMORE
Recorded: Jun 9 1857 - LEWELLEN MURPHY, Co Surv Parker Co Tx

Parker Co. TX - No. 34 - Before the undersigned authority this day came ASA GILMER as applicant and ["YOUNG" written first and lined through] YONG WARREN and MONROE UPTON, two disinterested and respectable witnesses. All of whom deposeth and saith that applicant was bonafide settled upon vacant land on the date of an act to authorize the location & settlement of the Mississippi & Pacific R. R. Reserve passed August 26th A D 1856 and has continued to reside upon the same
Signed: ASA GILMORE, MONROE UPTON, YONG "X" WARREN

[57] Sworn to & subscribed Feb 23 1857 before JOHN H PRINCE, Clerk Co Court Parker Co, by WM. M. GREEN, Dept

Denton Land Dist. TX - Field notes of survey of 160 acs. for ASA GILMER by virtue his preemption affidavit No. 34 - Situate in Parker Co. on waters of Grindstone Creek, tributary Brazos Riv.- Beg. SE from SE cor. YOUNG WARREN 160 ac. preemption survey -

[58] Surveyed: Mar 13 1857 - LEWELLEN MURPHY, Dept Surv Denton Land Dist
Chain Carriers: DUGAL CAMBELL, YOUNG WARREN
Recorded: Jun 9 1857 - LEWELLEN MURPHY, Co Surv Parker Co Tx

Parker Co. TX - No. 65 - Before the undersigned authority this day came JOHN W. BRASHERS as applicant and JOHN GRISHAM and WM. COFFEY, two disinterested and respectable witnesses. All of whom deposeth and saith that applicant was bonafide settled upon vacant land on the date of an act to authorize the location & settlement of the Mississippi & Pacific R. R. Reserve passed August 26th A D 1856 and has continued to reside upon the same

[59]   Signed: JOHN W. BRASHEARS, JOHN GRISHAM, WILLIAM COFFEY
Sworn to & subscribed Feb 26 1857 before JOHN H. PRINCE, Clerk Co. Co. Parker Co., by WM. M. GREEN, Dept

Parker Co. TX - Field notes of survey of 160 acs. for JOHN W. BRASHEARS by virtue his preemption affidavit No. 65 - Situate in Parker Co. on waters of Brazos Riv.- Beg. on W cor. ALEXANDER M. BRASHEARS 160 ac. preemption survey -

[60]   Surveyed: Feb 27 1857 - LEWELLEN MURPHY, Dept Surv Denton Land Dist
Chain Carriers: NATHAN GRISHAM, ALEXANDER M. BRASHEARS
Recorded: Jun 10 1857 - LEWELLEN MURPHY, Co Surv Parker Co Tx

Parker Co. TX - No. 7 - Before JOHN MATLOCK, Chief Justice Parker Co., personally appeared SOLOMON HINES as applicant and ROBERT GEORGE and THOMAS ALLEN, two disinterested and respectable witnesses. All of whom deposeth and saith that applicant was bonafide settled upon vacant land on the date of an act to authorize the location & settlement of the Mississippi & Pacific R. R. Reserve passed August 26th A. D. 1856 and has continued to reside upon the same

[61]   Signed: SOLOMON HINES, ROBERT GEORGE, THOMAS ALLEN
Sworn to & subscribed Feb 2 1857 before JOHN MATLOCK, Chief Justice Parker Co

Parker Co. TX - Field notes of survey of 160 acs. for SOLOMON HINES by virtue his preemption affidavit No. 7 -

[62]   Situate in Parker Co on waters of Walnut Creek, tributary West Fork Trinity Riv. - Beg. S of SW cor. THOMAS ALLEN 160 ac. preemption survey -
Surveyed: Apr 3 1857 - LEWELLEN MURPHY, Dept Surv Denton Land Dist
Chain Carriers: SAMUEL S. LEONARD, WILLIAM J. WOMACK
Recorded: Jun 10 1857 - LEWELLEN MURPHY, Co Surv Parker Co Tx

[63]   Parker Co. TX - No. 9 - Before the undersigned authority this day came JOHN F. PORTER as claimant and JOSEPH REEVES and R. S. PORTER, SR., two disinterested and respectable witnesses. All of whom deposeth and saith that applicant was bonafide settled upon vacant land on the date of an act to authorize the location & settlement of the Mississippi & Pacific R. R. Reserve passed August 26th A. D. 1856 and has continued to reside upon the same
Signed: JOHN F. PORTER, JOSEPH REEVES, R. S. PORTER, Sr.

Sworn to & subscribed Feb 25 1857 before   J. J. BEEMAN, Notary Public

Parker Co. TX - Field notes of survey of 160 acs. for JOHN F. PORTER by virtue his preemption affidavit No. 9 -

[64]   Situate in Parker Co. on waters of Grindstone Creek, tributary Brazos Riv.- Beg. E of NE cor. ROBERT S. PORTER 160 ac. preemption survey -
Surveyed: Mar 13 1857 - LEWELLEN MURPHY, Dept Surv Denton Land Dist
Chain Carriers: THOMAS M. CLAYTON, JOHN C. HIGHTOWER
Recorded: Jun 10 1857 - LEWELLEN MURPHY, Co Surv Parker Co Tx

[65]   Parker Co. TX - No. 33 - Before CHARLES GILDON, Notary Public in and for aforesaid co., personally   appeared ISAAC C. FLETCHER as applicant and   THOMAS GOLHIER and JNO.   BLACK, two disinterested and respectable witnesses. All of whom deposeth and saith that applicant was bonafide settled upon vacant land on August 26th A. D. 1856 and has continued to reside upon the same
Signed: ISAAC C. "X" FLETCHER [mark], THOMAS GOLHER,
JOHN "X" BLACK [mark]
Sworn to & subscribed Mar 7 1857 before CHARLES GILDON, Notary Public

[66]   Parker Co. TX - Field notes of survey of 160 acs. for ISAAC C. FLETCHER by virtue his preemption affidavit No. 33 - Situate in Parker   Co. on   waters of   Silver Creek,   tributary West   Fork   Trinity   Riv. - Beg. SW from NW   cor. EGBERT N. CLEMENT 160 ac. preemption survey -
Surveyed: Mar 24 1857 - LEWELLEN MURPHY, Dept Surv Denton Land Dist
Chain Carriers: JOHN E. RASH, THOMAS GOLHER

[67]   Recorded: Jun 10 1857 - LEWELLEN MURPHY, Co Surv Parker Co Tx

Parker Co. TX - No. 8 - Before the undersigned authority this day came ROBERT S. PORTER, Jr., as applicant and A.   J. DYCHE and C. C. PORTER, two disinterested and respectable witnesses. All of whom deposeth and saith that applicant was bonafide settled upon vacant land on the date of an act to authorize the location & settlement of the Mississippi & Pacific R. R. Reserve passed August 26th A. D. 1856 and has continued to reside upon the same
Signed: R. S. PORTER, A. J. DYCE, C. C. PORTER
Sworn to & subscribed Feb 25 1857 before J. J. BEEMAN, Notary Public

[68]   Parker Co. TX - Field notes of survey of 160 acs. for ROBERT S. PORTER by virtue his preemption affidavit No. 8 -

Situate in Parker Co. on waters of Grindstone Creek, tributary Brazos Riv.- Beg. E of NW cor. A. J. DYCHE 160 ac. preemption survey -
Surveyed: Mar 5 1857 - LEWELLEN MURPHY, Dept Surv Denton Land Dist
Chain Carriers: A. J. DYCHE, JAMES H. PORTER

[69]   Recorded: Jun 12 1857 - LEWELLEN MURPHY, Co Surv Parker Co Tx

Parker Co. TX - No. 33 - Before the undersigned authority this day came MONROE UPTON as applicant and MILTON IKARD and F. C. BROWN two disinterested and respectable witnesses. All of whom deposeth and saith that applicant was bonafide settled upon vacant land on the date of an act to authorize the location & settlement of the Mississippi & Pacific R. R. Reserve passed August 26th A D 1856 and has continued to reside upon the same
Signed: MONROE UPTON, M. IKARD, F. C. BROWN
Sworn to & subscribed Feb 23 1857 before JOHN H. PRINCE, Clerk Co Court Parker Co, by WM. M. GREEN, Dept

Parker Co. TX - Field notes of survey of 160 acs. for MONROE UPTON -

[70]   by virtue his preemption affidavit No. 33 - Situate in Parker Co. on waters of Grindstone Creek, tributary Brazos Riv.- Beg. W of NW cor. JOSEPH H. HEWETT 160 ac. preemption survey -
Surveyed: Mar 16 1857 - LEWELLEN MURPHY, Dept Surv Denton Land Dist
Chain Carriers: DAVID HERRING, ISAAC B. MAJORS
Recorded: Jun 12 1857 - LEWELLEN MURPHY, Co Surv Parker Co Tx

[71]   Parker Co. TX - No 107 - Before the undersigned authority this day came WILLIAM UPTON as applicant and MONROE UPTON and D. HERRING, two disinterested and respectable witnesses. All of whom deposeth and saith that applicant was bonafide settled upon vacant land on the date of an act to authorize the location & settlement of the Mississippi & Pacific R. R. Reserve passed August 26th A. D. 1856 and has continued to reside upon the same
Signed: WILLIAM UPTON, MONROE UPTON, DAVID HERRING
Sworn to & subscribed Mar 10 1857 before JOHN H. PRINCE, Clerk Co Court Parker Co

Parker Co. TX - Field notes of survey of 160 acs. for WILLIAM UPTON by virtue his preemption affidavit No. 107 - Situate in Parker Co. on -

[72]   of Grindstone Creek, tributary Brazos Riv.- Beg. SW of SW cor. ROBERT P. BAKER 160 ac. preemption survey -

Surveyed: Mar 16 1857 - LEWELLEN MURPHY, Dept Surv Denton Land Dist
Chain Carriers: MONROE UPTON, DAVID HERRING
Recorded: Jun 12 1857 - LEWELLEN MURPHY, Co Surv Parker Co Tx

[Page No. torn] Parker Co. TX - No. 24 - Before CHARLES [torn] Notary Public in and for aforesaid Co., personally appeared SAML S LEONARD [torn] applicant and THOS CULWELL and WILLIAM H ALLEN, two disinterested and respectable witnesses. All of whom deposeth and saith that applicant was bonafide settled upon vacant land on August 26th A. D. 1856 and has continued to reside upon the same
Signed: SAMUEL S. LEON[torn], THOS. "X" CULWELL [mark], W. H. ALLEN
Sworn to & subscribed Feb 23 1857 before CHARLES GILDON, Notary Public

Parker Co. TX - Field notes [page torn]

[?4] for SAMUEL S. LEONARD by virtue his preemption affidavit No. 24 - Situate in Parker Co. on waters of Walnut Creek, tributary West Fork Trinity Riv. - Beg. in NE cor. THOMAS CULWELL 160 ac. preemption survey - E boundary line of WM. H. ALLEN's preemption - THOMAS CULWELL's S boundary line - S boundary line ALLEN C. HILL's preemption -
Surveyed: Apr 1 1857 [remainder of page torn]

[75] Recorded: Jun 12 1857 - LEWELLEN MURPHY, Co Surv Parker Co Tx

Parker Co. TX - No. 17 - Before the undersigned authority this day came A. J. DYCHE as applicant and ANGUIS M. POE and JAMES HUDSON, two disinterested and respectable witnesses. All of whom deposeth and saith that applicant was bonafide settled upon vacant land on the date of an act to authorize the location & settlement of the Mississippi & Pacific R. R. Reserve passed August 26th A. D. 1856 and has continued to reside upon the same
Signed: A. J. DYCHE, A. M. POE, JAMES HUDSON
Sworn to & subscribed Feb 17 1857 before JOHN H. PRINCE, Clerk Co Court Parker Co, by WM. M. GREEN, Dept

[76] Parker Co. TX - Field notes of survey of 160 acs. for ALFORD J. DYCHE by virtue his preemption survey No. 17 - Situate in Parker Co. on waters of Grindstone Creek, tributary Brazos Riv.- Beg. NE of NE cor. CHRISTOPHER C. PORTER 160 ac. preemption survey -
Surveyed: Mar 5 1857 - LEWELLEN MURPHY, Dept Surv Denton Land Dist
Chain Carriers: GEORGE W. LIGHT, HOWELL R. MOSS

[77]   Recorded: Jun 12 1857 - LEWELLEN MURPHY, Co Surv Parker Co Tx

Parker Co. TX - No. 94 - Before JOHN MATLOCK, Chief Justice Parker Co., personally came WILLIAM C. BURTON as applicant and THOMAS S. BURTON and JAMES M. BURTON, two disinterested and respectable witnesses. All of whom deposeth and saith that applicant was bonafide settled upon vacant land on August 26th A. D. 1856 and continues to reside upon the same
Signed: WM. C. BURTON, T. S. BURTON, JAMES M. BURTON

[78]   Sworn to & subscribed Apr 1 1857 before JOHN MATLOCK, Chief Justice Parker Co. TX

Parker Co. TX - Field notes of survey of 160 ac. for WILLIAM C. BURTON by virtue his preemption affidavit No. 94 - Situate in Parker Co. on waters of Walnut Creek, tributary West Fork Trinity Riv. - Beg. SE of SE cor. WILLIAM D. FORE [?] 99 6/10 ac. preemption survey -

[79]   Surveyed: Apr 3 1857 - LEWELLEN MURPHY, Dept Surv Denton Land Dist
Chain Carriers: THOMAS S. BURTON, JAMES M. BURTON
Recorded: Jun 13 1857 - LEWELLEN MURPHY, Co Surv Parker Co Tx

Parker Co. TX - No. 59 - Before the undersigned authority this day came JANE MOSS as applicant and A. J. DYCHE and ROBERT S. PORTER, Jun., two disinterested and respectable witnesses. All of whom deposeth and saith that applicant was bonafide settled upon vacant land on the date of an act to authorize the location & settlement of the Mississippi & Pacific R. R. Reserve passed August 26th A. D. 1856 and has continued to reside upon the same
Signed: JANE "X" MOSS [mark], A. J. DYCHE, R. S. PORTER, Jr.

[80]   Sworn to & subscribed Feb 25 1857 before JOHN H PRINCE, Clerk Co Court Parker Co

Parker Co. TX - Field notes of survey of 160 acs. for JANE MOSS by virtue her preemption affidavit No. 59 - Situate in Parker Co. on waters of Grindstone Creek, tributary Brazos Riv. - Beg. on NW cor. A. J. DYCHE 160 ac. preemption survey

[81]   Surveyed: Mar 5 1857 - LEWELLEN MURPHY, Dept Surv Denton Land Dist
Chain Carriers: GEORGE W. LIGHT, HOWELL R. MOSS
Recorded: Jun 13 1857 - LEWELLEN MURPHY, Co Surv Parker Co Tx

Parker Co. TX - No 4. - Before the undersigned authority this day came OLIVER DAVIS as applicant and HENRY INNMAN and W. N. COZORT, two disinterested and respectable witnesses. All of whom deposeth and saith that applicant was bonafide settled

upon vacant land on the date of an act to authorize the location & settlement of the Mississippi & Pacific R. R. Reserve passed August 26th A. D. 1856 and has continued to reside upon the same
Signed: OLIVER "X" DAVIS [mark], HENRY INNMAN, W. N. COZORT

[82] Sworn to & subscribed Feb 10 1857 before JOHN H PRINCE, Clerk Co Court Parker Co

Parker Co. TX - Have Surveyed for OLIVER DAVIS 160 acs. by virtue affidavit No. 4 - Situate in Parker Co. S Fork Trinity Riv. about 1 mi. S 80° E from Weatherford - Beg. S from NE cor. & E boundary line of D. C. THOMAS 320 ac. survey - N boundary JOHN E. MILLER 160 ac. survey -
Surveyed: May 3 1857 - ISAAC O. HEADLEY, Dept Surv Parker Co
Chain Carriers: W. N. COZORT, ELSBERRY MILLER

"The JAMES A. YEOMEN 260 ac. survey is now substituted in place of D. G. THOMAS which became vacated" [right margin]

[83] Recorded: Jun 13 1857 - LEWELLEN MURPHY, Co Surv Parker Co Tx

Parker Co. TX - No. 31 - Before CHARLES GILDON, Notary Public in and for aforesaid Co., personally appeared THOMAS GOLHIER as applicant and JOHN BLACK and ISAAC C. FLETCHER, two disinterested and respectable witnesses. All of whom deposeth and saith that applicant was bonafide settled upon vacant land on August 26th A D 1856 and has continued to reside upon the same
Signed: THOMAS GOLHER, JOHN "X" BLACK [mark],
ISAAC C. "X" FLETCHER [mark]

[84] Sworn to & subscribed Mar 7 1857 before CHARLES GILDON, Notary Public

Parker Co. TX - Field notes of survey of 151 2/10 acs. for THOMAS GOLHER by virtue his preemption affidavit No. 31 - Situate in Parker Co. on waters of Ash Creek, tributary West Fork Trinity Riv. - Beg. N of SE cor. & the E boundary line of WILLIAM T. REYNOLDS 320 ac. preemption survey - W boundary of JAMES WITCHER 320 ac. preemption survey -

[85] Surveyed: Mar 7 1857 - LEWELLEN MURPHY, Dept Surv Denton Land Dist
Chain Carriers: PHILLIP S. BURROW, WILLIAM H. BURROW
Recorded: Jun 13 1857 - LEWELLEN MURPHY, Co Surv Parker Co Tx

Parker Co. TX - No. 55 - Before the undersigned authority this day came LEANNER LEE as applicant and LEVI KIDWELL and B. R. REYNOLDS, two disinterested and respectable witnesses. All of whom deposeth and saith that applicant was bonafide settled upon vacant land on the date of an act to authorize the loca-

tion & settlement of the Mississippi & Pacific R. R. Reserve passed August 26th A. D. 1856 and has continued to reside upon the same
Signed: LEANNER "X" LEE [her mark], LEVI KIDWELL, B. R. "X" REYNOLDS [mark]
Sworn to & subscribed Feb 24 1857 before JOHN H. PRINCE, Clerk Co Court Parker Co

Parker Co. TX - Field notes of survey of 160 acs. for LEANNER LEE by virtue her preemption affidavit No. 55 - Situate in Parker Co. on waters Brazos Riv. - Beg. N of SW cor. HARDIN LOGSDON 380 ac. survey -

[87] Surveyed: May 20 1857 - LEWELLEN MURPHY, Co Surv Parker Co Tx
Chain Carriers: SILAS BARNES, PERRY M. BARNES
Recorded: Jun 13 1857 - LEWELLEN MURPHY, Co Surv Parker Co Tx

Parker Co. TX - No. 76 - Before the undersigned authority this day came A. B. BROWN as applicant and J. B. MAJORS and ELEM MARTIN two disinterested and respectable witnesses. All of whom deposeth and saith that applicant was bonafide settled upon vacant land on the date of an act to authorize the location & settlement of the Mississippi & Pacific R. R. Reserve passed August 26th A. D. 1856 and has continued to reside upon the same

[88] Signed: A B BROWN, ELEM "X" MARTIN [mark], J B MAGORS
Sworn to & subscribed Feb 27 1857 before JOHN H. PRINCE, Clerk Co Court Parker Co, by WM. M. GREEN, Dept

Parker Co. TX - Field notes of survey of 160 acs. for ALBERT B. BROWN by virtue his preemption affidavit No. 76 - Situate in Parker Co. on waters Grindstone Creek, tributary Brazos Riv.- Beg. NW of N cor. JOHN W. BRASHEARS 160 ac. preemption survey -

[89] Surveyed: Mar 4 1857 - LEWELLEN MURPHY, Dept Surv Denton Land Dist
Chain Carriers: JAMES M. UPTON, ALLEN W. BROWN
Recorded: Jun 15 1857 - LEWELLEN MURPHY, Co Surv Parker Co Tx

Parker Co. TX - No. 32 - Before the undersigned authority this day came YOUNG WARREN as applicant and ASA GILMORE and J. H. HEWETT, two disinterested and respectable witnesses. All of whom deposeth and saith that applicant was bonafide settled upon vacant land on the date of an act to authorize the location & settlement of the Mississippi & Pacific R. R. Reserve passed August 26th A. D. 1856 and has continued to reside upon the same

[90] Signed: YOUNG "X" WARREN [mark], J H HEWETT, ASA GILMORE

Sworn to & subscribed Feb 23 1857 before JOHN H. PRINCE, Clerk Co Court Parker Co, by WM. M. GREEN, Dept

Parker Co. TX - Field notes of survey of 160 acs. for YOUNG WARREN by virtue his preemption affidavit No. 32 - Situate in Parker Co. on waters of Grindstone Creek, tributary Brazos Riv.- Beg. SW of SW cor. WILLIAM P. WILSON 160 ac. preemption survey -

[91] Surveyed: Mar 7 1857 - LEWELLEN MURPHY, Dept Surv Denton Land Dist
Chain Carriers: ASA GILMORE, ISRAEL BURROWS
Recorded: Jun 15 1857 - LEWELLEN MURPHY, Co Surv Parker Co Tx

[92] Parker Co. TX - No. 16 - Before the undersigned authority this day came JAMES JOHNSON as claimant and ISAAC PRICE and HENRY C. PRICE, two disinterested and respectable witnesses. All of whom deposeth and saith that applicant was bonafide settled upon vacant land on the date of an act to authorize the location & settlement of the Mississippi & Pacific R. R. Reserve passed August 26th A. D. 1856 and has continued to reside upon the same
Signed: JAMES "X" JOHNSON [mark], ISAAC "X" PRICE [mark], H. C. "X" PRICE [mark]
Sworn to & subscribed Feb 26 1857 before J. J. BEEMAN, Notary Public

Parker Co. TX - Field notes of survey of 160 acs. for JAMES JOHNSON by virtue his preemption affidavit No. 16 - Situate in Parker Co. on waters S Fork Clear Fork Trinity Riv. -

[93] Beg. SE from SE cor. of J. J. BEEMAN 160 ac. preemption survey -
Surveyed: May 2 1857 - LEWELLEN MURPHY, Dept Surv Denton Land Dist
Chain Carriers: WILLIAM B. GILLILAND, JAMES JOHNSON
Recorded: Jun 16 1857 - LEWELLEN MURPHY, Co Surv Parker Co Tx

[94] Parker Co TX - No 70 - Before JOHN MATLOCK, Chief Justice Parker Co., came EZEKIEL A. FLEMING as applicant and WILLIAM H. ALLEN and QUINTON N. ANDERSON, two disinterested and respectable witnesses. All of whom deposeth and saith that applicant was bonafide settled upon vacant land on August 26th A. D. 1856 and has continued to reside upon the same
Signed: EZEKIAL A FLEMING, QUINTON N ANDERSON, WILLIAM H ALLEN
Sworn to & subscribed Feb 27 1857 before JOHN MATLOCK, Chief Justice Parker Co.

Parker Co. TX, Denton Land Dist. - Field notes of survey of 160 acs. for EZEKIEL A. FLEMING -

[95] by virtue his affidavit No. 70 - Situate on waters of

Walnut Creek, tributary West Fork Trinity Riv. - Beg. NW of NE cor. A. C. HILLs 160 ac. survey - SW cor. G. W. DUNCANS 160 ac. survey -
Surveyed: May 5 1857 - R. J. BILLINGSLEA, D. S. D. L. D.
Chain Carriers: C. W. BLANTON, JAS. E. LEONARD
Recorded: Aug 31 1857 - LEWELLEN MURPHY, Co Surv Parker Co Tx

[96]   Parker Co. TX - No. 32 - Before CHARLES GILDON, Notary Public in and for aforesaid co., personally appeared JOHN BLACK as applicant and THOMAS GOLHIER and ISAAC C. FLETCHER, two disinterested and respectable witnesses. All of whom deposeth and saith that applicant was bonafide settled upon vacant land on August 26th A. D. 1856 and has continued to reside upon the same
Signed: JOHN "X" BLACK [mark], THOMAS GOLHER, ISAAC "X" C. FLETCHER [mark]
Sworn to & subscribed Mar 7 1857 before CHARLES GILDON, Notary Public

Parker Co. TX - Field notes of survey of 113 3/10 acs. for JOHN BLACK by virtue his preemption affidavit No. 32 -

[97] Situate in Parker Co. on waters of Silver Creek, tributary West Fork Trinity Riv. - Beg. N of NW cor. survey No. 29 of 160 ac. made in name of [blank - no name] -
Surveyed: Mar 25 1857 - LEWELLEN MURPHY, Dept Surv Denton Land Dist
Chain Carriers: AARON TUCKER, MOSES TUCKER
Recorded: Jun 22 1857 - LEWELLEN MURPHY, Co Surv Parker Co Tx

[98]   Parker Co. TX - No. 77 - Before the undersigned authority this day came WM. S. HERRING as applicant and A. B. BROWN and J. B. MAJORS, two disinterested and respectable witnesses. All of whom deposeth and saith that applicant was bonafide settled upon vacant land on the date of an act to authorize the location & settlement of the Mississippi & Pacific R. R. Reserve passed August 26th A. D. 1856 and has continued to reside upon the same
Signed: WM. S. HERRIN, A. B. BROWN, J. B. MAJORS
Sworn to & subscribed Feb 27 1857 before JOHN H. PRINCE, Clerk Co Court Parker Co, by WM. M. GREEN, Dept

Parker Co. TX - Field notes of survey of 160 acs. for WILLIAM S. HERRIN by virtue his preemption affidavit No. 77-

[99]   Situate in Parker Co. on Brazos Riv.- Beg. SW of S cor. Leon Co. School Land 960 ac. survey -
Surveyed: May 6 1857 - LEWELLEN MURPHY, Dept Surv Denton Land Dist
Chain Carriers: BENJAMIN K. BARTON, ALBERT B. BROWN

[100] Recorded: Jun 22 1857 - LEWELLEN MURPHY, Co Surv Parker Co Tx

Parker Co. TX - No. 75 - Before JOHN MATLOCK, Chief Justice Parker Co., personally came JOSEPH WALKER as applicant and EDWARD M. HARRIS and WILLIAM TAYLOR, two disinterested and respectable witnesses. All of whom deposeth and saith that applicant was bonafide settled upon vacant land on August 26th A. D. 1856 and has continued to reside upon the same
Signed: JOSEPH WALKER, EDWARD M. HARRIS, WILLIAM TAYLOR
Sworn to & subscribed Feb 28 1857 before JOHN MATLOCK, Chief Justice Parker Co.

[101] Parker Co. TX - Field notes of survey of 160 acs. for JOSEPH WALKER by virtue his preemption affidavit No. 75 - Situate in Parker Co. on waters Clear Fork Trinity Riv. - Beg. NW from NE cor. JONATHAN H. WALKER 160 ac. preemption survey -
Surveyed: Mar 23 1857 - LEWELLEN MURPHY, Dept Surv Denton Land Dist
Chain Carriers: ISAAC P. DAVIS, WILLIAM J. SILLIVENT

[102] Recorded: Jun 22 1857 - LEWELLEN MURPHY, Co Surv Parker Co Tx

Parker Co. TX - No. 19 - Before the undersigned authority this day came JOHN E. MILLER as applicant and LARKIN MC CARTY and G. W. HOLLINGSWORTH, two disinterested and respectable witnesses. All of whom deposeth and saith that applicant was bonafide settled upon vacant land on the date of an act to authorize the location & settlement of the Mississippi & Pacific R. R. Reserve passed August 26th A. D. 1856 and has continued to reside upon the same
Signed: JOHN E. "X" MILLER [mark], LARKIN M. [sic] CARTY, G. W. HOLLINGSWORTH
Sworn to & subscribed Feb 17 1857 before JOHN H. PRINCE, Clerk Co Court Parker Co

[103] Parker Co. TX - Have Surveyed for JOHN E. MILLER 160 ac. by virtue affidavit No. 19 - Situate in Parker Co. on S Fork Trinity Riv. about 1 1/2 mi. S 20° E from Weatherford - Beg. SE from NE cor. D. C. THOMAS 320 ac. survey -
Surveyed: Mar 31 1857 - ISAAC O. HEADLEY, Dept. Surveyor D. L. Dist.
Chain Carriers: DAVID STIMPSON, ELSBERRY MILLER

[104] Recorded: Jun 23 1587 - LEWELLEN MURPHY, Co Surv Parker Co Tx

Parker Co. TX - No. 19 - Before the undersigned authority this day came ANDREW SIMONS as claimant and JOHN TRIMBLE and A. G. [?] PISTOLE, two disinterested and respectable witnesses. All of whom deposeth and saith that applicant was bonafide settled

upon vacant land on the date of an act to authorize the location & settlement of the Mississippi & Pacific R. R. Reserve passed August 26th A. D. 1856 and has continued to reside upon the same
Signed: ANDREW SIMONS, A. J. PESTOLE, JOHN TRIMBLE
Sworn to & subscribed Feb 27 1857 before J. J. BEEMAN, Notary Public

[105] Parker Co. TX - Have surveyed for ANDREW SIMONS 160 acs. by virtue affidavit No. 19 - Situate in Parker Co. on S Fork Clear Fork Trinity Riv. about 2 1/2 mi. S 85° E from Weatherford Beg. E & S from SE cor. JOHN E. MILLER 160 ac. survey -
Surveyed: May 22 1857 - ISAAC O. HEADLEY, D. P. S. P. C.
Chain Carriers: JAMES SIMONS [?], VALINTINE SIMONS
Recorded: Jun 23 1857 - LEWELLEN MURPHY, Co Surv Parker Co Tx

[106] Parker Co. TX - Before the undersigned authority this day came ELSBERRY MILLER as applicant and DAVID STIMPSON and BERRY SPARKS, two disinterested and respectable witnesses. All of whom deposeth and saith that applicant was bonafide settled upon vacant land on the date of an act to authorize the location & settlement of the Mississippi & Pacific R. R. Reserve passed August 26th A. D. 1856 and has continued to reside upon the same
Signed: ELSBERRY "X" MILLER [mark], DAVID STIMPSON, BERRY SPARKS
Sworn to & subscribed Mar 30 1857 before JOHN H. PRINCE, Clerk Co. Co. Parker Co.

Parker Co. TX - Have surveyed for ELSBERRY MILLER 160 ac. by virtue affidavit No. [blank] - Situate in Parker Co. -

[107] about 2 mi. SE from Weatherford - Beg. SW from SE cor. JOHN E. MILLER 160 ac. survey -
Surveyed: Mar 31 1857 - ISAAC O. HEADLEY, Dept Surv Denton Land Dist
Chain Carriers: JOHN E. MILLR, DAVID STIMPSON
Recorded: Jun 23 1857 - LEWELLEN MURPHY, Co Surv Parker Co Tx

[108] Parker Co. TX - No. 29 - Before the undersigned authority this day came ABRAHAM PIPKIN as applicant and WM. OLINGER and R. P. BAKER [?], two disinterested and respectable witnesses. All of whom deposeth and saith that applicant was bonafide settled upon vacant land on the date of an act to authorize the location & settlement of the Mississippi & Pacific R. R. Reserve passed August 26th A. D. 1856 and has continued to reside upon the same
Signed: ABRAHAM PIPKIN, WM. T. OLINGER, R. P. BAKER
Sworn to & subscribed Feb 23 1857 before JOHN H. PRINCE, Clerk Co Court Parker Co, by WM. M. GREEN, Dept

Parker Co. TX - Have surveyed for ABRAHAM PIPKIN 160 acs. by virtue affidavit No. 29 - Situate in Parker Co. waters of Clear Fork Trinity Riv. about 4 mi. S 80° E from Weatherford -

[109] Beg. SW from SW cor. E. [?] J. EDDLEMAN 320 ac. survey
Surveyed: May 25 1857 - ISAAC O. HEADLEY, Dept Surv Parker Co
Chain Carriers: OLIVER DAVIS, JOSEPH M. INNMAN
Recorded: Jun 23 1857 - LEWELLEN MURPHY, Co Surv Parker Co Tx

[110] Parker Co. TX - No 155 - Before the undersigned authority this day came T. J. SHAW as applicant and SAMUEL R. BARBER and J. A. GARDNER, two disinterested and respectable witnesses. All of whom deposeth and saith that applicant was bonafide settled upon vacant land on the date of an act to authorize the location & settlement of the Mississippi & Pacific R. R. Reserve passed August 26th A. D. 1856 and has continued to reside upon the same
Signed: T. J. SHAW, SAM. R. BARBER, J. A. GARDNER
Sworn to & subscribed May 16 1857 before JOHN H. PRINCE, Clerk Co Court Parker Co

Parker Co. TX - Have surveyed for THOMAS J. SHAW 143 acs. by virtue affidavit No. 155 - Situate in Parker Co. on Spring Creek, tributary Brazos Riv.- Beg. NE from NW cor. Leon Co. survey -

[111] Surveyed: May 16 1857, I. O. HEADLEY, D. S. D. L. D.
Chain Carriers: ROBERT GALE, THOMAS J. SHAW
Recorded: Jun 24 1857 - LEWELLEN MURPHY, Co Surv Parker Co Tx

Parker Co. TX - No. 88 - Before JOHN MATLOCK, Chief Justice Parker Co. TX, personally came JAMES E. LEONARD as applicant and WILLIAM J. ELLIS and QUINTON N. ANDERSON, two disinterested and respectable witnesses. All of whom deposeth and saith that applicant was bonafide settled upon vacant land on August 26th A. D. 1856 and has continued to reside upon the same

[112] Signed: JAMES E LEONARD, W J ELLIS, QUINTON N ANDERSON
Sworn to & subscribed Mar 21 1857 before JOHN MATLOCK, Chief Justice Parker Co. TX

Parker Co. TX - Field notes of survey of 160 acs. for JAMES E. LEONARD by virtue his preemption affidavit No. 88 - Situate in Parker Co. on waters of Walnut Creek, tributary West Fork Trinity Riv. - Beg. at SW cor. MARY LEONARD 160 preemption survey -

[113] SE cor. QUINTON N. ANDERSON 160 ac. preemption survey -
Surveyed: Apr 1 1857 - LEWELLEN MURPHY, Dept Surv Denton Land Dist
Chain Carriers: SAMUEL S. LEONARD, ROBERT A. HENDERSON
Recorded: Jun 24 1857 - LEWELLEN MURPHY, Co Surv Parker Co Tx

[114]   Parker Co. TX - No. 64 - Before the undersigned authority this day came JOHN GRISHAM as applicant and ALEXANDER M. BRASHERES and JOHN W. BRASHERS two disinterested and respectable witnesses. All of whom deposeth and saith that applicant was bonafide settled upon vacant land on the date of an act to authorize the location & settlement of the Mississippi & Pacific R. R. Reserve passed August 26th A. D. 1856 and has continued to reside upon the same
Signed: JOHN GRISHAM, ALEXANDER M. BRASHERS, JOHN W. BRASHERS
Sworn to & subscribed Feb 26 1857 before JOHN H. PRINCE, Clerk Co Court Parker Co, by WM. M. GREEN, Dept

Parker Co. TX - Field notes of survey of 160 acs. for JOHN GRISHAM by virtue his preemption affidavit No. 64 -

[115]   Situate in Parker Co. on waters of Grindstone Creek, tributary Brazos Riv.- Beg. SW of SW cor. WILLIAM UPTON 160 ac. preemption survey -
Surveyed: Mar 13 1857 - LEWELLEN MURPHY, Dept Surv Denton Land Dist
Chain Carriers: WILLIAM BRASHERS, ALEXANDER M. BRASHEARS
Recorded: Jun 24 1857 - LEWELLEN MURPHY, Co Surv Parker Co Tx

[116]   Parker Co. TX - No 129 - Before the undersigned authority this day came JOHN SQUIRES as applicant and ANDERSON GREEN and A. W. GREEN, two disinterested and respectable witnesses. All of whom deposeth and saith that applicant was bonafide settled upon vacant land on the date of an act to authorize the location & settlement of the Mississippi & Pacific R. R. Reserve passed August 26th A. D. 1856 and has continued to reside upon the same
Signed: JOHN SQUIRES, ANDERSON GREEN, A. M. [?] GREEN
Sworn to & subscribed Mar 28 1857 before JOHN H. PRINCE, Clerk Co Court Parker Co, by WM. M. GREEN, Dept

Parker Co. TX - Field notes of survey of 160 acs. for JOHN SQUIRES by virtue his preemption affidavit No. 129 - Situate in Parker Co. on waters Clear Fork Trinity Riv. -

[117]   Beg. SW of NW cor. J. T. SMITH 320 ac. survey -
Surveyed: Mar 30 1857 - LEWELLEN MURPHY, Dept Surv Denton Land Dist
Chain Carriers: THOMAS J. GREEN, JOHN W. MURPHY
Recorded: Jun 24 1857 - LEWELLEN MURPHY, Co Surv Parker Co Tx

[118]   State of Texas
        County of Parker | Before me, J. H. PRINCE, Clerk Co. Court Parker Co., personally appeared JOHN SHEEN, to me known and who being duly sworn says on oath that DAVID STIMSON settled and made improvements upon the tract of land situated in Parker Co. which he claims by virtue of then existing preemption Law previous to the 21st

Dec A. D. 1853 and that JAMES COOK, and JAMES H. MAYS prevented said STIMSON from having a survey of said land completed on the 21st March A. D. 1854 by forbidding the survey and by force and arms accompanied by violent threats of the said STIMSON. Said SHEEN further states that JAMES COOK and JAMES H. MAYS did not settle upon the respected tract of land which they now claim by virtue of the preemption Laws until after the 13th of Feb A. D. 1854.
Signed: JOHN SHEEN
Sworn to & subscribed before me on this the 1st day of Dec A D 1856 - JOHN H. PRINCE, C. C. P. C. Texas

State of Texas
County of Parker | Before me, JOHN H. PRINCE, Clerk Co. Court of Parker Co., personally appeared JAS. H. SEWELL and who being duly sworn says on oath that DAVID STIMSON settled upon the tract of land for which he claims 320 acs. as a preemption under the act of Jan 22 1845, prior to the 21st of Dec 1853 and that he believes that he is entitled to the same under said act. Said SEWELL further states that JAMES COOK is not entitled to a preemption under the act of Jan 22 1845 as he did not settle upon the tract of land upon which he now resides and which he claims under said act until after the passage of the

[119] act of Feb 13 1854 which granted to actual settlers 160 acs. of land.
Signed: JAMES H. SEWELL
Sworn to & subscribed before me this 29th June A. D. 1857 - JOHN H. PRINCE, C. C. C. P. C. Texas

State of Texas
County of Parker | Before me, R. C. HART, an acting Justice of the Peace in and for the state and county aforesaid, personally appeared THOMPSON MASON, who being duly sworn says that DAVID STIMSON settled upon the tract of land which he claims as a preemption prior to the 21st day of Dec 1853 and that he was prevented from having a survey of the same completed on the 21st of Mar 1854 by JAMES COOK and others by forbidding the survey and by force and arms. He also states that JAMES COOK did not settle upon the tract of land which he claims as preemption until after the 13th of Feb 1854.
Signed: THOMPSON "X" MASON [mark]
Sworn to & subscribed before me, R. C. HART, Esqr., this June 23rd 1857

State of Texas
County of Parker | I, JOHN ADAMS, do Solemnly swear that DAVID STIMSON settled upon land he claims as a preemption survey of 320 acs. before the 21st of Dec A D 1853 and that at time of said STIMSONs settlement there was no con-

flicting claim.
Signed: JOHN "X" ADAMS [mark]
Sworn to & subscribed before me this 13th Jul A. D. 1857 -
JOHN H. PRINCE, Co. Clerk Parker Co., TX

[120] State of Texas
County of Parker | Before me, R. J. BILLINGSLEE, Dept Surveyor of Denton Land Dist., personally appeared DAVID STIMSON, who being duly sworn says on oath that he settled and improvement [sic] on a certain tract of land previous to the 21st day of Dec 1853 which he believed to be vacant public domain of the state and that he is entitled to 320 acs. of land under the provisions of an act authorizing persons to hold 320 acs. of land. Given under my hand and seal using a scroll for seal this 25th day of March A. D. 1857
Signed: DAVID STIMSON
Sworn to & subscribed before me, R. J. BILLINGSLEE, Dept Surv of Denton Land Dist., on the day and date above written R. J. BILLINGSLEE, Dept Surv Denton Land Dist

Parker Co. TX, Denton Land Dist. - Field notes of survey of 320 acs. for DAVID STIMSON by virtue foregoing affidavit hereunto attached No. 2nd, issued 25th Mar 1857 - Situate on waters of Clear Fork tributary of the West Fork Trinity Riv. - Beg. on SW cor. JOHN SHEENs 320 ac. survey -

[121] Surveyed: Mar 25 1857 - R. J. BILLINGSLEE, Dept Surv Denton Land Dist
Chain Carriers: ISAAC PRICE, BALEY HILL
Recorded: Jul 15 1857 - LEWELLEN MURPHY, Co Surv Parker Co Tx

Parker Co. TX - No. 170 - Before JOHN H. PRINCE, Clerk Co Court Parker Co TX, personally came E. A. S. L. IKARD as applicant and MILTON IKARD and L. J. GILBERT, two disinterested and respectable witnesses. All of whom deposeth and saith that applicant was settled upon vacant land in June 1856 and remained there 1 month, building a house - but was absent from his claim at date on an act to authorize the location and settlement of Mississippi & Pacific Rail Road Reserve passed Aug 26th 1856 for the purpose of procuring bread from another county and makes this affidavit to avail himself of the provisions of the act above recited
Signed: E. A. S. L. IKARD, M. IKARD, L. J. "X" GILBERT [mark]
Sworn to & subscribed Jun 27 1857 before JOHN H. PRINCE, Clerk Co Court Parker Co TX

[122] Parker Co. TX - Field notes of survey of 160 acs. for E. A. S. L. IKARD by virtue his preemption affidavit No. 170 - Situate in Parker Co. on Brazos Riv. about 16 mi. S 65° W from Weatherford - Beg. on SW bank of Brazos Riv. W & S of W cor. L D MEEK 160 ac. preemption survey - E boundary line L J GILBERT

preemption survey -
Surveyed: Jun 29 1857 - LEWELLEN MURPHY, Co Surv Parker Co
Chain Carriers: WILSON LITTLEFIELD, MILTON IKARD

[123]   Recorded: Jul 25 1857 - LEWELLEN MURPHY, Co Surv Parker Co Tx

Parker Co. TX - No. 75 - Before the undersigned authority this day came LARKIN MC CARTY as applicant and A. G. PISTOLE and J. B. BILLINGSLY, two disinterested and respectable witnesses. All of whom deposeth and saith that applicant was bonafide settled upon vacant land on the date of an act to authorize the location & settlement of the Mississippi & Pacific R. R. Reserve passed August 26th A. D. 1856 and has continued to reside upon the same
Signed: LARKIN MC CARTY, A. G. PISTOLE, J. B. BILLINGSLY
Sworn to & subscribed Feb 27 1857 before JOHN H. PRINCE, Clerk Co Court Parker Co TX

[124]   Parker Co. TX - Have surveyed for LARKIN MC CARTY 160 ac. by virtue affidavit No. 75 - Situate in Parker Co. 1 mi. S from Weatherford - Beg. SW from SE cor. Parker Co. 320 ac. survey -
Surveyed: May 25 1857 - ISAAC O. HEADLEY, Dept Surv Parker Co
Chain Carriers: B. F. POLK, JACKSON FIDLER

[125]   Recorded: Jul 25 1857 - LEWELLEN MURPHY, Co Surv Parker Co TX

Parker Co. TX - No. 4 - Before the undersigned authority this day came N. H. PITTILLO as applicant and JAMES C. STROUD and WILEY STROUD, two disinterested and respectable witnesses. All of whom deposeth and saith that applicant was bonafide settled upon vacant land on the date of an act to authorize the location & settlement of the Mississippi & Pacific R. R. Reserve passed August 26th A. D. 1856 and has continued to reside upon the same
Signed: N. H. PITTILLO, JAMES C. STROUD, WILEY STROUD
Sworn to & subscribed Feb 27 1857 before R. A. EDDLEMAN, Notary Public Parker Co TX

[126]   Parker Co. TX - Have Surveyed for N. H. PITTILLO 160 acs. by virtue affidavit No. 4 - Situate in Parker Co. on Spring Creek, tributary stream of Brazos Riv. - Beg. SW from SE cor. R. C. EDDLEMAN 160 ac. survey -
Surveyed: Apr 14 1857 - ISAAC O. HEADLEY, D. S. D. L. D
Chain Carriers: J. W. PITTILLO, R. C. EDDLEMAN

[127]   Recorded: Jul 29 1857 - LEWELLEN MURPHY, Co Surv Parker Co TX

Parker Co. TX - No. 7 - This day personally came WILEY STROUD

as applicant and N. H. PITTILLO and RICHARD C. EDDLEMAN, two disinterested and respectable witnesses. All of whom deposeth and saith that applicant was bonafide settled upon vacant land on the date of an act to authorize the location & settlement of the Mississippi & Pacific R. R. Reserve passed August 26th A. D. 1856 and has continued to reside upon the same
Signed: WILEY STROUD, N. H. PITTILLO, R. C. EDDLEMAN
Sworn to & subscribed Feb 27 1857 before R. A. EDDLEMAN, Notary Public Parker Co.

[128] Parker Co. TX - Have surveyed for WILEY STROUD 160 acs. by virtue affidavit No. 7 - Situate in Parker Co. on Spring Creek, tributary Brazos Riv. - Beg. SE from NW cor. N. H. PITTILLO 160 ac. survey -
Surveyed: Apr 15 1857 - ISAAC O. HEADLEY, D. S. D. L. Dist.
Chain Carriers: J. C. STROUD, J. S. STROUD

[129] Recorded: Jul 30 1857 - LEWELLEN MURPHY, Co Surv Parker Co TX

Parker Co. TX - No. 5 - Before the undersigned authority this day came R. C. EDDLEMAN as applicant and JAMES C. STROUD and JOHN S. STROUD, two disinterested and respectable witnesses. All of whom deposeth and saith that applicant was bonafide settled upon vacant land on the date of an act to authorize the location & settlement of the Mississippi & Pacific R. R. Reserve passed August 26th A. D. 1856 and has continued to reside upon the same
Signed: R. C. EDDLEMAN, JAMES C. STROUD, JOHN S. STROUD
Sworn to & subscribed Feb 27 1857 before R. A. EDDLEMAN, Notary Public Parker Co.

[130] Parker Co. TX - Have surveyed for R. C. EDDLEMAN 160 acs. by virtue affidavit No. 5 - Situate in Parker Co. on Spring Creek, tributary Brazos Riv. - Beg. W & S from SW cor. JESSE THOMAS 320 ac. survey -
Surveyed: Apr 14 1857 - ISAAC O. HEADLEY, Dept Surv Denton Land Dist
Chain Carriers: C. A. EDDLEMAN, J. W. PITTILLO

[131] Recorded: Jul 30 1857 - LEWELLEN MURPHY, Co Surv Parker Co TX

Parker Co. TX - No. 2 - This day personally came JAMES C. STROUD as applicant and N. H. PITTILLO and R. C. EDDLEMAN, two disinterested and respectable witnesses. All of whom deposeth and saith that applicant was bonafide settled upon vacant land on the date of an act to authorize the location & settlement of the Mississippi & Pacific R. R. Reserve passed August 26th A. D. 1856 and has continued to reside upon the same
Signed: JAMES C. STROUD, N. H. PITTILLO, R. C. EDDLEMAN

Sworn to & subscribed Feb 27 1857 before R. A. EDDLEMAN, Notary Public Parker Co.

[132] Parker Co. TX - Have surveyed for JAMES C. STROUD 89 acs. by virtue affidavit No. 2 - Situate in Parker Co. on Spring Creek, tributary Brazos Riv. - Beg. SW from SW cor. WILEY STROUD 160 ac. survey -
Surveyed: Apr 15 1857 - ISAAC O. HEADLEY, Dept Surv Denton Land Dist
Chain Carriers: J. C. STROUD, J. S. STROUD

[133] Recorded: Jul 30 1857 - LEWELLEN MURPHY, Co Surv Parker Co TX

Parker Co. TX - No. 3 - Before the undersigned authority this day came JOHN S. STROUD as applicant and N. H. PITTILLO and R. C. EDDLEMAN, two disinterested and respectable witnesses. All of whom deposeth and saith that applicant was bonafide settled upon vacant land on the date of an act to authorize the location & settlement of the Mississippi & Pacific R. R. Reserve passed August 26th A. D. 1856 and has continued to reside upon the same
Signed: JOHN S. STROUD, N. H. PITTILLO, R. C. EDDLEMAN
Sworn to & subscribed Feb 27 1857 before R. A. EDDLEMAN, Notary Public Parker Co.

[134] Parker Co. TX - Have surveyed for J. S. STROUD 113 acs. by virtue affidavit No. 3 - Situate in Parker Co. on Spring Creek, tributary Brazos Riv. - Beg. NE from SW cor. & S boundary of J. C. STROUD 89 ac. survey -
Surveyed: Apr 15 1857 - ISAAC O. HEADLEY, Dept Surv Denton Land Dist
Chain Carriers: J. C. STROUD, J. S. STROUD

[135] Recorded: Jul 31 1857 - LEWELLEN MURPHY, Co Surv Parker Co TX

Parker Co. TX - No. 6 - Before JOHN MATLOCK, Chief Justice Parker Co. TX, personally appeared SAMUEL R. BARBER as applicant and ZEBADEE P. SHURLEY and ROBERT P. BAKER, two disinterested and respectable witnesses. All of whom deposeth and saith that applicant was bonafide settled upon vacant land on the date of an act to authorize the location & settlement of the Mississippi & Pacific R. R. Reserve passed August 26th A D 1856 and has continued to reside upon the same
Signed: SAMUEL R. BARBER, ZEBEDEE P. SHURLEY, ROBERT P. BAKER

[136] Sworn to & subscribed Jan 31 1857 before JOHN MATLOCK, Chief Justice Parker Co.

Parker Co. TX - Have surveyed for SAML. R. BARBER 160 acs. by virtue affidavit No. 6 - Situate in Parker Co. about 3 1/2 mi.

from Weatherford on waters of Brazos Riv. - Beg. E & N from NE cor. HANIBAL GOOD 320 ac. survey -

[137] Surveyed: May 10 1857 - ISAAC O. HEADLEY, Dept Surv Denton Land Dist
Chain Carriers: S. F. JONES, A. J. HUNTER
Recorded: Aug 3 1857 - LEWELLEN MURPHY, Co Surv Parker Co TX

Parker Co. TX - No. 124 - Before the undersigned authority this day came R. P. BARTON as applicant and SAML. LITTLEFIELD and G. W. GUEST, two disinterested and respectable witnesses. All of whom deposeth and saith that applicant was bonafide settled upon vacant land on the date of an act to authorize the location & settlement of the Mississippi & Pacific R. R. Reserve passed August 26th A. D. 1856 and has continued to reside upon the same
Signed: R. D. BARTON, SAMUEL LITTLEFIELD, G. W. GUEST

[138] Sworn to & subscribed Mar 28 1857 before JOHN H PRINCE, Clerk Co Court Parker Co.

Parker Co. TX - Field notes of survey of 160 acs. for R. P. BARTON by virtue his preemption affidavit No. 124 - Situate in Parker Co. on Brazos Riv. about 15 or 16 mi. S 55° W from Weatherford - Beg. in bed of Brazos Riv. W & S of SW cor. MARY MEEK 160 ac. preemption survey -

[139] Surveyed: Jul 1 1857 - LEWELLEN MURPHY, Co Surv Parker Co
Chain Carriers: WADDY THOMPSON, J. W. GUEST
Recorded: Aug 3 1857 - LEWELLEN MURPHY, Co Surv Parker Co TX

Parker Co. TX - No. 185 - Personally before me came C. F. BOWMAN as applicant and D. H. SISK and J. M. WEST, two disinterested and respectable witnesses. All of whom deposeth and saith that applicant was bonafide settled upon vacant land on the date of an act to authorize the location & settlement of the Mississippi & Pacific R. R. Reserve passed August 26th A. D. 1856 and has continued to reside upon the same

[140] Signed: C. F. BOWMAN, J. M. WEST, D. H. SISK
Sworn to & subscribed Aug 3 1857 before JOHN H. PRINCE, Clerk Co Court Parker Co.

Parker Co. TX - Field notes of survey of 160 acs. for C. F. BOWMAN by virtue his preemption affidavit No. 185 - Situate in Parker Co. on waters of Red Bear Creek, tributary Clear Fork Trinity Riv. about 10 mi. SE from Weatherford - Beg. NW from NW cor. DAVID SPEAR 160 ac. survey -

[141] Surveyed: Aug 4 1857 - LEWELLEN MURPHY, Co Surv Parker Co

Chain Carriers: WILLIAM C. MC KAMY, MILES ALBERT BEACH
Recorded: Aug 5 1857 - LEWELLEN MURPHY, Co Surv Parker Co TX

Parker Co. TX - No. 20 - Before the undersigned authority this day came ISAAC ANDERSON as applicant and JAMES H. MAYS and JAMES COOK, two disinterested and respectable witnesses. All of whom deposeth and saith that applicant was bonafide settled upon vacant land on the date of an act to authorize the location & settlement of the Mississippi & Pacific R. R. Reserve passed August 26th A. D. 1856 and has continued to reside upon the same

[142] Signed: ISAAC ANDERSON, JAMES COOK, JAMES H. MAYS
Sworn to & subscribed Feb 20 1857 before JOHN H. PRINCE, Clerk Co Court Parker Co.

Parker Co. TX - Have surveyed 160 acs. for ISAAC ANDERSON by virtue affidavit No. 20 - Situate in Parker Co. 6 mi. N 60° W from Weatherford on S Fork waters of Clear Fork Trinity Riv. - Beg. SE from SW cor. JAMES H. MAYS 320 ac. survey -

[143] Surveyed: Jul 15 1857 - ISAAC O. HEADLEY, D. S. P. C.
Chain Carriers: ISAAC ANDERSON, JAMES KIDWELL Seign. [sic]
Recorded: Aug 6 1857 - LEWELLEN MURPHY, Co Surv Parker Co TX

Parker Co. TX - No. 119 - Before the undersigned authority this day came WILSON LITTLEFIELD as applicant and L. J. GILBERT and SAMUEL LITTLEFIELD, two disinterested and respectable witnesses. All of whom deposeth and saith that applicant was bonafide settled upon vacant land on the date of an act to authorize the location & settlement of the Mississippi & Pacific R. R. Reserve passed August 26th A. D. 1856 and has continued to reside upon the same

[144] Signed: WILSON "X" LITTLEFIELD [mark], SAMUEL LITTLEFIELD, L. J. "X" GILBERT [mark]
Sworn to & subscribed Mar 28 1857 before JOHN H. PRINCE, Clerk Co Court Parker Co.

Parker Co. TX - Field notes of survey of 160 acs. for WILSON LITTLEFIELD by virtue his preemption affidavit No. 119 - Situate in Parker Co. on Brazos Riv. about 16 mi. S 65° W from Weatherford - Beg. SW from -

[145] W cor. LEMUEL J. GILBERT 160 ac. preemption survey -
Surveyed: Jun 29 1857 - LEWELLEN MURPHY, Co Surv Parker Co
Chain Carriers: JAMES M. GILBERT, LEMUEL J. GILBERT

[146] Recorded: Aug 7 1857 - LEWELLEN MURPHY, Co Surv Parker Co TX

Parker Co. TX - No. 120 - Before the undersigned authority

this day came L. J. GILBERT as applicant and WILSON LITTLE-
FIELD and SAMUEL LITTLEFIELD, two disinterested and respectable witnesses. All of whom deposeth and saith that applicant
was bonafide settled upon vacant land on the date of an act to
authorize the location & settlement of the Mississippi & Pacific R. R. Reserve passed August 26th A. D. 1856 and has continued to reside upon the same
Signed: L. J. "X" GILBERT [mark], SAMUEL LITTLEFIELD, WILSON
"X" LITTLEFIELD [mark]
Sworn to & subscribed Mar 28 1857 before JOHN H. PRINCE, Clerk
Co Court Parker Co.

[147] Parker Co. TX - Field notes of survey of 160 acs. for
LEMUEL J. GILBERT by virtue his preemption affidavit No. 120 -
Situate in Parker Co. on Brazos Riv. about 16 mi. S 65° W from
Weatherford - Beg. W & N of W cor. L. D. MEEK 160 ac. pre-
emption survey -
Surveyed: Jun [torn] 185[torn]

[148] Chain Carriers: JAMES M. GILBERT, WILSON LITTLEFIELD
Recorded: Aug 7 1857 - LEWELLEN MURPHY, Co Surv Parker Co TX

Parker Co. TX - No. 123 - Before the undersigned authority
this day came SAML. LITTLEFIELD as applicant and J. W. GUEST
and R. P. BARTON, two disinterested and respectable witnesses.
All of whom deposeth and saith that applicant was bonafide
settled upon vacant land on the date of an act to authorize
the location & settlement of the Mississippi & Pacific R. R.
Reserve passed August 26th A. D. 1856 and has continued to
reside upon the same
Signed: SAMUEL LITTLEFIELD, R P BARTON, J W "X" GUEST [mark]

[149] Sworn to & subscribed Mar 28 1857 before JOHN H PRINCE,
Clerk Co Court Parker Co.

Parker Co. TX - Field notes of survey of 160 acs. for SAMUEL
LITTLEFIELD by virtue his preemption affidavit No. 123 - Situate in Parker Co. on Brazos Riv. about 15 or 16 mi. S 65° W
from Weatherford - Beg. N of E cor. LEMUEL J. GILBERT 160 ac.
preemption survey -

[page no. torn] Surveyed: Jun 30 1857 - LEWELLEN MURPHY, Co
Surv Parker Co
Chain Carriers: FRANCIS M. ELLISON, LEMUEL J. GILBERT
Recorded: Aug 7 1857 - LEWELLEN MURPHY, Co Surv Parker Co TX

Parker Co. TX - No. 57 - Before the undersigned authority this
day came JAMES KIDWELL as applicant and LEVI KIDWELL and BENJ.
R. REYNOLDS, two disinterested and respectable witnesses. All
of whom deposeth and saith that applicant was bonafide settled
upon vacant land on the date of an act to authorize the location & settlement of the Mississippi & Pacific R. R. Reserve

passed August 26th A. D. 1856 and has continued to reside upon the same

[151] Signed: JAMES "X" KIDWELL [mark], LEVI KIDWELL, B. R. "X" REYNOLDS [mark]
Sworn to & subscribed Feb 24 1857 before JOHN H. PRINCE, Clerk Co Court Parker Co. TX

Parker Co. TX - Have surveyed 160 acs. for JAMES KIDWELL by virtue affidavit No. 57 - Situate in Parker Co. on Clear Fork Trinity Riv. about 6 mi. N 60° W from Weatherford - Beg. E from SE cor. ISAAC ANDERSON 160 ac. survey -

[152] Surveyed: Jul 15 1857 - ISAAC O. HEADLEY, Dept Surv Parker Co
Chain Carriers: STEPHEN KIDWELL, B. R. REYNOLDS
Recorded: Aug 10 1857 - LEWELLEN MURPHY, Co Surv Parker Co TX

[153] Parker Co. TX - No 171 - Before JOHN H. PRINCE, Clerk Co. Court Parker Co. TX, personally appeared AMESLEY PARSONS as applicant and R. E. BYRD and TILMON BOYD, two disinterested and respectable witnesses. All of whom deposeth and saith that applicant was bonafide settled upon vacant land on the date of an act to authorize the location & settlement of the Mississippi & Pacific R. R. Reserve passed August 26th A. D. 1856 and has continued to reside upon the same
Signed: AMESLEY PARSONS, T. BOYD, R. E. BYRD
Sworn to & subscribed Jun 27 1857 before JOHN H. PRINCE, Clerk Co Court Parker Co.

Parker Co. TX - Have Surveyed: for AMESLEY PARSONS 160 acs. by virtue affidavit No. 117 [?] - Situate in Parker Co. on E prong Red Bear Creek, waters of Brazos Riv. -

[154] Beg. NE from N cor. ALEXANDER W. PATTON 738 ac. survey
Surveyed: Aug 12 1857 - ISAAC O. HEADLEY, Dept Surv Parker Co
Chain Carriers: JAMES C. HEFFINGTON, AMESLEY PARSONS
Recorded: Aug 22 1857 - LEWELLEN MURPHY, Co Surv Parker Co TX

[155] Parker Co. TX - No. 16 - Before the undersigned authority this day came LORENZO D. SKIDMORE as applicant and JOSHUA BARKER and J. J. BEEMAN, two disinterested and respectable witnesses. All of whom deposeth and saith that applicant was bonafide settled upon vacant land on the date of an act to authorize the location & settlement of the Mississippi & Pacific R. R. Reserve passed August 26th A. D. 1856 and has continued to reside upon the same
Signed: L. D. SKIDMORE, JOSHUA BARKER, J. J. BEEMAN
Sworn to & subscribed Feb 17 1857 before JOHN H. PRINCE, Clerk Co Court Parker Co.

Parker Co. TX - Have Surveyed for L. D. SKIDMORE 160 acs. by

virtue affidavit No. 16 - Situate in Parker Co. on waters
Clear Fork Trinity Riv. -

[156] Beg. NW from NE cor. PETER KIRK 320 ac. survey -
Surveyed: Jul 3 1857 - ISAAC O. HEADLEY, Dept Surv Parker Co
Chain Carriers: J. M. JONES, J. S. [?] THORNSBURG
Recorded: Sep 2 1857 - LEWELLEN MURPHY, Co Surv Parker Co TX

Parker Co. TX - No. 175 - Before the undersigned authority
this day came JAMES R. CAMPBELL as applicant and THOMAS
JACKSON and -

[157] JAMES C. EDWARDS, two disinterested and respectable
witnesses. All of whom deposeth and saith that applicant was
bonafide settled upon vacant land on the date of an act to
authorize the location & settlement of the Mississippi & Pacific R. R. Reserve passed August 26th A. D. 1856 and has continued to reside upon the same
Signed: JAMES R. CAMPBELL, THOMAS JACKSON, JAMES C. EWARDS
Sworn to & subscribed Jul 4 1857 before JOHN H. PRINCE, Clerk
Co Court Parker Co., by WM. M. GREEN, Dept

Parker Co. TX - Have Surveyed for JAMES R. CAMPBELL 160 acs.
by virtue affidavit No. 175 - Situate in Parker Co. on waters
Clear Fork Trinity Riv. about 5 mi. N 45° E from Weatherford
- Beg. E & N of NE cor. of 320 ac.-

[158] survey of JOHN ADAMS -
Surveyed: Jul 7 1857 - ISAAC O. HEADLEY, Dept Surv Parker Co
Chain Carriers: W. B. GILLILAND, JOSEPH C. GILLILAND
Recorded: Sep 2 1857 - LEWELLEN MURPHY, Co Surv Parker Co TX

"The SW cor. of J. R. CAMPBELL's survey is situated 1633 vs. N
41° E from NE cor. of 320 ac. in name of JOHN ADAMS" [left
margin this sheet]

Parker Co. TX - No. 23 - Before CHARLES GILDON, Notary Public
in and for aforesaid co. personally came

[159] WM. H. ALLEN as applicant and THOS. CULWELL and S. S.
LEONARD, two disinterested and respectable witnesses. All of
whom deposeth and saith that applicant was bonafide settled
upon vacant land on August 26th A. D. 1856 and has continued
to reside upon the same
Signed: WILLIAM H. ALLEN, THOS. "X" CULWELL [mark], S. S.
LEONARD
Sworn to & subscribed Feb 23 1857 before CHARLES GILDON, Notary Public

Parker Co. TX - Field notes of survey of 160 acs. for WILLIAM
H. ALLEN -

[160] by virtue his preemption affidavit No. 23 - Situate in Parker Co. on waters of Walnut Creek, tributary West Fork Trinity Riv. about 13 mi. N 17° E from Weatherford - Beg. NW cor. THOMAS CULWELL, Junr., 160 ac. survey - N. boundary line THOMAS CULWELL, Senr., 160 ac. preemption survey - E. boundary line JAMES CULWELLs preemption -

[161] Surveyed: Aug 1 1857 - LEWELLEN MURPHY, Co Surv Parker Co
Chain Carriers: THOMAS CULWELL, MERRICK BARTLETT
Recorded: Sep 2 1857 - LEWELLEN MURPHY, Co Surv Parker Co TX

Parker Co. TX - No. 169 - Before JOHN H. PRINCE, Clerk Co. Court Parker Co. TX, came CALVIN LYNCH as applicant and JAMES L. EDWARDS and MASON Y. NOLAND, two disinterested and respectable witnesses. All of whom deposeth and saith that applicant was bonafide settled upon vacant land on the date of an act to authorize the location & settlement of the Mississippi & Pacific R. R. Reserve passed August 26th A. D. 1856 and has continued to reside upon the same

[162] Signed: CALVIN LYNCH, N. Y. NOLAND, JAMES L. EDWARDS
Sworn to & subscribed Jun 4 1857 before JOHN H. PRINCE, Clerk Co Court Parker Co.

Parker Co. TX - Field notes of survey of 160 acs. for CALVIN LYNCH by virtue his affidavit No. 169 - Situate on waters Clear Fork tributary West Fork Trinity Riv. - Beg. on NE cor. of L. P. MC DONALD's 320 ac. preemption survey -

[163] Surveyed: Aug 9 1857 - R. J. BILLINGSLEA, Dept Surv Parker Co
Chain Carriers: WILLIAM COALMAN, S. MAY [?] JONES
Recorded: Sep 2 1857 - LEWELLEN MURPHY, Co Surv Parker Co TX

Parker Co. TX - No. 93 - Before JOHN MATLOCK, Chief Justice Parker Co. TX, personally came TIMOTHY H. LUCKY as applicant and ANDREW JONES and CHARLES N. GARRET, two disinterested and respectable witnesses. All of whom deposeth and saith that applicant was bonafide settled upon vacant land on August 26th A. D. 1856 and has continued to reside upon the same

[164] Signed: TIMOTHY H LUCKY, ANDREW JONES, CHARLES N GARRET
Sworn to & subscribed Mar 31 1857 before JOHN MATLOCK, Chief Justice Parker Co.

Parker Co. TX - Field notes of survey of 160 acs. for TIMOTHY H. LUCKY by virtue his preemption affidavit No. 93 - Situate in Parker Co. on waters of Walnut Creek, tributary West Fork Trinity Riv. about 17 1/2 mi. N 27° E from Weatherford - Beg. NE from NE cor. GEORGE W. WILKERSON 160 ac. survey -

[165] W boundary line CALVIN M. CRISWELL 160 ac. preemption survey - W boundary line SARAH BLYTHE preemption survey - E boundary line ABRAHAM S. BIRDWELL 160 ac. preemption survey - Surveyed: Aug 15 1857 - LEWELLEN MURPHY, Co Surv Parker Co
Chain Carriers: WILLIAM C. FARRIS, ARTHUR M. GRAHAM

[166] Recorded: Sep 3 1857 - LEWELLEN MURPHY, Co Surv Parker Co TX

Parker Co. TX - No. 35 - Before the undersigned authority this day came JAMES M. UPTON as applicant and MONROE UPTON and F. C. BROWN, two disinterested and respectable witnesses. All of whom deposeth and saith that applicant was bonafide settled upon vacant land on the date of an act to authorize the location & settlement of the Mississippi & Pacific R. R. Reserve passed August 26th A. D. 1856 and has continued to reside upon the same
Signed: JAMES M. UPTON, F. C. BROWN, MONROE UPTON
Sworn to & subscribed Feb 23 1857 before JOHN H. PRINCE, Clerk Co Court Parker Co., by WM. M. GREEN, Dept.

[SEVERAL PAGES MISSING - FOLLOWING PAGES HAVE THE PAGE NUMBER TORN OFF - NEXT PAGE BEGINS WITH THE END OF A SURVEY]

[next sheet]
Surveyed: Aug 5 1857 - ISAAC O. HEADLEY, Dept Surv Parker Co
Chain Carriers: J. D. WATSON, WILLIAM GILLILAND
Recorded: Sep 8 1857 - LEWELLEN MURPHY, Co Surv Parker Co TX

Parker Co. TX - No. 6 - Before the undersigned authority this day came C. A. EDDLEMAN as applicant and N. H. PITTILLO and WILEY STROUD, two disinterested and respectable witnesses. All of whom deposeth and saith that applicant was bonafide settled upon vacant land on the date of an act to authorize the location & settlement of the Mississippi & Pacific R. R. Reserve passed August 26th A. D. 1856 and has continued to reside upon the same
[remainder of sheet torn]

[reverse side of previous sheet]
Sworn to & subscribed Feb 27 1857 before R. A. EDDLEMAN, Notary Public

Parker Co. TX - Have surveyed 97 ac. for C. A. EDDLEMAN by virtue his affidavit No. 6 - Situate in Parker Co. on Spring Creek, waters Brazos Riv. about 7 mi. S 25° E from Weatherford - Beg. SE from SW cor. JESSE THOMAS 320 ac. survey - E. line R. C. EDDLEMAN 160 ac. survey -
Surveyed: Apr 15 1857 [torn]
Chain Carriers: J. F. PITTILO, [remainder of page torn]

[next sheet - begins middle of a survey]

Surveyed: Aug 28 1857 - ISAAC O. HEADLEY, Dept Surv Parker Co
Chain Carriers: JOHN TRIMBLE, J. M. INMAN
Recorded: Sep 21 1857 - LEWELLEN MURPHY, Co Surv Parker Co TX

Parker Co. TX - No. 151 - Before the undersigned authority this day came W. B. FONDREN as applicant and DANIEL V. KIRBIE and ISAM CRANFIELD, two disinterested and respectable witnesses. All of whom deposeth and saith that applicant was bonafide settled upon vacant land on the date of an act to authorize the location & settlement of the Mississippi & Pacific R. R. Reserve passed August 26th A. D. 1856 and has continued to reside upon the same
Signed: W. B. FONDREN, DANIEL V. KIRBIE, ISAM CRANFIELD
[remainder page torn]

[reverse side last sheet]
Sworn to & subscribed May 4 1857 before JOHN H. PRINCE, Clerk Co Court Parker Co., by WM. M. GREEN, Dept.

Parker Co. TX - Have surveyed for W. B. FONDREN 160 acs. by virtue affidavit No. 151 - Situate in Parker Co. in Upper Cross Timbers on Dry Creek, tributary Brazos Riv. - Beg. SW from SW cor. DANIEL KIRBY 160 ac. survey -
Surveyed: Jul 1 1857 - ISAAC O. HEADLEY, Dept Surv Parker Co
Chain Carriers: JAMES YOUNGBLOOD, SPAIN FONDREN
[remainder sheet torn]

[Page numbers begin again]

[193] Parker Co. TX - No. 73 - Before JOHN MATLOCK, Chief Justice Parker Co. TX, personally came JOSEPH RASH as applicant and HOWARD HAYS and JAMES WIMBLEY, two disinterested and respectable witnesses. All of whom deposeth and saith that applicant was bonafide settled upon vacant land on August 26th A. D. 1856 and has continued to reside upon the same
Signed: JOSEPH RASH, HOWARD HAYS, JAMES WIMBLEY
Sworn to & subscribed Feb 27 1857 before JOHN MATLOCK, Chief Justice Parker Co.

Parker Co. TX - Field notes of survey of 160 acs. for JOSEPH RASH by virtue his preemption affidavit No. 73 - Situate in Parker Co. on waters [remainder page torn]

[194] ? cor. & E. boundary line JESSE R. CLIFTON survey -
Surveyed: Apr [?] 8 1857 - LEWELLEN MURPHY, Co Surv Parker Co
Chain Carriers: CHRISTOPHER [?] BEDWELL, WILLIAM D. CALLAWAY
Recorded: Oct 15 1857 - LEWELLEN MURPHY, Co Surv Parker Co TX

[195] Parker Co. TX - No. 99 - Before JOHN MATLOCK, Chief Justice Parker Co. TX, came FRANCIS M. HARRIS as applicant and WM. J. SILLIVENT and F. M. SILLIVENT, two disinterested and respectable witnesses. All of whom deposeth and saith that

applicant commenced settlement and improvement in month of Nov 1855 as a single man over the age of 17 and has continued to reside and improve to present date and claims same by an act to authorize the location & settlement of the Mississippi & Pacific R. R. Reserve passed August 26th A. D. 1856
Signed: FRANCIS M. 'X' HARRIS [mark], WILLIAM J. SILLIVENT, FRANCIS M. 'X' SILLIVENT [mark]
Sworn to & subscribed Sep 18 1857 before JOHN MATLOCK, Chief Justice Parker Co.

Parker Co. TX - Field notes of survey of 160 acs. for FRANCIS MARION HARRIS by virtue [remainder of page torn]

[196] Parker Co. on waters of Clear Fork Trinity Riv. about 12 mi. N 3° E from Weatherford - Beg. at SE cor. EDWARD M. HARRIS 160 ac. preemption survey -
Surveyed: Sep 19 1857 - LEWELLEN MURPHY, Co Surv Parker Co
Chain Carriers: CLEMENT BLACKWELL, EDWARD M. HARRIS
Recorded: Oct 15 1857 - LEWELLEN MURPHY, Co Surv Parker Co TX

[END OF BOOK "D"]

APPENDIX I

TARRANT COUNTY: PETITION FOR NEW COUNTY

"Petition of the Citizens of the Territory of Tarrant County, asking a New County - Refered [sic] to Com. on Co. Bond No 18 - ISAAC PARKER -

"To the honorable Senate and House of Representatives of the State of Texas in general yearly __?__, your petition's legal voters of Tarrant County respectfully represent to your honorable body that Settlement have Spread all over the Country and are daily increasing. They furthermore state that they are laboring under a great disadvantage in attending to their County business on account of their __?__ from the County Seat of Tarrant County. They therefore pray your honorable body that you pass an act creating a new county out of the Territory West of Tarrant County, bounded as follows to wit:

"Beginning at the North West corner of Tarrant County running Thence West 30 miles, Thence South 30 miles, Thence East to the North West corner of Johnson County and with the North boundary of the same 30 miles to the South West corner of Tarrant County, Thence North with the West boundary of the same 30 miles to the place of beginning.

"For which your petitions all in duty bound will ever pray Bedford County is the wish and Covington for the County Seat."

1. Daniel Waggoner
2. Wm. P. Clatterbuck
3. T. J. Duval
4. W. G. Williams
5. E. M. Curtiss
6. R. S. Porter
7. James H. Porter
8. Lewellen Murphy
9. A. J. Dyche
10. J. C. Hightower
11. James H. Mayes
12. William J. Mayes
13. S. Bevins
14. Benj. Reynolds
15. James H. Sewell
16. Lewis P. McDonald
17. W. ?. Gillalan
18. Tilman --?--
19. Samuel L. Gilliland
20. J. B. Gillaland
21. James Johnson
22. B. J. W. French
23. John D. Watson
24. James R. Campbell
25. M. M. [?] Rucker
26. David Eddleman
27. James F. Earnest
28. Calvin Lynch
29. Lewis White
30. John Jones
31. Wesley White
32. Preston White
33. Stephen Kidwell
34. James Tinsley
35. Aser Pipkin
36. Phillip B. Pipkin
37. Abraham Pipkin
38. Levi Kidwell
39. Joseph Reeves
40. A. I. Duke
41. W. I. Duke
42. William Bonds

43.	A. McKensiz	92.	A. B. Smith
44.	J. M. J--?--	93.	[marked out]
45.	M. H. Casbier	94.	J. ---?---
46.	James M. Gibson	95.	James C. Jones
47.	Wm. Boil	96.	W. H. Green
48.	John Trimble	97.	G. B. Jones
49.	Nathan Y. Nolan	98.	J. P. Cole
50.	L. D. Skidmore	99.	J. T.[M. marked out]Oxer
51.	?. ?. Thornburg	100.	Ch--- Durrett
52.	W. C. Joiner [?]		
53.	Johnson Woosley		2ND COLUMN
54.	John McCulley		
55.	Lisey [?] Lewis	101.	Wesley [?] Franklin
56.	Wm. Woosley	102.	Wesley Franklin
57.	D. H. Sisk	103.	Isaac O. Headley
58.	A. M. Gary	104.	John P. Smith
59.	B. R. Mitchell [?]	105.	N. Underwood
60.	C. Larimore	106.	Thomas Hill
61.	Stephen Trimble	107.	Richard Dannel [?]
62.	Wm. Trimble	108.	Thos. C. Darrett [?]
63.	Noah S. Barns	109.	I. [or J.] Blackwell
64.	J. C. Casslin [?]	110.	James Davis [?]
65.	Eli Lee	111.	G. K. Elkins
66.	Haleden Walters	112.	W. W. Ware
67.	Daniel Lee	113.	A. H. Onstot
68.	Oliver Childers	114.	P. L. [or T.] Stroud
69.	W. N. Cozort	115.	Amesley Parsons
		116.	R. A. Eddleman
[2ND PAGE - 1ST COLUMN]		117.	R. C. Eddleman
		118.	H. L. Dyer
70.	Israel [?] Headley	119.	Wm. H. Sheley
71.	John H. Phelps	120.	A. Gregory
72.	M. N. [?] Toler	121.	J. A. Baker
73.	Robert Elkins	122.	R. E. Byrd
74.	? Bright	123.	A. B. Brown
75.	W. C. Coldman	124.	J. ?. Spruill
76.	Wm. P. McCarver [?]	125.	Jacob Sealy
77.	James N. Bright	126.	J. T. Coffman
78.	John Snyder	127.	Lemuel Franks
79.	James Kidwell	128.	James Franks
80.	S. Stephen F. Jones	129.	J. G. Robbins
81.	Joshua Hollman	130.	Wm. M. Eubanks
82.	S. R. Barber	131.	D. B. Hayens
83.	L. McCarty		
84.	John Durkee		3RD COLUMN
85.	Noah Staggs		
86.	Jeremjiah [sic] Shumaker	132.	T. W. Eubanks
87.	T. J. Fidler	133.	S. M. Woods
88.	G. T. S--ltigge	134.	D. Herring
89.	John M. McEarly	135.	J. W. Blackwell
90.	George Staggs	136.	J. W. Roberts
91.	Isaac Ledbetter	137.	J. Upton

138. R. B. Ash
139. J. Higgins
140. John Jimison
141. James Coline
142. S. Blevins
143. W. Baty
144. W. C. H---
145. C. [or E.] Gilliand
146. A. Dodson
147. H. D. Roberts
148. L. B. Richeson
149. J. Neal
150. James Maulding [Waulding?]
151. John Sidwell, Sen
152. T. J. Shaw
153. Wm. C. Baker
154. Richard Blevins
155. Moses Pinkson
156. Wm. N. Heath
157. ILLEGIBLE
158. John Poyntess
159. J. Barton
160. J. H. Csop [sic]

3RD PAGE - 1ST COLUMN

161. Samuel T. Crum
162. B. M. [?] Emerson
163. M. Upton
164. F. Sanchess
165. J. J. Hamilton
166. Wiley Stroud
167. Martin [?] Baker
168. Egbert Grant
169. D. B. Koen
170. Z. P. Shirley
171. Simeon Meek
172. F. M. Bates
173. Thos. S. McKnight
174. A. W. Brown
175. John Sidwell [Tidwell ?]
176. D. T. Brogdon
177. J. Matthews
178. Hugh M. McCullon [?]
179. Eom Boothe
180. Isaac Sela
181. L. Luther [?] P. [marked out]
182. Luke Blevins
183. T. [or J.] Blevins
184. L. D. Meek
185. Washington Meek
186. Wesley Meek

187. John Meek
188. L. Meek
189. Jacob Shipman
190. Adam Santo
191. Joseph Walker
192. W. D. Weaver

2ND COLUMN

193. Stepen Jones
194. Josua Holman
195. J. F. Webb
196. Wm. Coffee
197. R. Coffee
198. Thos. Bandey
199. J. B. Pinkson
200. Joseph Jackson
201. John Holden [Molden ?]
202. Wm. P. Ramsey
203. Aderson Green
204. J. M. Froman
205. G. W. Prutt
206. Johatan [sic] Alen
207. B. F. Williams
208. J. B. Robinson
209. J. B. --ggs
210. J. Campbell
211. T. J. Spilman
212. Stephen Heffington
213. Joel Crain
214. T. [?] A. O. Nuchols
215. A. P. Hoffman [Huffman]
216. Edward Alston
217. E. A. Daniel
218. Levi Spilman
219. Egbert Grant
220. John Parker
221. Daniel McCord
222. Soloman Durrett
223. Edward Welborn
224. James F. Cole

3RD COLUMN

225. Stephen Kidwell

[NO DATE]

APPENDIX II
LEGISLATIVE ACT CREATING PARKER COUNTY, TEXAS

"CHAPTER 1

"An Act to create the County of Parker

"SECTION 1. Be it enacted by the Legislature of the State of Texas, That all the territory comprised within the following limits, to wit: beginning at the north-west corner of Tarrant County; thence south with the western boundary line of Tarrant County 30 miles to the south-west corner of Tarrant County; thence west with the northern boundary of Johnson county 30 miles; thence north 30 miles; thence east 30 miles to the place of beginning, be, and the same is hereby constituted a new county, by the name of the county of Parker.

"SECTION 2. That the Chief Justice of Tarrant county shall, within three months after the passage of this act, lay off the said county of Parker in suitable election pricincts [sic] in accordance with law, and shall within the said three months order an election for county officers, which election shall be advertised at three public places in the county of Parker, stating the times and places, which places shall be the different election precincts laid out by the Chief Justice of Tarrant county as herein before provided, which election shall be conducted in all other respects in accordance with the general laws governing elections, and in accordance with, 'an act to provide for organizing new counties,' approved, March 20th, 1848; and the said Chief Justice of Tarrant county shall qualify the person elected to the office of Chief Justice of the county of Parker, who, when qualified by the Chief Justice of Tarrant county, shall qualify the other officers elected for said county of Parker.

"SECTION 3. That it shall be the duty of the county court of said new county, so soon as they are duly qualified, to proceed to locate the county seat of said county, by selecting at least three eligible sites, not exceeding three miles from the center of said county, having respect for any donation of land that may be made for that purpose, as well as convenience of wood and waters, and when so selected, the Chief Justice shall order an election which shall be conducted according to the general laws governing elections for county officers, and if at the first election neither of the sites so selected shall receive a majority of all the votes cast, the place receiving the smallest number of votes shall be thrown out, and the Chief Justice shall order another election as before, and so continue to do, throwing out the site receiving the smallest number of votes, until some one of the sites selected shall receive a majority of all the votes cast, which shall be declared to be the county seat of said county and shall be

186

called Weatherford. That all settlers 21 years old who have resided within the limits of said county sixty days prior to said election, shall be entitled to vote for the location of the county seat.

"SECTION 4. That in case the site which shall be declared to be the county seat of said county, shall prove to be vacant and unappropriated domain, then the State does by this act relinquish and donate to the said county of Parker all her right and title to 320 acres of the same, and the Commissioner of the General Land Office is hereby authorized to issue a patent in the name of the said county for the said 320 acres upon a return, according to law, of the plot and field notes of the same to the General Land Office, duly certified, and the said county court of said new county shall have the power to purchase, if necessary, land not to exceed 320 acres for the use of said county, (should the site selected as above provided prove to be appropriated land,) and shall lay off the site so selected into suitable lots, and after selecting and setting apart such suitable lots as may be necessary for a Court House, Jail, Clerk's Offices, Churches, School-houses and burying grounds, they shall proceed to sell the remainder, or such portion thereof, as they may deem necessary, at public auction at such time and upon such terms as will most conduce to the interests of the county, and shall apply the proceeds thereof to the erection of necessary public buildings for the use of said county.

"SECTION 5. That the Chief Justice of Tarrant county shall be entitled to three dollars per day for every day that he is necessarily employed or detained in holding said elections and organizing said county of Parker.

"SECTION 6. That all that territory west of the county hereby created and which was heretofore included within the limits of Tarrant county, shall be attached to and form a part of the territorial limits of said new county, and for all the county and general purposes shall form a part of the same after the organization of said county and the location of the seat of Justice thereof.

"SECTION 7. That this act take effect and be in force from and after its passage.

"Approved, December 12th, 1855."
(H. P. N. GAMMEL, The Laws of Texas 1822-1897 [Austin, The Gammel Book Co., 1898] IV, pp 183-185)

INDEX

AARON, Jacob 130
ADAMS, John 8 46 73 91 114 130 169 170 178 Whory 1 Wm 7 8 73
ADKINS, Bartley 31
AL(L)EN, Geo 1 72-73 J P 49 Jas 49 Jas A 50 Johathan 185 John P 144-45 John Perry 60 61 144 146 R W 7 8 10-13 15-23 25-43 45-47 51-70 Rubin 55 56 Thos 146 156 W H 159 W R 44 W W 55 Wm 55 62 97 100 Wm H 97 100 145 159 163 178
ALMON, Jas 12
ALSTON, Edward 185
AMOS, Jos S 83
AND, ? L 49 Ignatius L 67
ANDERSON, P H 73 Quinten N 99 100 163 167 Isaac 175 177 W B 122
ANGELY/ANJELY, Ambers 89 147
ARMSTRONG, Wm 1-3
ASBERRY, Sally 52
ASH, R B 185
AUEL, Ignatius L 67
AUSBURN, J A 34 Jas A 24 34 John Jas 125

BABINSON, Wm M 75
BAGLEY, Wm H 49
BAKER, J A 184 Martin 185 R P 20 72 154 166 Robt P 20 21 65 153-54 158 173 Wm 101 106 Wm C 20 21 25 65 72 95 151 153-54 185
BALEMAN, Jas 72
BALES, Hiram 1
BALIMAN, J 106 T 106
BANDEY, Thos 185
BANDY, Calvin L 105-107
BANNER, Mahala 72
BARBAR/BARBER, G P 81 S P 31 67 S R 67 128 184 Saml R 31 122 126 128 134 167 173 Solomon P 31
BARKER, Jas J 131 145 Joseph 72 131 144 Joshua 83 177
BARN(E)S, Noah S 17 184 Perry

BARN(E)S (Cont) M 17 162 S 17 Silas 16 17 47 72 162 Wm 118
BARTEM, Reuben B 89
BARTEN, M O 104 Manelies Oliver 93 R P 93 Reuben P 93 W T 93 104
BARTLETT, Merrick 60 61 144 145 179
BARTON, Benj K 164 J 185 M O 93 R P 174 176
BASHERS, John W 91
BASS, W A 5
BATES, F M 185
BATY, W 185 Walter 33 134
BAWCOM, G W 24 J W 31
BAWSCOM, J W 31
BAYLEY, W H 11 Wm 11 Wm H 58 70
BAYLOR, W H 11
BEACH, Miles Albert 175
BEADLE, Henry 63 65 104
BEADLE/BEEDLE, Henry 49 63 65 104
BEALL, Richd 8 9
BEDFORD, Jas 136-7 Stephen 136-7 Thos 120 126 134 136 137
BEDFRED, Jas 120
BEDWELL, Christopher 11-13 45 72 87 104 181 Stephen 18
BEEMAN, Jas J 46 80 J J 81 91 108 112 124-26 134 147-8 150-51 157 163 166 177
BERGES, Elijah 72
BERLINAN, J 5
BETTY, Isaac 102 105 110 R C 101 102
BEULEU, John B 6
BEVERLY, Jas 124 138
BEVINS, S 183
BIBBES, H 2
BICHARELS, Jas 1
BIDIORNEL, L M 72
BIDWELL, Jas 18
BILLINGSLEA/BILLINGSLEE/ BILLINGSL(E)Y, J B 171 J R 85 Jas 72 R J 78 79 83 84 92 129 131 164 170

188

BILLINGSLEA/BILLINGSLEE/
  BILLINGSL(E)Y (Cont) 179
  Robt 12 72 Robt J 12 79
  111 115
BIRDWELL, Abraam 103 Abraham
  S 180
BLACK, John 138 157 161 164
BLACKWELL, Clement 59 60 182
  I 184 J 184 J W 184 Josiah
  F 127 Upton C 101 103
BLAIN, C C 126
BLAIR, Wm N 92
BLAN, C C 126
BLANTON, C W 164 Chas Wesley
  51
BLASSINGAME, W T 102 Wm L 109
BLEVINS, J 185 Luke 185 Richd
  185 S 185 T 185
BLODGET, Francis S 100 108
  Jas D 108
BLYTHE, Sarah 138 139 180
BOGGS, 117 Miyamin M 97
BOIL, Wm 184
BOLES/BOWL(E)S, Hiram 2 3
BONDS, Wm 54 183
BOOKER, S R 31
BOOTHE, Eom 185
BOSWELL, B F 110 116 121
BOWMAN, C F 72 174
BOYD, John 122 128-9 P H 93
  Robt H 122 T 177 Tillman
  129 Tilmon 90 177 Will A
  121 Wm A 120
BRADFORD, H E 3
BRANNAN, Stephen 107
BRASHEARS/BRASHER(E)S, Alex M
  156 168 Alex N 153 John W
  91 106-7 153 155-6 162 168
  Wm 168
BRENT, W B 115
BREWSTER, H P 6
BRIGHT, 184 Jas 136 Jas N 100
  184
BRISCO(E), Isaac 23 52 72 101
  103 107 129 Isom 108 J J
  128 Jacob 97 John 97
BROGDEN/BROGDON, D T 125 185
BROUMLEY, Evlyn v
BROWN, A B 162 164 184 A W
  185 Albert B 162 164 Allen
  W 162 David 141 Eli 24 35
  41-2 140 F C 94 154 158

BROWN (Cont) 180 Harrison 141
  Hugh 113 143 Jas R 135-6
  John 65 79 81 86 N 42 R W
  49 R W Jr 49 Robt 81-2 111
  140 T C 93
BULLION(S), Thos 49 57 62 64
  65
BURKE, Wm E 101
BURRIP, E 49
BURRIS, 64 121 Elias 55 Jas L
  56 Jas M 82 83 Tarleton 78
  Thos 56 83 89 147 Zacha-
  riah 89 99 147 150
BURROW(S), Isaac 108 Israel
  24-26 80 127 151 163 John
  140 P H 121 P J 110 Philip
  J 110 Phillip S 161 W H 58
  Wm 11 58 70 Wm H 161
BURTON, Jas M 160 T S 160
  Thos S 160 Wm C 160
BUSTER, John 97
BUT(T)LER, Jas 35 John H 102
  105 110
BUTTON, Thos 63
BYERS, J L 85
BYRD, R E 33 134 177 184

CA__ELL, H S 49
CABBINESS, Chas A 121 Eliz
  98 W H C 121 Wm H C 98 99
CADDELL, J C 3
CAFFFMAN, J B 37
CALAWAY, Wm D 13
CALDEROUS, Jas 35
CALDWELL/CALWELL, Andrew
  Jackson 30 Hezekiah 49 61
  62 144 Jas 49 60-62 144-5
  John 49 55 Joshua 49 50 60
  61 144 145 Robt W 5 6
  Thos 49 55 61 62 97
CALLAWAY, Wm D 12 87 181
CAL__Y, Wm D 11
CAMP, L E 42 53-57 85 138-9
CAMBELL/CAMPBELL, Dugal 155
  J 185 J R 24 45 178 Jas R
  120 178 183
CAN(N)AFAX, E N 42 Elijah N
  77 Elizah B 77 Elizah
  Newton 86 Ezra N 77 Ezra
  Jasper 54 66 Jno A 120
  John A 66 77 99 Newton 81
CANCLIFF, Wm H 66

189

CANTRELL/CANTRIL, A G 57 H E 78 H G 62 Hazael 62 Hazael E 78 Hezael G 62 Shade 110
CAPP(S), J 49 Jeremia 70 Jeremiah 69
CARR, Jas 136 Jas D 100
CARRINGTON, A L 2
CARTY, Larkin M 165
CASBIER, M H 184
CASSLIN, J C 184
CATSIN(G)ER, Danl 120 Saml 120
CAUTRSLK, H G 118
CENTON, D C 12
CHAMBERS, B J 5-7
CHAPMAN, John C 63 64 67 133 134
CHENAWORTH, John 1
CHILDERS, 24 Oliver 46 113 114 184
CHILMAN, Levi 123
CLARY, Abaslam W 124 John 101 102 104 105
CLATTERBUCK, Wm P 183
CLAYTON, Jas 5 6 134 136 137 Thos M 157
CLEMENT, Egbert N 157
CLGTON, Thos M 19
CLIFTON, Jesse R 4 11 44 53 181 Loving 104 110 Lurans 63
CLOYES, A 1
COALMAN/COLEMAN, Wm 112 179
COCKBERN/COCKBURN, Jermiah 62 Jeremiah 78
COFFEE/COFF(E)Y, R 185 Wm 24 44 155 156 185
COFFMAN, J B 38 J P 24 38 39 139 J T 184 T P 38
COGBURN, 64
COLDMAN, W C 184
COL(D)WELL, Jas 144 146 Joshua 144 146 Thos 100
COLD, J F 100 108 J P 108 141 184 Jas F 100 108 185 John P 100 Wm 28 29
COLINE, Jas 185
COLLIE, Jane 132
COLLIN, Jane 114
COOK, Jas 7 8 169 175
COOPER, C W 54 Wm C 1 3
COPELAND, Geo 105 122 141 Wm

COPELAND (Cont) 24 30 42 99 147
COTTRELL, G W 8 9
COTTON, Fred vii
COWAN, Saml W 52
COZART/COZORT, W N 24 135 160 161 184 Wm M 38 Wm N 39 133
CRAIN, Joel 185
CRANFIELD/CRANFIELL/CRANFIL, Isam/Isom 105 122 147 148 181
CRETSINGER, 118 Danl 136 137 Saml 123
CRISWELL, C M 85 139 Calvin M 85 139 180 Davis 90 92 Davis S 92 W D 138 139 Wm 90 93 Wm W 122
CROMPTON, E H 103 Enoch H 104
CROP, J H 24 28 Rebecca 24
CROSS, J H 28 95 96
CRUM, Geo 28 Saml T 28 185
CRUMPTON, E H 40 135
CSOP, J H 185
CUL(L)WELL, Hezekiah 145 Jas 144 145 179 Joshua 146 Thos 145 159 178 Thos Jr 145 179 Thos Sr 179
CUNCLIFF, Wm H 66
CURRANT/CURRENT, Levi 95 151 152
CURTISS, E M 183

DANIEL, E A 185
DANNEL, Richd 184
DARRETT/DERRETT, R W 27 S 27 Solomon 141 Thos C 184
DAVID, Isaac P 42
DAVIDSON, E B 109 139
DAVIS, ? P 49 Isaac P 54 66 165 J P 50 Jas 184 Oliver 39 160 161 167 Wm 49 66
DEASON, Jas 33
DENNISON, Wm 49 50 53 54
DENTON, Ashley N 21 153 Ashly N 20
DICKENSON, Noah 1 Noah Jr 2
DOBIE, R N 115
DODIONS, A 65
DODSON, A 185 Alderson 35
DOLLARHIDE, J P 33
DOSS, Eliz 18

DOYLE, Russell H 44
DRAPER, Thos 137 Thos R 137
DUBIEL, Laura v
DUKE, A I 183 W I 183
DULAN(E)Y, Wm P 92 98 140
DULANTY, Wm P 97
DULENS, Jas 19
DUNCAN, G W 78 164 Geo W 77
   John 103
DUNKIN(S), J 10 John 10 Jos 8
DUNNAGAN, B S 138
DURKEE, John 184
DURRETT, Ch-- 184 Soloman 185
DUVAL, T J 183
DYC(H)E, A J 25 146 147 149
   150 151 157-60 183 Alford
   J 18 159
DYEKE, A J 19
DYER, A J 19 H L 184 Henry H
   126 134
DYET, Alford J 19

EARNEST, Jas F 183 Jas H 73
EDDLEMAN, C A 33 172 180
   Columbus J 73 David 29 73
   183 E J 167 I C 29 R A 123
   171-3 180 184 R C 27 33 73
   171-3 180 184 Richd C 21
   22 172
EDWARDS, Jas C 108 117 120
   178 Jas L 179
ELKINS, G K 28 64 67 184 Geo
   K 133 Robt 184
ELLIS, W J 167 Wm J 83 99 167
ELLISON, F M 89 Francis M 176
EMBERSON, B V 34 E S 35
EMERRY, Wm R 129
EMERSON A W 86 B M 185 E A W
   86
ENSEY, D C 50 Denes C 55
   Dennis C 52 56 E 131
   Ezekiel L A 55 56 130 131
   Ezekiel S A 52 I C 49 S A
   49 Sally Asberry 56 150
ERAIN, J W 57
ERATH, G B 2
ERWIN, Jas W 117 S L 119
   Stephen ? 117 Stephen L
   117 Stephen S 119 Wm A 119
EUBANK(S), T W 184 Wm 118 120
   123 Wm M 184
EVANS, Benj 45 53 J M 118

EVANS (Cont) Robt 6 73
EWARDS, Jas C 178

F__CHER, G C 15
FALDER, John E 17
FANNIN, J W ix
FARRIS, Wm C 180
FEATHERKILE, Geo 88
FELKISON, Benj 89
FERGSON, Jos 124
FID(D)LER, Jackson 134 171
   T J 184
FIELDS, Noah 1 73
FISHER, Jas 26 27
FLETCHER, Wm R 53
FLEMING, Ezekiel A 163
FLETCHER, Isaac C 157 161 164
   John R 116 Wm F 12 Wm K 13
   73 86 87
FOLDER, M F 37
FOLLY, G W 36 Lydia 36 132
FONDEN, W B 68
FONDREN, Spain 181 W B 68 86
   87 147 181 Wm B 81 86 147
FORD, Wm D 83
FORE, Wm D 160
FOX, G W 36 114 132 Geo W 36
FRANCES/FRANCIS, H E 49 Henry
   E 62 63 Jno 49 John 14 62
   64 L D 82 L J 82 131
   Leftridge J 131 R L 14
   Ramey L 64 82 Ramy L 49
   Raney L 82 Rarney L 64
   Reighney L 14
FRANKLIN, Hiram 114 132 J W
   80 96 150 Jesse 78 Jesse W
   30 43 80 89 96 99 150
   Jesse Wright 89 Wesley 36
   73 132 184
FRANKS, Jas 184 Lemuel 115
   149 184
FREEMAN, John 73 John A 73
FRENCH, B J W 183
FROMAN, J M 28 185 John M 73

GALE, Benj 27 Robt 167
GARDNER, J A 134 167 Jerome A
   120 134
GARRET, Chas N 179
GARRISON, J 51
GARY, A M 79 86 90 92 94 184
GATTERY, Thos 121

GELDON, Chas 98 99 109 110
GEORGE, C 64 Robt 51 156
GIBSON, J M 124 Jas M 184
GILBERT, Jas M 175 176 L J 112 124 170 175 176 Lemuel J 113 175 176 Singleton 112 113
GILDAN, C 12
GILDON, Chas 82-85 92 116-19 122 123 138-40 145 149 157 159 161 164 178
GILLALAN(D), J B 183 W ? 183
GILLETT, Jas S 66
GILLIAND, C 185 E 185
GILLILAND, Elijah 45 J B 130 Jas B 91 Jos C 45 178 S L 102 Saml L 183 W B 45 178 Wm 180 Wm B 46 163
GILLISPEE, Wm C 135
GILMER/GILMORE, Asa 149 155 162 163
GILP(H)IN, Geo W 125 126 J W 125
GLASS, Isaac 46 47 101 121 131 140 141
GLENN(E), J A 123 Jas A 73 Walter B 73
GODBEHERE, Martha J 109 Martha Jane 109
GODBEKERE, Richd D 78
GODFREY, J W 82 131 145 John W 82 144 145
GODLYHENE, Richd D 62
GOLH(I)ER, Thos 59 157 161 164
GOMER, F 73
GONZALAS/GONAZLES, D 1 Dinnses 73 Dinnsez 73
GOOD, Hanibal 174
GORDON, Alfred 101 John 101 107 Jerome 126
GORE, Liddy 103
GRAHAM, Arthur M 180
GRANT, Egbert 185
GREEN, A W 168 Aderson 185 Alfred 120 Anderson 119 120 168 Geo 1 6 73 Thos J 168 W H 184 Wm 66 Wm M 79 91 94 102 111 118 141 148 149 151-56 158 159 162-4 166 168 178 180 181
GREGORY, A 184

GRISHAM, Elijah 121 John 91 153 155 156 168 Nathan 153 156
GUEST, G W 174 J W 89 174 176
GUITON, Wm D 81
GULKER, Thos 18
GUTTERY, John 110 Thos 110
GUTTIREC, Thos 110
GUYTON, W D 68 87 88 Wm D 81

HAILEY/HALEY, W D 73 Wm D 116
HAINES/HAYNES, B 95 Bluford 73 95 123 135
HALFELL, J C 39
HALFULL, H 38
HALL, P S 133 Peter S 74 Wm 12 Wm C 80 109 126 127
HALLER, Francis 73
HAMILTON, J J 35 185 John J 65
HAND, Saml 111
HANPIS, John 101
HANTE, John 109
HARRIS, A 10 B 123 Edward 52 Edward M 23 60 84 165 182 F M 60 Francis M 181 182 Francis Marion 144 182 J 51 M E 10
HARRISON, J A J 99 J T 117 Jos 97 M E 10 W D 10 Wm D 10 73
HART, Gabriel 32 Jos 32 129 Mahala 31 32 R C 32 129 169 Robt 32 Robt C 126 129 Stephen 32 129
HAUPE/HAWPE, John 101 John W 73 112
HAWKINS, R A 123 R H 114
HAWTER, Jas 1-3
HAYENS, D B 184
HAY(E)S, Howard 12 110 111 115 181
HAZARD, Jas 11
HEADLEY, I O. 67 102 122 134 139 167 Isaac O. 15-18 22 23 26-42 45-7 66-9 73 80 87 88 90 92 95 96 102 105 107 111 114 116 122 128-9 132-37 139-41 161 165-7 171-5 177-8 180 181 184 Israel 184
HEALLN, N B 38

HEATH, Wm N 185
HEAVENSMITH, L 73
HEFFINGTON, Jas C 177 Stephen 73 185
HEFLEY, J M 96 150 John 96 John M 80 96
HEIFRIN, Geo vi Geo N v
HEINES/HINES, Solomon 146 156
HENDERSON, Robt A 100 167
HENDIRCK(S), A 123 Albert 123
HENRY, Woodson 138 Woodson D 85 103 138 139
HERNDON, Jas 56
HERREN/HERRIN(G), D 158 184 David 53 67 93 94 154 158 159 Wm S 53 164
HERRINGTON, Wm 3
HEWETT, J H 93 94 154 162
HEWETT/HEWITT, J H 93 94 154 162 Jos 74 Jos H 20 21 65 66 67 94 154 158
HIBBERT, I B 26 J B 26 John B 73 R C 133
HIGANS/HIGGINS, J 185 Wm 73 96 144
HIGHTOWER, J C 183 John C 19 20 25 147 150 151 157
HILL, A C 164 A L 118 119 Allen C 100 159 Bailey 92 98 Baley 97 140 170 Baly 92 98 Bayle 98 Ben F 1 2 Thos 184
HITTSON, John 19 73
HIUSTAN, Walter 73
HODGES, Henry 73
HOFFMAN, A P 185
HOFFORD, Jas 45
HOGGAN, Jas 116 Wm 116
HOGGARD, Jas 118 Wm 118
HOLDEN, John 185 Peter B 73
HOLDER, M J 37 N B 38 136 139 N J 38 109 Nathan B 139 W B 38 39
HOLLINGSWORTH, G W 40 135 165
HOL(L)MAN, Jos(h)ua 184 185
HOPKINS, Jas 121 Wm 124
HORRIS, Edward M 59
HORTON, G H 37 Jas 132 Jas W 132 T W 37
HOWARD, Emry A 81 Wm 82 140 153
HUDSON, Jas 29 39 146 149-51

HUDSON (Cont) 155 159 Thos 45
HUFFMAN, A P 185
HUNT, M 73 Memucan 116 138 Momucan 13
HUNTER, A J 174 Abram M 93 Martha 93 Shadrack V 93

IKARD, E A S L 89 170 M 158 170 Milton 20 21 65 66 154 158 170 171
IN(N)MAN, Henry 24 39 40 135 160 161 J M 24 40 181 Jos M 167
IOLA, Isaac 120
IRBY(E), Benj F 136-7 Wm 123

JACKSON, 49 Andrew 149 C 69 Calvin 69 Jas 106 Jos 185 Thos 120 121 178 Wm 107
JAMES, Grant ix John 111
JAMESON/JAMISON/JEMASON/ JIMISON, John 24 35 89 90 95 185
JENKINS/JINKINS, J C 10 J E 7 8 10-2 21-2 50-1 57-8 63-4 67 70 74 123 144-5 J M 108 Jas M 74 John 30 Mr 52
JIM(M)ERSON, J 34 John 34-5 90
JOHNSON, Benj 19 F W ix Geo M P 74 Jas 24 45-6 98 149 163 183 Jas P 13 138 John J 13 M L 14 Richd N 114 132
JOINER, W C 184
JONAS, John 81
JONES, Andrew 179 G B 24 184 Hezekiah 5 74 J M 178 Jas 74 Jas C 184 John 30 81-2 95 130 183 S F 135 174 S May 179 S Stephen F 184 Stephen 185 Stephen F 30-1 67 93 T F 135
JUNKIN, Jos 9

KEARBY/KERBY/KIRBIE/KIRBEE/ KIRBY, Danl 181 Danl V 105 110 147-8 181 John B 105 107 Saml J 122
KEEL, Jas 123
KEEN, A M 44 56

KERR, Nathl G 5
KIDWELL, Jas 18 30 111 148
    175-7 184 Jas Jr 67 Jas Sr
    67 Levi 82 161-2 176-7 183
    Lewis 29 30 Stephen 24 47
    81 90 94-5 177 183 185
KING, Saml W 109 W D 24 37
    109 W S 24 W T 37 Wm D 109
KINNEDE, H 68
KINSLEY, A M 41
KIRK, Peter 74 111 178 Wm 74
KOEN, D B 185

LACY, Chas C 13-15 22-3 48 69
    70 72 Wm Y 66
LADGSDON, Jos 74
LANG, Edward 13 74
LANTZ, H 78 Henry 78-9 John G
    44 78-9
LARIMORE, C 184 Canumel 17
LAW, D A 79 80
LAYNE, Wm T 125
LEACH, F A vi
LEAK(E), Saml 74 108
LEDBETTER, Isaac 184 J A 108
    L B 22
LEE, Danl 91 113-4 130 184
    Eli 46 91 113-4 184 Geo
    74 129-30 148 Jno 148 L D
    49 55-6 Leanner 161-2 N G
    84 101 129 Nicholas G 107
    Nicolas G 119
LEELA, Isaac 137
LEFTLET(T), Francis 106-7
LEONARD, G L 10 49 Geo L 57
    H R 10 J L 10 51 Jas E 164
    167 Louisa 99 100 Mary 100
    167 S S 178 Saml S 55 83
    100 145 156 159 167 Saml
    Sevier 100
LEWIS, Linzy 74 129 130 Lisey
    184 Thos J 51 96 Thos John
    51
LIDDY, Francis 52 56
LIGHT, G W 151 155 Geo W 92
    146 150-1 155 159 160
LINCE/LINCH/LYNCH(E), Calvin
    46-7 106 109 141 179 183
    John 74 91
LITTLEFIELD, Saml 89 113 174
    175-6 Wilson 112-3 124 171
    175-6

LITTL(E)TON, Chas 54 Correll
    117 J ? 64 J W 54 Jos H 81
LIVELY, Jas W 69 70 Wm 130
    Wm L 130
LLOYD, A P 23 48 71-2
LODGSDON, Jos 74
LOGSDON, Hardin 162 J 63
LONG, Alfa 138 Alsa 138 Edwd
    13 Jas 78 138 Wm 6 35 74
    90
LORANCE, Jason 27
LOW, D A 68 87-8 David A 87-8
    W M 68 87 Wm M 87-8
LOWDERS, Adam L 74 115
LUCK(E)Y, T H 138-9 Timothy H
    179
LUTHER, L 185
LYNN, Isaac 16 Peter 16-7

MC ADAMS, W C 15 104-5 110
    Wm C 15
MC ANNEELY/MC ANNELLY, Peaset
    74 Pleasant 8
MC CARTY, L 135 184 Larkin 74
    165 171 Wm 135
MC CARVER, Adm 74 C C 29 74
    135 Wm P 184 Wm Pitts 74
MC CARY, P J 69
MC CLAREN/MC CLERRAN/
    MC CLERRIN, John 13-5 22
MC CORD, Danl 185
Mc CULLAH, John 74
MC CULLEY, John 184 L M 63
MC CULLON, Hugh M 185
MC DONALD/MC DONNAL, L P 46-7
    141 179 Lewis P 74 102 106
    109 183
MC EARLY, John M 184
MC EWIN, Nancy 74
MC KAMY, Wm C 175
MC KENNEY, Una 1
MC KENSIZ, A 184
MC KNIGHT, Thos S 185
MC LAREN, John 74
MC MAHAN J L 49 50 John L 52

MAGERS/MAGORS/MAJORS, Isaac B
    154 158 Isaac Barton 53
    Isaac Benton 53 J B 50 162
    164 Pleasant H 16 53 Seton
    101 109
MANLEY, Jos 142

MARKLEY, Wm 114
MARTIN, Elem 162 Ephraim 153
 T B 131 Thos B 88 91 94-5
 148 Wm H 123
MASON, Thompson 7 8 67 74 169
MASSEGEE, G B 11
MATLOCK, John 43-4 56 62-3
 78-80 82-7 89 96-7 99 100
 103-4 109-11 113 115 117
 119 121 129-31 138-9 143-7
 150 156 160 163 165 167
 173 179 181-2
MATTHEWS, B ? 13 J 13 185
 John 125 R H 75 Richd H 14
 15 22 Z G 14
MAULDING, Jas 185
MAY(E)S, J H 7 47 Jas H 7 8
 17 74 169 175 183 Wm J 7 8
 74 183
MAYO, W J 102 129
MAYORS, Seton 101 112
MEADOR, R M 92 132 Reason M
 140
MEDLAN, Peter 16
MEEK, G W 93 104 Henry 152-3
 Isaac H 44-5 52-3 J H 50
 Jacob 104 153 John 185
 John W 151-2 John Wesley
 104 152 L 185 L D 151-2
 170 176 185 Mary 104 152
 174 Simeon 185 Washington
 185 Wesley 185
METORD, Danl 96
MILES, John H 2 74
MILLAND, N 2
MILLER, 49 A O 75 Artetious O
 14 15 22 E 85 Ebenezer 85
 Elsberry 161 165-6 Geo 65
 Jas A 52 84 102 129 John
 29 John E 161 165-6 Mary A
 57 Mrs 57 W 35
MILLR, John E 166
MILLS, Milton 27-9 Wm Jr 6 74
MILLSAPP, Mary 6
MILRONS, Edder Boxion 56
MITCHEL(L), B R 184 J B 17
 John B 17 J R 47 75 John R
 17
MOLDEN, John 185
MONTGOM(E)RY, Jesse F 80 96
 Jesse Franklin 51 John 51
 80 96 150 John P 50-1

MONTRY, Wm 74
MOORE, David 34 128 F A 40
 F C 79 J M 29 36 John 128
 John H 74 115 T C 79 90
 Thos C 79 W G 79 Wm C 102
 112 Wm G 79
MORE, A 136 G C 94 T C 90-1
 94-5 Thos C 94-5 W G 94-5
 Wm G 91 94
MORRIS, A 58 Achil(l)es 10 74
 H R 56 58 J A 85 Jas 49 66
 M E 58 M R 10
MOSS, Howell R 146 159 160
 Jane 146 160
MT GOMERY, J P 50 John 50
MULKEN/MULKIN(S), Ezra 28-9
 100 133 Isaiah 26 John 26
 28 John W 133 Jno H 54 S P
 26
MULLERS, Nancy 51
MURPHY, John W 119 120 168
 Jno W 121 Lewellen 4 11-13
 16-21 23 25-6 30 42-6 51-6
 59-67 77-168 170-83 Milton
 44
MYERS, Wm J 7

NATIONS, Wm 104
NEAL/NEILL, J 185 Jno A 131
NELIWS, C C 75
NEWLY, John H W 23
NEWSON, John 45 John A 44
 Stephen 104
NIX, Wm 114-5 119
NOLAN(D), Mason Y 179 Nathan
 Y 184 N Y 179
NORTON, D C 91
NUCHOLS, T A O 185

OBENCHAIN, A F 63
OLINGER, Wm 166 Wm T 166
ONSTOT(T), A H 128 184
ORR, Geo 1 3
OTIER, Eliza 141
OWEN, J H 36 J W 132 John W
 114 Thos M 36
OXER, J T 184
OXIER, Eliza 141 Elza 75 Jas
 28 Jas S 75

PARKER, Cinnt-- 50 Isaac vi
 183 John 66 96 185

PARKINSON, Thos 126
PARSONS, Amesley 129 177 184
    G W 95
PASCHAL(L), J C 14 50 J T 75
    Jas C 57 John T 14 M T 118
    R T 14
PATILLO, N H 33
PATISON, Wm 146
PATRICK, John 5-7 Wm W 6 75
PATTEN/PATTON, Alex W 177
    Columbus R 122 David W 88
PATTERSON, Jno M 99 Wm 108
    111-2 147
PATTESON, Wm 112
PEACH, Miles A 133
PEARCE/PEIRCE/PIERCE, Cabele
    123 Cebea 123 Jas 10 11 58
    75
PENNINGTON, Wm 4 44 63 104
PEPKIN, A 39 Aser 39 40 H 39
    Silas 1
PERRY, Amos 31
PESTOLE, A J 166
PETERS, W S 69 Wm 70 Wm S 69
PETTILLO, Jefferson W 90
PHELPS, John H 27 108 135 141
    184
PHILPOTT, J P 6 9
PHYMER, A 2
PINKNEY, John L 75
PINKSON, J B 185 John B 35
    Moses 185
PINKSTON, J B 90 95
PINNEL(L), H 16 79 Hiram 75
    79 131-2 148 Hyram 16
PIPKIN, A 29 Abraham 133 166
    167 183 Aser 39 133 135
    183 P B 39 Phillip B 133
    183
PISTOLE, A G 165 171
PITIL(L)O, J F 180 J W 171-2
    N H 171-3 180
PLOWMAN, Geo vi
PLUMLEE, Isaac Denton 147
POE, A M 149 159 Anguis M 149
    152-3 159 Asa 124 John W
    149
POLK, B F 171 B K 75
PORSEN, G W 90
PORTER, C C 75 151 157
    Christopher C 151 159 J F
    75 Jas H 25 88 148 150 158

PORTER (Cont) 183 John F 147
    151 156-7 R S 25 112 147
    151 183 R S Jr 108 R S Sr
    150 156 Robt F 109 Robt S
    25-6 80 112 146-7 150 157
    Robt S Jr 111 157 160
    Robt S Sr 151
POSEY, J 81 Jeremiah 81 92
    140
POTER, Christopher C 19 20
    John F 19 20 Robt S 18
POYNTESS, John 185
PREWETT, J C 33
PRICE, A 82 Anger 111 140
    Auger 81-2 111 H C 163
    Henry C 149 163 Humphrey
    32 Isaac 117 139 140 163
    170 J 70 Jas 70 Jno A 140
    John A 139 140 Pleasant 42
    Umphrey 32
PRINCE, J 58 J H 89 90 168
    John H 66 79-82 86-95 97-8
    101-2 104-7 109-14 116 118
    120-6 128-9 131-7 139-41
    146-9 151-6 158-71 174-81
    T M Sr 116 Wm 116 Wm C 116
PROCTOR, Ira 6
PRUTT, G W 185

RAMSEY, John C 65 Wm P 185
RASH(E), J N 83 Jno N 24
    John E 157 John N 45 53 83
    86-7 Jos 11-2 75 86-7 181
    S P 83 Thos N 104
RAY/REY, John S 128 John G 22
REAVES/REEVES, Jos 18 80 108
    111-2 126-7 146-7 150 156
    183 Jos C 80
REER, Nathl G 5 6
REYNOLD(S), 50 B R 111 161-2
    177 Benj 30 111 183 Benj R
    111 176 J C 75 Jas 57-8
    John G 11 Jno G 118 Jno Y
    118 M A 11 50 58 Mark A 58
    Reynold 30 67 W J 58 Wm T
    161 Wm Thos 18 59
RHODES, Thos L 138
RICHARDS, Jas 2 3
RICHARDSON, Dan 2
RICHESON, L B 185
RIDDLE, Saml 5 6 75
RIDER, Wm 69 70

RIGGINS, Wm 82
RIGHTMER, E 24 Edwin 35
RILEY, Thos 149
RIPP(E)Y, E M 50 67-8 80 87-8
    Edward 86 Edward M 88
ROB(B)INS, J G 184 John 24 33
    34 Wm R 33
ROBERTS, H D 185 J W 184
ROBERTSON, A E 117 139 140
    A M 99 Asher E 97 117
ROBINSON, J B 185 Jos 31 34
    127-8 Thos J 66
RODENALL, L M 119
RO(W)LAND, P 24 Pleasant 34
ROLY, Moses 47
ROSE, D C 141 David 101 David
    C 101-2 112
ROY, Washington 106
RUCKER, M M 183

S----ELL, Jas H 75
S--LTIGGE, G T 184
SA--AT, Thompson D 75
SAMOND, E 84
SANCHES(S), F 24 33 185
    Francis(c)o 118 123
SANTO, Adam 85
SEALA/SEELA/SEILA/SELA, I 137
    Isaac 120 136 185
SEALY, Jacob 184
SEE, Michel 91-2
SENALDEUR, A R 83
SEWELL, J H 112 Jas H 149 169
    183 Wm 8
SHANKS, J C 39 John 39 136
SHANNON, vi
SHAW, T J 24 27 90 128 167
    185 Thos J 167
SHEEN, John 16 168-70
SHELEY, Wm H 184
SHELTON, J 1 75
SHEPPARD, L P 83 L T 83-4
    S T 85
SHIPMAN, Jacob 185
SHIRLEY/SHURLEY, B P 41 John
    43 W V D 24 41 Z P 24 41-2
    90 185 Zebadee P 173
SHORT, Robt 111
SHULTS/SHULTZ, Martin 116
    Martin B 118 Martin V 116
    Wade Hampton 116
SHUMAKER, Jeremjiah 184

SIDWELL, John 185 John Sr 185
SIL(L)IVANT/SILLIVENT/
    SILLIVINT, Carrale 119
    Carroll 119 F M 181 Franis
    M 86 113 182 Jas 118 Jas W
    42 M J 50 60 Wm 24 42 85-6
    97 113 117 119 143 Wm J
    143-4 165 181-2 Wm Jas 60
    Wm S 113
SIMONS, Andrew 165-6 Jas 166
    Valintine 166
SINCLAIR, Wm 5-7
SISK, D H 24 32-3 45 125 127
    137 174 184 Danl H 134 137
    138 H S 134 Henry S 134
    S H 125
SKIDMORE, G W 47 L D 24 177
    184 Lorenzo D 177 S 78
SMITH, A B 22 75 184 J T 168
    Jas H 103 138-9 John 5-7
    John P 184 L E 124 Richd B
    103 SILAS 126 134
SMYMS, Geo 75
SMYTH, Geo W 65
SNOW, J 50 Jeremiah 67 75
SNYDER, John 75 106 121 184
SOWELL, J M 8
SPARKS, A 29 39 75 139 Absa-
    lom 136 139 Berry 166 Wm
    24
SPEAR, David 174
SPEARMAN, J W 22 John M 133
    John W 75
SPILMAN, Levi 185 T J 185
SPROULS, Jas 24 30 43 78 89
    99 147
SPRUILL, J ? 184
SQUIRE(S), John 97 119-21 168
STACKS, Benj J 143
STAGGS, A F 63 G W 134-5 Geo
    135 184 Geo W 124 Miller
    50 Noah 124 184
STANL(E)Y, Chas J 59 Chas T
    84
STARR, Richd 6 75
STEEL, T 69
STEPHENS, J A 15 J S 15 68-9
    110
STERGGS, Noah 63
STIM(P)SON, D 92 David 92 98
    144-5 165-6 168-70
STINSON, David 66

STREET, T 69 Thos 70 W H 69
  Wm H 69
STROUD, J C 172-3 J S 128 172
  173 Jas C 171-3 John S 172
  173 P L 184 P T 184 Wiley
  171-3 180 185
STULTS/STULTZ, Adam 98 John
  97 98
STWLTS, John 75
SWALLOW, A R 84 John W 82

TACKETT/TACKITT, J H 84 129
  Josephus H 86 M D 84 102-3
  129
TANDIAN, W B 122
TANKERSLEY, Sarah 76
TARPLEY, Green H 76
TATE, J G 15 J H 15 68-9 76
TAYLOR, Geo 54 66 76 John M
  105 142 148 Wm 50 54 77 85
  86 143 165
TEETER(S), G G 50 Geo G 68-9
  Isaac 15 50 68-9 Robt P 82
THARP, Wm 76
THERILL, DE--- 11
THOMAS, D C 76 161 165 D G
  161 J 112 J B 85 J T 50
  J W 50 Jesse 90 134 172
  180 John B 103 John W 51
THOMASON, W D 76 Wm D 76
THOMPSON, Jas 8-9 76 Jeremiah
  141 Robt 46-7 Waddy 174
THORNBURG, 184
THORNHILL, A 50 Achilles 69
THORNSBURG, J S 178
THORP, S T 85
THROGM-RTON, Robt M 76
THURMEN, John M 76
TIDWELL, John 185
TIMMONS, E S 84
TINDAUS, J A 58
TINSLEY, Jas 133 183
TOLEN, A E 28 Thos H 27
TOLER, M N 184
TRAVIS, W B ix
TRIMBLE, Jo 67 John 23-4 40-1
  64 67 165-6 181 184 Jos
  23 40 41 Stephen 22 67 76
  184 Wm 22 41 47 134 184
TUBB, M M T 36 W M T 24 36-7
TUCKER, Aaron 164 Jas M 79
  Moses 164

TURNER, F B 9 76
TURREN, John 149
TYLER, John 116

UNDERWOOD, N 184 Norman 76
UPTION, Monroe 65
UPTON, J 184 Jas M 16 65 154
  162 180 M 185 Monroe 20-1
  66 94 153-5 158-9 180 Wm
  16 66 76 158 168

VARDY, John 114
VEAL, W G 83 Wm G 82
VERNON, Thos 150

W---D, Christopher C 51
WAGGONER, Danl 183
WALDEN/WALDON, Peter 16 92
WALDREN, Jos B 76
WALDRON, Chas S 2 Jos B 2
WALKER, B F 80 106 C P 50
  Chas 56 Chas L 44 Chas P
  56 Jno H 42 85-6 143 165
  Jos 42 54 84 113 143 165
  185 Jos L 9 76 Martin 125
  126 Peter 92 Robt M 103
  Robt Milton 43 Saml 119
  Saml H 43 103-4 Saml L 54
  Saml S 54
WALTERS, Haleden 184 Hallden
  91 Walden 91 129-30
WAMPLER, J F 124 M F P 123
  M J S 33-4 118 125 R R 34
  Volentine S 124 W J S 34
WARD, Henry 77-8 Jos 50 64 77
  78 Thos Wm 67
WARE, W W 184
WARFIELD, Jas H 106
WARREN, Yong 155 Young 26 155
  162-3
WATSON, J D 180 John D 183
WAUGH, T G 50 60 Thos G 59-60
  84 Thos Geo 59 Thos J 23
WAULDING, Jas 185
WEAVER, W D 185
WEBB, J F 185 J T 41
WEBER, ? C 1
WELBORN/WILBURN, Edward 185
  F C 76
WELCH, Wm 106
WELDEN/WELDON, P 131 148
  Peter 79 94 98 131-2 148

WELMITH, J T 124
WEST, J M 174
WHITE, Benj J 76 David 105 122 141-2 Jas 18 44 50 56 59 62-3 82 Jesse 76 John D 31 John S 31 67 Lewis 17-8 30 183 Preston 18 183 Priston 30 Thos 47 51 Wesley 30 41 183
WHITTEN, J A 102 Jacob A 101 105 110
WILCOX, J 119 Jacob 9 76
WILKERSON, Geo W 179
WILKIN, John 29
WILLIAMS, B F 185 J T 92 Jas 76 109 132 Jeremiah T 92 K P 26 R P 26 28 W G 183 Wyatt 92
WILMETH, Jas A 124
WIL(L)SON, Crain 76 E-viny 5 W T 76 Wm 83-4 106 146 150 151 155 Wm L 140 Wm P 26 92 155 163
WIMBERLY, Jas 111
WIMBL(E)Y, Jas 12 110-1 115 149 181
WINN/WYNN, G B 37 J B 36-8 Jos B 76 T B 37-8
WISON, Wm P 18
WITCHER, J 58 Jas 110 161
WOMACK, L J 52 T J 50 52 131 Thos J 55 130 131 Thos Jefferson 55-6 Wm J 130-1 156
WOOD, C C 50 Ira R 46 Wilson 136
WOODALL, J A 118 Jos A 115 119
WOOD(E)S, S M 184 Spence M 90 Wilson 28 Wm 76
WOOD(E)Y, B 57 Brice 58 Jas 18 59 Sam 14 57 85 Wm 44 76 78 82
WOODROME, Nicolas J 115
WOOSLEY, Johnson 76 121 184 Wm 76 184
WRAY, J G 27 76 100
WRIGHT, Robt 12 110-1 115 149 S 12

YEOMEN, Jas A 161
YOAKUM, Volentine 85
YOUNG, J M 13 Jos M 15 22
YOUNGBLOOD, Jas 141 181

www.ingramcontent.com/pod-product-compliance
Lightning Source LLC
Chambersburg PA
CBHW050145170426
43197CB00011B/1976